The Sweet Cherry Ranch

Frank King
July 29, 2001

The Sweet Cherry Ranch

A Memoir

Frank King

Writer's Showcase
San Jose   New York   Lincoln   Shanghai

The Sweet Cherry Ranch
A Memoir

Writer's Showcase
an imprint of iUniverse.com, Inc.

For information address:
iUniverse.com, Inc.
5220 S 16th, Ste. 200
Lincoln, NE 68512
www.iuniverse.com

ISBN: 0-595-18153-8

Printed in the United States of America

Dedication

This book is dedicated to my family; The King, Smith, Wittliff, Matavia, Van De Graaff, Tromp Van Holst, Jackson, Morrison, Sellers and Hansen clans. I wrote it especially for my grandchildren, and great-grandchildren.

Epigraph

One faces the future with one's past.
-Pearl S. Buck

About 90 percent of what I say is true, about ten percent bullshit. And I
don't know which is which.
-Gary Lowe

Contents

Acknowledgements

My facts, figures, and recollections were authenticated by a host of friends and family members. My grateful thanks to author M. K. Wren, whose real name is Martha Kay Refroe, for publishing advice. Janis Homlberg, who copy edited my manuscript, saved me from many a blunder. Betsy Cherednik, the reference librarian at the Lincoln City, Oregon Driftwood Library, was a great help in finding book titles, dates and events. Friend Sharon Cox, with Oregon Coast Community College assisted with computer software solutions. My ham radio friends, Carl Schmauder, K7EWG; Bryce Spence, N7LQQ; Jim Hawley, W7VTW; John Nicholson, K7FD; Joe Novello, KB7FYZ, Hobie Clark, W6TCA; Phil Smith, W7BFX; John Wilson, Wl0ND, Carol Moore, WA6THI, Charlie Smith, K7GI, and Carol Dorning, N7HEH, were generous with support and advice. Jan Riedberger and Glenna Barney, at the Café Roma Bookstore and Coffeehouse, were unflagging in their encouragement. Carma, my wife, son Mike, and daughters Melanie and Lisa, gave me their love, time and advice. My brothers, Tony and Pete, filled in some of the blanks and hazy areas of when we were boys together. My niece, Dolores Theresa King Lowery, a computer whiz, bailed me out with important computer program advice and help. And a special "thank you" to Luciele Van De Graaff Rackham, my loving sister-in-law. Her great memory helped me write this book, and relive a most dear part of my life. I am indeed lucky to such great friends and family.

Chapter 1

Our Way Out West

They were forever talking about Michigan-how green the landscape, how blue Lake Huron, how good the food, how great the friends and family. If it was so great, why did they leave? Dad said it was because of the weather.

"Michigan is beautiful three months out of the year," he said. "The rest of the time it's hotter than the mill tails of hell, cold enough to freeze the balls off a brass monkey, or tornadoes will carry off your house."

The job situation after the First World War looked a lot better in the balmy climate of Southern California, but I suspect that Dad wanted to get away from the place that haunted him-scenes of grinding poverty and booze-addicted Grandpa King who deserted his wife and young son. My mother's and my health had a lot to do with the move. Mother had some sort of breathing trouble that was later mistakenly diagnosed as tuberculosis, but later found to be some sort of chronic bronchitis. I had eczema and was sick most of the time with asthma and all kinds of infections.

Their reasoning was that we would be a lot healthier in the drier and warmer climate of Southern California.

My direct family, my mother and father and their parents, except for my mother's mother and my dad's father, were born in Port Huron, Michigan. All of their families settled there generated a lot of talk about the decision to move. But move we did in 1923 when I was one year old.

I was born October 1, 1922, at home, with a doctor and midwife helping my mother, Catherine Theresa Smith King. My mother married my father, William Ernest King, in 1920. Mom and Dad met shortly after he was discharged from the U.S. Navy following World War I. They both grew up in Port Huron. Mother was the eldest of two girls born to my grandfather, Frank Smith, and my grandmother, Rosalia Wittliff Smith. My aunt, Leola Cecelia, was born two years after my mother. My dad's father, Nelson George King, and my grandmother, Ellen Matavia, had a big family. My father was the youngest, and his brothers and sister who survived devastating childhood illnesses were Frank, Jim and Dolly. Three other children died. No one talked much about Grandma King's side of the family. My Dad always said that he was "three-quarters French, and a quarter Irish," but we found that not quite true. Great-grandfather Matavia was French Canadian, but Great-grandmother Matavia is listed in Port Huron records as Indian Mary. My Grandpa King was born in New York state, and his father's name was John Baptiste King. We don't know who Great Grandmother King was. Family legend has it that old John Baptiste had a family in New York, deserted them, moved to Michigan where he sired my dad's side of the family, deserted them, and ended up in the Chicago area where he married again and raised another brood.

Leaving that colorful bunch wasn't too difficult for my father, but Mother felt differently. She said that leaving Port Huron permanently was stressful because she loved her Grandma Wittliff very much, but she and Dad were looking forward to a new home on the West Coast.

After getting out of the Navy, my father had several jobs, including one at a foundry and working for Grandpa Smith in his saddle, harness and shoe repair shop. He said that anything was better than what he did in the Navy during the Great War. He was in the Black Gang, a fireman who shoveled coal into the troop transport boilers. Dad made three trips across the North Atlantic on the USS George Washington, a former German luxury liner converted into a troop transport that carried American and Canadian troops from the United States to France.

"Only a thin sheet of steel separated us from the German torpedoes that were fired at our ship," he said.

Grandpa Smith's family had been in Port Huron for a long time also. His father, William J. Smith, had a big harness, saddle and buggy whip store and was a very successful businessman. Family reports conflict on his origin. Grandpa Smith always said that he was "English, Scotch and Irish." Aunt Leola said Great-grandpa Smith told her he was born in Ireland, but some reports indicate he was born in Montreal. His wife, my grandfather's mother, Catherine Ford Smith, died shortly after the second child, Maude Estelle, was born. Great-grandfather Smith remarried, and it caused a lot of friction in the family. Grandpa Smith hated his stepmother and refused to mention her name.

The other side of my mother's family, the Wittliffs, were all German stock. My great grandparents, Joseph Wittliff and Theresa Lindamann Wittliff, immigrated to the United States in 1869. They settled near Port Huron, moved to St. Joseph, Missouri, for a short time where my grandmother was born, then moved back to Port Huron. It was a second marriage for my great grandmother. Her first husband died and left her with a little girl, Aunt Annie. Annie was called "The Black One," because she had a dark Mediterranean-type complexion. As was the custom in German Catholic families then, the eldest bachelor son was required to marry the widowed sister-in-law and care for the family. Great-grandfather Wittliff was in a seminary studying to be a priest. He left his studies, married Theresa Lindamann, and they immigrated to the United States. He was a tailor. In 1927 Great-grandma Wittliff, who was born in 1838, was honored as one of the pioneers of the city of Port Huron. When she settled there 6,000 people were living in the town. By 1927 that number had grown to 30,000.

So it was with hope, and some regret, that my family set out on the great adventure. My mother, grandmother and aunt were sad because they were leaving their families, while Dad and Grandpa were looking forward to opportunities. Things were bound to get better in California.

Chapter 2

Los Angeles

Grandpa and Grandma Smith, Mom and Aunt Leola, whom I called "Lada," knew California well. In 1914 they had moved to Los Angeles for a short stay, and remained for three years. Grandpa had a job as a harness maker with a Michigan timber company that was working near Flagstaff, Arizona. Grandpa would work in Arizona for a while, and then take the train back to Los Angeles. My Mother and Lada tell stories of the garden that Grandma Smith cultivated at their shotgun bungalow in the Watts area. Grandma's fruits and vegetables were what they lived on, until Grandpa sent them money from Arizona. That lasted until World War I broke out, and they moved to St. Louis, Missouri, where Grandpa worked as a leather goods inspector for the U.S. Army's Quartermaster General. In 1918 they moved back to Port Huron. Their early travels were all by train, so traveling across the country in a car would be a new experience.

Our automobile trip west was like a motorized covered wagon trek. Grandpa Smith had a 1922 Maxwell touring sedan, a fine vehicle. I remember it as being sort of a dark brownish color with a canvas light tan colored top. To me it was a huge thing. I was only one year old, and, of course, I can't remember that, but Grandpa had the old Maxwell for seven or eight more years before he sold it to my dad. It was in that fine piece of machinery that we made our way across the county. My folks described the trip in fine detail, over and over, and it became family legend.

I can remember sitting in the Maxwell with my Grandpa, and him crying when Lada married Uncle Louie. Louis Hubbard was the offspring of a Protestant missionary family. Poor Uncle Louie. At the wedding he was as popular as a bordello madam in church with most of the staunch German-French-Irish Roman Catholic members of the family. It was the first time I saw a man cry, my Grandpa. I thought he was crying because Uncle Louie wasn't Catholic. I was puzzled. Grandpa wasn't Catholic. His family was Methodist, and he didn't convert to Catholicism until I was 12 years old. I didn't know what to do, so I hugged him and tried to wipe the tears away. He crushed me to him so hard I thought my ribs would break. Then he released me, sat up straight, tugged at his vest, pulled out a cigar, lit it, and became calm.

Grandpa said that it took six weeks to make the journey. We stayed in hotels and roadside inns most of the time, but when night fell and there were no close towns, we camped out. We had a big tent, pads to sleep on, blankets, cooking gear, and supplies-all stuffed in the Maxwell with the driver and five passengers.

"There were only a couple hundred miles of hard-surfaced roads between Port Huron and Los Angeles," Grandpa said. "All the rest were over 2,000 miles of rough gravel, plain dirt, sand and potholes. You could prove it by the calluses on your butt."

After untold flat tires and a major repair job in New Mexico, we arrived in The City of the Queen of Angels. We moved into a house on West 51st Place, between Vermont and Hoover Avenues. It was just south of the huge Los Angeles Coliseum where the University of Southern California played all of their home football games. I remember we could hear the crowd roaring when touchdowns were made. We never went to the games, but would all gather around the radio. We would enthusiastically cheer on Notre Dame when the Fighting Irish came to play the Trojans of USC. Grandpa set up his shoe repair business, and Dad began looking for work. After a few weeks he was hired by the Southern California Gas Company in Los Angeles where he would drive around in a truck and fix gas lines and kitchen stoves.

After we set up housekeeping in California things got a lot better. Grandpa tried selling real estate as a sideline, but didn't do too well in that endeavor. Dad had a good job and we were doing fine except for the health thing. I was sick most of the time, and Mother would periodically have one of her spells. One of the first memories I have of my Grandma King-Ellen Matavia King-was her caring for me for a short time when I was sick. She was a tiny woman with a deformed back-a hump back. Dad told the story of how she got it from an injury when she was a child. She was playing on a tall fence around a pig pen when she fell off and landed on her back and shoulder. It was never set right and she had the deformity the rest of her life. Legend also has it that she and Thomas Alva Edison were playmates when the Edisons lived in Port Huron. My grandmother said that she and Edison were considered the odd ones, she with her deformity and he with his odd, quirky personality that drew them together. My Grandma King was a kind, gentle person and I can remember her soft hands, soothing voice and the great stories she told. About three years later, after we moved to Beaumont, California, I remember the phone call from Uncle Frank telling my Dad of Grandma King's death in Santa Monica. My father broke down, sobbing. My mother had to pry the telephone out of his hand and hang it on the wall hook after Uncle Frank said goodbye. I always remember when the dominant male figures in my life showed their humanity by weeping. The last time was when my father died, and Grandpa Smith cried out to me, tears pouring down his leathery cheeks, "Why, Billy? Why not me? He was like my son. I am so much older than he."

Life on 51st Place was like an amorphous, fuzzy, fairytale where early events were burned in my memory. I remember eating an apricot, taking the seed and planting it out next to the back fence. When I visited years later there was a young apricot tree growing in the same spot I planted the seed. I can recall my first encounter with the hydra-headed monster of sex on 51st Place. I was out in the back yard, near the fence by the garage, when one of the neighbor kids had to pee. He took out his weenie and started spraying on the garage, then the little girl said she had to go, pulled down her pants, squatted, and let go.

The boy said to me, "Why don't you go."

"I will not," I hollered, "I don't want to go to hell!"

Prude that I was, I knew that what the kids were doing was forbidden. I wanted to pee too and see what the girl had, but I didn't. Dire promises of what would happen to a good Roman Catholic kid who exposed himself to others ricocheted around my brain, and I became a sanctimonious little prig I didn't like.

I remember going to the big church on Vermont Ave, and the motion picture theater on the same street. The kids' and the Saturday matinees with the western and adventure serials were tops on my list. A big thing happened in 1925. On January 21 my younger brother Peter Leo drew his first breath at the house on 51st Place. He was called Leo, or Pete, depending on who was talking to him. Grandma Smith always called him Leo, because she had a brother named Leo. My Dad called him Pete, because he liked the name. No matter what he was called, Peter Leo always came running. He was a happy, bouncy, plump kid, affectionate and talkative.

We moved from 51st Place to 88th Street further south, just Mom, Dad, Pete and I. I don't know why we moved, but I imagine the house on 51st Place was getting pretty crowded and they were suffering from cabin fever. Pete remembers the dirt roads out at 88th Street, and I remember a big feed, seed and farm supply store that was down on the corner from our house. It was an interesting place with the great smells of hay and livestock feed. Grandpa and Grandma Smith and Lada stayed on at 51st Place. Moving those three miles was like going to another planet. The thing that I remember most about 88th Street was being sick, and the horrible remedies that our mother forced upon us. One instrument of torture involved onions. Mother heard of some folk remedy-I think it came from Grandpa Smith. He came up with some great, but distorted, ideas of what was sure to cure us. Nasty head and chest colds had struck Pete and I. Mom bought us long, black cotton stockings. Into the black stockings, at the soles, around the feet, and up the legs, were stuffed huge slices of fresh, reeking onions. We had to wear them for three days. At first the smell gagged us. Pete threw up on the bed because of the smell. Our noses became numb, then the tactile horror of squishy onions made us crawl on hands and knees. I don't know if the onions-in-the-stockings treatment cured us or made us sicker. We did live to tell about the horror.

My Grandpa and Grandma Smith, and my mother, were great on home remedies. I can remember the bread and milk, and the soap-always Fels Naptha-and sugar poultices. If you had a splinter, or a boil, out came the soap and sugar and the clean rag bandages. When Pete, and my baby brother Tony and I got into a bunch of old redwood planks we came home loaded with splinters in all parts of our bodies. When Mother got through with us we looked like a trio of mummies. The infernal mixtures worked. It was very embarrassing to go out to play with your friends and get teased because you were a mummy. Then there were the tonics in the spring time. Sulfur and molasses and other noxious mixtures designed to torture children. I don't know why we had to take that stuff. We had fresh vegetables and fruits year round in Southern California. But old habits die hard.

Because I was so skinny, my folks wanted to fatten me up. Grandma Smith, true to her good German stock, believed that if you were skinny you were sick. So out came the cod liver oil and the beef, iron and wine tonic. I had a great appetite, but I used to hate meals because that was when I had to take all of the horrible stuff that would make me eat more so I would grow fat.

I had started first grade at the 51st Street Grammar School, but again I got a bad chest infection and lost a lot of time from school. About this same time my mother was also having bronchial problems, and our doctor recommended that we move to a dry climate. There was a gas company pumping plant in Beaumont, about 80 miles east of Los Angeles, between the Riverside-San Bernardino area and Palm Springs, right on the edge of the Colorado Desert. In 1929 we moved to Beaumont, and that is the place I really call home, my Camelot-a very dry Camelot.

Chapter 3

Beaumont

Like a horny toad basking in the warm, rock strewn sand, surrounded by grease wood, sagebrush and cactus, Beaumont, California lies on its belly in San Gorgonio Pass, towered over by the mountains peaks of the San Bernardino mountains to the north, and the rocky San Jacintos to the southeast. Like human Beaumont residents, the horny toad doesn't look toward the west, to the boiling smog rising into the sky of frantic bustling cities, but to the north and southeast. The horny toad and residents ignore things to the west, hoping that they will not be infected by the brownish plague of smog creeping eastward. Mount San Gorgonio and San Jacinto Peak soar two miles into the crystal blue desert skies. Both have nick-names-like loved or hated friends or family members-San Gorgonio is Old Grayback and San Jacinto is San Jack.

When we moved to Beaumont Lada came with us to take care of my mother, who was pretty sick. I can't remember being really sick after we made the move. So I guess the climate and dry air was good for me. We fitted comfortably into the life of a small town. Beaumont boasted a population of 1,500 then. I started first grade again, and my teacher was Mrs. Merrill. I was one of the oldest kids in the class, seven years old. I didn't complete the year in Los Angeles because of being sick so much.

I remember some of the children from the first and second grade: Fred Fierro, Henry Mendoza, Dolores Swearingin, Gretchen Coy, Mable Fly, Marjorie Schmidt, George Humphries, Winifred Brown, and Joaquin Lara. Most of them are still alive and I see them most of them at school reunions and when I visit Southern California.

When we first moved to Beaumont, we lived on Wellwood Ave. down near Fifth Street. Fifth Street was called the "main drag" by Dad and Grandpa. After a year or so we moved to our house a block north on Wellwood, across the street and south of the Wellwood Grammar School. I only had to run across the street to go home for lunch. And run I did. Everywhere. Dad and Mom bought the house for $2,400. It had two bedrooms and a big alcove off of one bedroom. Brother Pete and I slept in the same double bed in one bedroom and our parents had the bigger bedroom. A feature of the house was another alcove built off of the living room. Dad made it into a combination office, library and music room. He had his desk in there, along with a well-stocked bookcase, and Mom had her piano. She was an enthusiastic, by-the-book pianist who would bang out "Whispering Hope," "The Skater's Waltz" and "Beautiful Dreamer" in measured, unaccented notes.

Mom had a weight problem. We would never, ever dare to call her fat. It would have been a good way to ensure a lightening-quick swipe across your bottom with the wire handle of the fly swatter. We became defensive over Mom's weight with those outside the family. If a kid asked you, "Why is your mother so fat?" you automatically had to bust him in the chops. If a girl alluded to Mom's obesity you couldn't hit her unless she was a head taller than you. So you beat up her little brother. If she didn't have one you kicked her dog. Everybody had a dog in Beaumont. So no evil word about

Mom's weight went unpunished. Our dog's name was Bozo, but more about him later.

One day we were sitting on the porch when a young man and his date drove by our house in a Model A roadster with the top down. The girl pointed at my mother, giggled, and nudged her escort. He looked, laughed, and drove on. Mom began crying, went into the house and closed the door to her bedroom. When Dad got home that night, we told him what had happened, and we called a war council at the kitchen table. We mapped out a strategy for revenge that would have made the Hatfields and McCoys proud. We would set the guy's roadster on fire, flatten his tires, throw horse manure on the seats, and so on. We bided our time until Halloween. We didn't know where the girl lived, but we had the address of the guy who owned the roadster. Six paper bags of fresh manure were placed on his porch, gently moistened with gasoline, and set on fire. You would have thought that family was a bunch of grape-stomping, wine-making maniacs the way they went at those flaming bags.

We were a close family. My happiest memories are of being held by my Dad after we moved to Beaumont. When he held me I could smell the tobacco, sweat, the after shave lotion he used and the sharp chemical odors of paint, natural gas and lamp black. I have never felt as safe as when my father was holding me, nor as loved when hugged and kissed by my mother. Most of the times Mom was patient and loving, but when really aggravated she would blow and we would run for cover. As children we were nurtured within the shell of family, church and the town. The family loved us and helped us grow, church and school opened doors to learning, and the community gave us safety. My Grandmother Smith was a lot like my mother; caring, loving and affectionate. She made her own clothes, and hats, dressed like an artist or gypsy in colorful dresses with lots of beads and jewelry. She painted, did beautiful needlework, sculpted and was always busy with an arts and crafts project. When excited, or angry, German expletives would erupt from her. My favorite was, *"Scheis der poop!"* Translation: "Aw shit!" Grandpa Smith was dignified most of the time, but he had a boisterous, direct, earthy and loud sense of humor. He had an explosive temper, but would cool down quickly after throwing his tools on the bench and swearing at length. He loved sports, particularly baseball, and did everything he could to see that my brothers and I joined in the sports.

In those early grade school days my best friend was Fred Fierro. The Fierro family, Mr. And Mrs. Fierro, Mike, Lalo, Juanita, Joe, Fred and Frances, lived a block away from us. Fred and I, my brother Pete and Frances Fierro soon became fast friends. An abandoned house, a small one, between our homes, became our playground. We sent away for the Little Orphan Annie secret decoder rings, and became great detectives modeled on Inspector Post, of FBI and Post Toasties fame. We were cowboys, Indians, pirates, buccaneers, adventurers, soldiers and heroes. Pete and I spent as much time at the Fierro's home as we did in our own. Fred's mother was so gentle and patient with us. We were always invited to the midday meal, or the evening dinner during the long days of summer. As I remember, the Fierro's home was in three small buildings. Two of the buildings housed the sleeping rooms and the living room, or sala. The kitchen was a separate one room building in the back. The floor was hard-packed earth. Mrs. Fierro or Juanita swept it with a damp broom three or four times a day. It was as shiny, hard and clean as fresh-washed concrete. The black wood-fired kitchen stove was In one corner. Fresh white-flour tortillas were baked on top of the stove each day. Salsa was a staple on the kitchen table, and pinto or red beans were the course of the day. Pete and I loved it. I developed a strong appetite for prickly pears after Mrs. Fierro fed me one. A huge prickly pear cactus grew at the rear of their property. The cactus had always given me problems, usually after I ended up in the clump when racing in on my bike. The long sharp stickers would painfully pierce your skin, but the nasty things were the tiny hair-like stickers that raised hell anywhere they touched you. Mrs. Fierro carefully pared the rind away from the prickly pear fruit and gave it to me. I had never tasted anything like it; subtle, fresh, faintly sweet. Mrs. Fierro could not speak

English, but we did not have any communication problem. With a few words of English and Spanish and sign language we understood each other. One of the saddest days of our lives was when Frances Fierro died. I heard that she had been sick, but I didn't know how bad it was. We all took it pretty hard, especially Peter Leo who was devastated when he heard of his playmate's death.

My youngest brother, Stephen Anthony King, came squalling into our world on November 13, 1932. Some neighbor had taken me up to the ball park behind the high school to watch a baseball game. In the middle of the game my father came rushing up to us.

"Frankie, you have a new baby brother at home," he said.

"That's nice."

"Don't you want to come home and see him?" Dad asked.

"Can't I wait until the game is over?"

Dad said that he named his three sons after the Popes, but we were called Frank, Pete and Tony.

"It sounds like I have sired a bunch of Italian banana peddlers," Dad said.

I was called Frankie, and my grandfather answered to Frank. It made things a lot simpler in our family.

After Tony was born the household changed. Mom got a washing machine. As far back as I can remember she would do all of the family washing at two stationary tubs on the back porch. The clothes, towels and bed linen all got a vigorous workout on a wash board, with plenty of soap. Then they were rinsed and wrung out. It was my job to turn the crank on the clothes wringer for Mom as she fed the washed laundry between the wringers. The new washing machine was a modern marvel. It even had wringers on it so I didn't have to turn the crank. Sometimes, with badly soiled work clothes, Mom would boil them in a wash tub in the back yard. Pete and I had all sorts of chores to do. That included helping Mom with the laundry, doing the dishes when we were older, helping with the house-work, feeding the chickens and rabbits and raking the yard. With a new baby brother, more chores came along.

"I don't have any girls," Mom would say, "so it is up to my boys to help me."

I hated it when she said that. She was putting skirts on me. I learned to cook, iron clothes, clean house and sew on buttons, all things my mother taught me, but duties that my Dad also took part in. He never considered it demeaning to hang out clothes, cook a meal, watch us kids, or help with the canning during harvest time. My new chores also included changing my baby brother's diaper. After gagging over his messy bottom, putting a clothespin on my nose, and completing the first diaper assignment, the job got easier. I was a happy boy when Tony started going to the bathroom on his own.

Shortly after the new washing machine came the refrigerator. Before the refrigerator the ice man would come every other day. He would park his Union Ice Company truck at the side of the house and ask Mom how big a block of ice she wanted. We usually got a 25- or 50-pound block. The ice man had big tongs that he used to grip the ice, sling it over his shoulder-protected by a large leather pad, tote the ice into the house and lower it into the ice box. Pete and I had the job of emptying the big pan from under the ice box. Mom couldn't get down to do it. When the ice would melt the water would drain down a tube at the bottom of the ice box and run into a large dish pan. We had to lift up a hinged door at the bottom of the ice box and slide out the dish pan full of water. We always waited until the pan was too full, and we would stagger with it to the kitchen sink, slopping water out all over the floor on the trip from the ice box to the drain. Then we would have to mop the floor after that operation. As I remember, we had to empty the ice pan once or twice a day.

When the new Electrolux gas refrigerator came life changed for the better, but Mom and Dad found ways to keep us busy. A hated chore was cleaning the chicken coop and rabbit hutches. We had to shovel the manure on the floor of the coop out the door into a pile. After a thorough cleaning, the inside was whitewashed cut down of the bugs. Working in the dusty, foul-smelling coop was a job from hell. The chickens provided us with eggs and Sunday dinner, with rabbit meat for the table.

Every other Sunday or so, Grandpa and Grandma Smith would drive up from San Gabriel Valley, where they had moved, to spend a Sunday with us. They usually arrived after Mass, in plenty of time for dinner. Most of the time we had chicken-roasted, stewed or fried. It was my job to butcher the chicken for Sunday dinner. I held that honor until Pete took over later. We would chop the head off the chicken with a hatchet over a big block of wood in the back yard. Mother dictated that we chop the head off, then drop the chicken into a big bucket where it thrashed about for about four minutes. It was a lot more fun to chop the head off, drop the chicken into the dirt and watch it flop around the back yard. Mom didn't want any extra dirt on the chickens, so we were threatened with the fly swatter handle until we promised to mend our ways. I really hated plucking the damn birds. We had a big bucket of scalding water into which we plunged the headless fowl. After a brief dousing the feathers were plucked out in big clumps. When most of the feathers had been pulled out, a painstaking search for smaller feathers was done. When plucking was finished Mom would singe the bird over an open burner on the gas range in the kitchen to burn off all of the pin feathers. It is a smell I remember, and hate.

Pete, Tony and I thrived in Beaumont. When I was in grade school, many of us would go to classes barefoot. In the early grade school days, the shoes would come off in March and didn't go back on until October. Beaumont has an elevation of 2,630 feet. In the winter, about every three or four years, we would get a sprinkling of snow. When the first frosts hit, and the mud puddles would freeze, in late October or early November, the shoes would come back on. In March when the tender, new leaves emerged and the cheat grass greened the hills around town, the shoes came off. The only time shoe wear was mandatory was when we went to mass on Sunday. Cramming tough feet that seemed to have grown two sizes over the week into shoes for church was sheer torture. After mass the shoes came off. The soles of our feet became so hardened that we could run at full speed over rock, sand and gravel of the desert earth and not flinch. And run we did. We were either asleep or running full tilt.

Rocks and stones didn't hurt our feet, but one pesky weed did. We called it the "puncture weed." Its burrs could flatten bicycle tires in seconds. The weed, that grew flat and close to the ground, had stickers that resembled a cattle skull with two, sharp horns. One time I heard them referred to as goat head burrs, and that is an appropriate name.

Summer was freedom. We had our work to do, but there was baseball; Run Sheep, Run; Kick the Can; Hide and Seek at twilight until dark when the parents would call us in. We would play under the street light in front of our house, and the air was thick with June bugs buzzing around us. After a barefoot day, Mom would make us wash our feet every night before climbing into bed. Before bed there were prayers we said on our knees: The Our Father, Hail Mary and blessing all the family. After the Sign of the Cross it was a jump into the bed, and we were asleep when our heads hit the pillow. Only Saturday night was different. That was bath night when we had to be scrubbed clean for mass the next morning.

Summer was when we had daily catechism classes at Our Lady of Guadalupe chapel across the tracks in the south part of town where most of my Mexican friends lived. I had made my first communion at San Gorgonio Church. There were 21 brown little faces in that communion class. I had the only light one, a true gringo pale face. Our summer uniform, for boys, at Our Lady was overalls, no underwear and bare feet. We had classes at long tables in the church yard, under a huge pepper tree, next to the Gonzales home. One year we had a craft project, to make a crucifix. The nuns, Franciscan Sisters, showed us how. They came from St. Boniface Indian School in Banning, a town seven miles east of Beaumont. Our priests, Franciscans, were also from St. Boniface. Our church, San Gorgonio, was a mission serviced by the priests and sisters from St. Boniface. I carefully cut and sanded the two pieces that made the cross and the base, then painted it a soft brown. They gave us the Christ figure to attach to the cross, and it was a moving experience for me. I kept that crucifix for years and then packed it away when I went into the Marine Corps in WWII. Years later I unpacked that gear, found the cross, and wondered where my faith had gone. I had packed it away with the crucifix.

One summer my Mother did something that resulted in a dark period in our childhood. Grandpa Smith said Pete and I should have all of our hair cut off. It would be good for us, we wouldn't catch any bugs in our hair, and it would give our scalps a chance to breathe. Mom went along with it. After a visit to the barber we were a great looking pair. Those white, bald heads were a great invitation to our Mexican colleagues at the Our Lady summer school. Bernardo Lozano, Pifi Hernandez, Pampo Valdivia, Joaquin Lara and Henry Mendoza would thump us with their knuckles on our bare sunburned heads. That hurt. Not only the pain, but our pride, too. Our pates became sunburned. It was sheer hell having a sun-blistered head with bumps on it from being hit with knuckles.

We had our first encounter with death on the walk from home to Our Lady for summer classes one day. We had to walk south by the depot, cross the Southern Pacific Railroad tracks, and then to the chapel. We often had to wait for a train to pass. One day a long freight train was slowly headed east and we stopped and waited for it to pass. A spotted black and white dog was about 25 feet away from us, nervously walking around, wanting to get at something on the other side of the tracks. Suddenly it dashed forward, tried to run under one of the cars, and the huge wheels ran over it. The dog's legs on one side had been cut off. It was on the far side of the train and we couldn't get to it. It lay yelping and crying as the blood drained out. We were frozen in place as we watched the dog die. After the train passed, we quickly ran past the dead dog to the chapel. I remember praying for the poor dead dog's soul.

Gray-white, then sunburned, hairless heads topped sun-browned faces, necks and shoulders, with bib overalls, no shirts or underwear and bare feet; we fit in great with the rest of the town characters. Mrs. Coultas, the barber's wife, made a dignified walk to town every day. A large woman with a big bust, she always wore a tan, pongee silk outfit with a full skirt, jacket and white blouse topped by a huge fawn-colored hat with a veil. She powdered her entire face until it was a white mask, with a black beauty mark on her cheek. She made her way down the sidewalk, with a big, black, walking stick. I thought she resembled a full-masted schooner sailing through the Pacific Ocean. We gave her lots of room. Then there was the guy who wore all white: white shorts, white shirt, white socks and white tennis shoes. It didn't matter what time of year it was, he was always in white, including his white hair. My dad said that he came to Beaumont many years before as a tubercular invalid. He wasn't given much time to live. He started walking in the mornings, and gradually regained his strength and lengthened his walks. When I was young he walked from two to three hours a day, always in white.

Outstanding town characters were Spittin' Jinny and The Colonel. They lived in a big white house next to the railroad tracks. The building had been a hotel at one time. The Colonel didn't do much more than sit on the porch. He also was dressed in white, had a black tie, and a big white plantation hat. It was rumored that he and Spittin' Jinny were man and wife, or shacking up. Shacking up was an evil thing, living with each other without benefit of matrimony. Spittin' Jinny was the active one. She did a lot of walking and spitting. Walk five steps, spit, five steps, spit. Her thin figure could not be mistaken, in a gingham dress, wearing a sun bonnet, striding and spitting between the hotel and Ray's Place, a tavern in the main part of town. After a few hours in Ray's Jinny would come out staggering on her way back to the big white house. Walk, stagger, spit; walk, stagger, spit. Some brash, daring kids tried to tease her, but she was a lot quicker than she looked. She nailed a couple of them, and she was given a wide berth from then on. When she was alive every Beaumont generation had its confrontations with Spittin' Jinny. She was a sort of a town monument.

Cipriano Rangel was a larger-than-life figure in my youth. He was a street sweeper. Mr. Rangel was in his late middle years, stockily built, with a huge black mustache. He was usually dressed in jean pants and a jacket with a large white sombrero. Every day he would sweep the downtown streets and keep them clean. He always had time for us kids. We would practice speaking Spanish with him, and his coaching and concern had an effect on many of us. He gave me a Spanish language primer, "El Maestro Infantil." I thought I was special. It wasn't until I went to my 50th Beaumont Union High School class reunion that I discovered he had given copies of that same book to several of my friends. My dad said that Mr. Rangel had at one time been a university student in Mexico City where he was a musician. The town thought so highly of Cipriano Rangel that they have named a park after him.

We even had a drunk dentist, the only tooth doctor in town. When my new incisors replaced by baby teeth, the front of my mouth looked lopsided. The place where the left front tooth should be was partially filled by a stub that looked like a little fang. They took me to the drunk dentist. He said a good tooth was up in the channel waiting to come down, and that he should pull the fang. He did, and it worked. There wasn't enough room so the second front tooth came in crooked. I thought the drunk dentist had placed a curse on me. I had a drunken tooth.

The dentist came into some money, and died soon after. I heard the folks talking about how he drank himself to death.

Ed McKinley lived in a small house near the north side of the Wellwood School grounds. He was a retired merchant mariner, and he looked like Popeye, except that he had both eyes and didn't squint. He was covered with tattoos, and he was hard to understand. Ed was a very talkative fellow, and loved to discuss current events and politics with my father. Like most sailors, he was a great storyteller, and the kids in the neighborhood thronged to his place when he told about his life at sea. Ed was a great reader, but didn't understand many of the words. He refused to use a dictionary. Ed said that he couldn't understand the words describing the word he didn't understand. After a conversation with Ed, my Dad would come in shaking his head and muttering that he couldn't make out what Ed was talking about. Ed's fractured speech resulted in a new vocabulary for us. In 1939 Germany marched into Czechoslovakia and occupied that small country. Ed ran down to our house and shouted for my father. Dad came out into the yard.

"Bill, did you hear what those damn Krauts did? They marched into *Shovoslovaski!*"

"Where?"

"*Shovoslovaski!*"

"You mean Czechoslovakia."

"That's what I said, *Shovoslovaski!*"

Downtown became my stomping ground. I wanted to earn some of my own money so I began selling magazines, *The Saturday Evening Post, Colliers, Liberty* and *Country Gentleman*. That grew into a newsboy job. Every day I would pick up my papers at DePeel's Drugstore when the Greyhound Bus dropped them off. We called it the "Greyhound Stage," probably because Beaumont was a stop on the Butterfield Overland Stage line in the late nineteenth century, and the name hung on. I sold the *Los Angeles Evening Herald* and *Express*, the afternoon Hearst newspaper. Every day I could be found delivering papers to five of my regular customers, and trying to sell the other five. I haunted the drugstore, and Chadsey's Variety Store. It was at Chadsey's that I could buy a good amount of candy for one or two cents. I made a penny for each paper I sold. I would sell from five to seven of them. If I sold all ten, candy here I come!

Highway 90, the federal highway that runs from Los Angeles to the east, was the main street in town. All of the major businesses were in the downtown area along the highway. Trucks from Imperial Valley hauling hay, melons, dates and vegetables made their way through downtown. Also, so did the rich people from Los Angeles and Hollywood on their way down to the desert, particularly Palm Springs. We used to get glimpses of the movie stars-Clark Gable, Wallace Beery, Carole Lombard, Myrna Loy,

Jean Harlow, Rudolph Valentino. We had a sure way to slow them down when they came through town in the springtime. There were many beautiful lilac bushes throughout the town. When the lilacs were in full bloom we would pick bunches of them and put them in buckets of water. We would haul the flowers down to the highway where traffic slowed going through town, and hold out bunches of lilacs for sale. We sold them for 50 cents a bunch, and we could make good money. The folks from L.A.-we called it "down below"-oohed and aahed over the gorgeous blooms, and we pocketed the money.

The affluence of the few driving east to Palm Springs emphasized the poverty of the dust bowl migrants coming into Southern California fleeing the drought and dust storms. By the time they reached San Gorgonio Pass, many of the migrants were penniless, out of food and fuel for their cars and trucks. Dad had continued his job with the gas company, and was the compressor plant operator in Beaumont. He had entered into the life of the small community in a big way. He was elected to the city council and chosen to be the commissioner of the police and fire department. He was involved in veterans' affairs, those who had served in World War I and the Spanish American War. He was a member of the American Legion and the Veterans of Foreign Wars. For a few years, Dad would bring home a stranded, destitute family, let them stay in the little one-room house we had behind our home, get them food and money to get to their destination. Many of them stayed on in town,the men getting jobs in the orchards or other places in the surrounding area. Many of my classmates were from families who migrated to Beaumont because of the Dust Bowl disaster. It was the time of the Great Depression.

In this period thousands of veterans and their families drove in caravans, hitched rides or rode empty railroad boxcars to Washington, D.C., for the Veterans' Bonus March. Back in 1924, Congress passed the Federal Bonus Law. The law granted World War I veterans a bonus certificate that would be paid off in 1945. Because of the poverty brought on by the depression, the veterans demanded that the bonus be paid immediately, and they tried to pressure Congress. The veterans and their families were camped out in the capital. President Herbert Hoover ordered General

Douglas MacArthur, the Army chief of staff, to drive the veterans from the city. Dad and his veteran friends listened to the radio, and reacted with horror as tear gas was shot at the bonus marchers and they were herded out of the city at bayonet point. Dad became violently anti-Republican, and hated Hoover and MacArthur until he died. It wasn't until 1936 that Congress approved the veterans bonus to be paid immediately.

For almost 15 years Dad served as a volunteer service officer for the American Legion. He would interview applicants for veteran benefits, then labor mightily at his little portable typewriter, banging out the data on the forms in a quick hunt-and-peck typing style. When the bonus bill was approved, hundreds of forms had to be filled out for the veteran applicants, and Dad worked tirelessly at that mission. When we would go to bed, he would be in his little office in the music room working over the Veterans Administration forms. When we got up in the morning he would be long gone and working at the gas plant. Many of the veterans were severely disabled, and several had been gassed in the French trenches of the Great War. They were thin, breathed with difficulty, wheezed and gasped for breath. Dad would introduce me to them, but I would quickly leave. It was too difficult watching them fight for breath.

Tramps, or hobos, were the norm. Usually men, or boys, they would stop by the house and ask for a meal. My mother never turned anyone away. There was always something in the icebox or refrigerator or on the stove that could be dished up for someone who was hungry. The men would usually eat their meal sitting on the steps of the back porch, and when finished would ask if there was anything they could do in exchange for the meal.

"Sometimes I would get the back yard raked 10 times a day, because I always thought it was the proper thing to do-to offer someone work for feeding them," Mom said.

Poverty wasn't new to my father. When his father abandoned him and Grandma King, life was very hard for them. Dad recalled living on a houseboat on the Black River in Port Huron. It was a shack on a raft really, not like the fancy, upscale craft moored in the affluent marina on the Black River now. Dad only went to the sixth grade, left school and he and Grandma King worked to support themselves. Grandma King developed a good reputation as a baker and cook, and they ended up one time at a resort at Island Lake, Michigan, where they worked for several years. Dad served as a bellboy and porter.

"I can remember days when all I had to eat were stale doughnuts Mother would bring home from work," Dad said.

Times were tough in the early 1930s, not only for the Okies, Arkies, Texans and Jayhawkers from the Dust Bowl, but for some of our family. The folks had heard from my Grandpa, Nelson George King, in Port Huron. My Dad called him "Old Nels."

"Everything about my father was backwards," my Dad said. "Even his name. He was named after Horatio Nelson, the English admiral and hero. His folks got his name wrong."

Grandpa King had been out of work for a long time, was getting old, and his health wasn't all that good. I had heard that my folks, Uncle Frank and Uncle Jim all pitched in to buy him a ticket west. I think that he spent a little time down in Santa Monica with Uncle Frank and Uncle Jim, then he came to Beaumont. Grandpa King took over the little house in our back yard. Dad and Grandpa King got along okay, but there wasn't any affection between them. My mother and Grandpa King hated each other. Mom thought that he should be helping with some of the household chores, but Grandpa King would not touch a broom, mop, the carpet sweeper or the washing machine. Those were women's tools, and he would "be damned if I will do women's work!" I think that the resentment my mother had for Grandpa King was more than his refusal to work around the house. Mom hated what he had done emotionally to Dad-the abandonment and the booze. My mother never forgot. If you did something bad to her, or her loved ones, God help you. You could never get back in her good graces.

Grandpa King had worked in the shipyards at Port Huron all of his life. When asked what his father did for a living, my Dad would say, "He was a ship builder."

"Ship builder, Hell!" Uncle Frank laughed, "He was a boat corker."

A "boat corker" was a shipyard worker who would caulk the seams between the planking and decks on the lake steamers. The caulkers would use a chisel-type tool and a maul to pound the caulking material into the seams to keep the water out.

I got along great with Grandpa King. He was a great storyteller, and he would whittle out boats from soft, white pine for Pete and me. He had a great eye for the shape and scale of a boat hull. Pete and I would dig holes and canals in the back yard, fill them with water, and sail the boats that Grandpa King made for us. We didn't have any brooks, creeks, rivers or lakes nearby, so we made our own.

The ditches and holes for the model boats were one more thing for Mom to get mad about in her stormy relationship with Grandpa King. But what really got her angry was the time he was spending down at Ray's Place. From tales I heard, I guess he frequently would come in at night, his scuppers awash in beer, and stagger into the little house. My mother, with her elephant memory for resentments, wasn't quiet on voicing all of Grandpa King's shortcomings to him. So Grandpa King's stay with us ended when he scraped enough money together to go back to Michigan. He said that he missed all of his old friends and the place where he had lived all his life. My younger brother Tony said that he can remember Mom getting mad at Grandpa King when he came home drunk one day, chasing him out of the house, taking up the garden hose, and spraying the old man with water. She thought it would sober him up, but it only hastened his return to Port Huron.

In June 1937 Dad received a call from back east saying that Grandpa King had died.

In 1985 my wife, Carma, and I made a train journey from Vancouver, B.C., to Montreal, Quebec, and back. On the return trip we stopped for a visit in Port Huron. We went to the cemetery looking for Grandpa King's grave, but couldn't find it. The cemetery manager took us to the gravesite marked with a round, brass, numbered tag. Carma and I ordered a gravestone, and Grandpa King no longer lies in an unmarked grave. The irony of Grandpa King's death from alcoholism, the date and the circumstances made me sad. It was in June of 1935 that two drunks trying to sober up in Akron, Ohio, founded Alcoholics Anonymous. I wonder if my Grandpa King would have made it in such a program. He was nice to me, gave me much, and I loved him.

The first death in the family that I remember was when we were living on 51st Place. My Grandma Smith's brother's wife, Aunt Ola, had died and we went to the funeral. All I remember was all of these grown-up people crying like babies. Then there was seeing the dog being killed by the train. Next came serving as an altar boy. When I was about 10 years old I began serving at mass on Sundays. One day, the priest assigned to our church from St. Boniface Indian School, Father Arthur, came by the house and wanted me to go with him to give the last rites to a parishioner who was dying. He brought cassock and surplice for me to wear, and he put on vestments, too. We went to the house where the sick person was quietly lying in bed, surrounded by lit candles. There wasn't any other person there, just the man in the bed. Father Arthur gave me a response card and I followed him in the rite that was said in Latin. I kept sneaking peeks at the man in the bed. I could tell he was breathing, but that was all. Father anointed him and then we said some more prayers. When we were back in the car, Father told me that the man was very sick, and they didn't expect him to live through the night. The man looked as if he were already dead. That night in bed after saying my prayers, I felt guilty. I felt sorrier for the poor dog in agony when his legs were cut off than for the poor man dying alone in bed.

Becoming an altar boy in the Catholic Church was sort of a rite of passage. Men made comments such as, "Are you sneaking into the altar wine, Frankie?" "Do you get to finish off the wine when the priest is through?"

and so on. It became tiresome, because I didn't swipe the wine. I had no taste for it then. But I did have a taste for beer.

My Dad, like most of his friends, made home-brewed beer and cherry wine. Beaumont had many cherry orchards around town. Almost every lot in town had a cherry tree or two, along with apricots and almonds. The peaches, pears and apples were grown at higher altitudes in nearby Cherry Valley and Oak Glen on the foothills of San Gorgonio. Dad would serve his home brew to his friends and family in one-pound coffee cans. They would hold about a pint of beer. Early on I discovered that there was beer left over in the cups. Being the nice, helpful lad that I was, I would volunteer clean up after the beer drinking sessions. Some of the cans still had an inch or two of brew left by the drinkers. I would sneak the cans to kitchen, quickly gulp the remaining beer, and get a nice little buzz on. I don't think my folks suspected a thing. But swipe the sacramental wine? Never! I didn't want to end up in blazing hell. Later on I developed a taste for the fine, sweet cherry wine Dad made. When I was in high school, I used to run home for lunch. Dad always kept a jug of cherry wine under the kitchen sink. I would take a couple of big mouthfuls, gulp it down, and run back to school, and have a great buzz on for the first period of the afternoon. But steal sacramental wine? Never!

Despite his wine and beer making activities, my Dad was a light drinker.

"I know what the stuff can do to you, after seeing my father and his problem," he said. "I like the stuff too much, so I have to be very careful of how much I drink."

Grandpa Smith was a great drinker, too. He had a shot of whiskey and a raw egg every morning, but I never saw him get drunk, or even tipsy. When I was about 12 years old he came down with pneumonia and was very sick. This followed a time when my Grandma Smith had been run over by a car in Monrovia. She spent a long time in the hospital recuperating, and then Grandpa fell ill. The doctors said Grandpa should go to the desert to recover, and get out of the damp area and air contamination in the Los Angeles Basin. The grandparents ended up in 1000 Palms down by Salton Sea. When Grandpa got sick in Monrovia he promised Grandma that he would become a Catholic if he got better. She couldn't take his word for it, so she brought Monsignor Moclare over from the church and had him witness Grandpa's promise. After a lengthy stay in the desert, Grandpa got well, went back to Monrovia, opened the shoe shop again, and life resumed it normal pattern. Except Grandma didn't forget Grandpa's conversion oath. About six months after his recuperation, the whole family came up to Beaumont for a weekend. Grandma, my mother, and Lada ganged up on me before church. They warned: "If you see something unusual at mass today, don't do anything drastic! O.K?" I was a little puzzled, but didn't think anything of it until just before mass started. My aunt knocked at the outside door of the sacristy and asked for me. She said Grandpa had been baptized and was making his first communion that day. Lada said she warned me because she didn't want me shouting at the priest not to give my Grandpa communion because he wasn't a Catholic. So Grandpa Smith, the man who I admired so much because he could swear for five minutes straight without using the same cuss word twice, became a rosary-carrying, novena-saying Catholic, but he would still get mad and swear mightily.

It was about this time that my folks decided that Pete and I needed good Catholic teaching. We had been getting a great education at Wellwood Grammar School, but when my folks made up their mind about something religious, particularly my mother, they couldn't be swayed. So Pete and I began daily classes seven miles away at St. Boniface Indian School. I was in the sixth grade. Everyday Mr. Calmus would drive us over and pick us up. Two families went in on the deal, the Calmuses and us. My classmate, Jack Calmus and I were the oldest; then there was Pete and the younger Calmus kids.

Life that first week was hard at St. Boniface. I had a fight almost every day. Jack wasn't very combative, and Pete was a lot smaller than I, so when anyone would get picked on by the resident kids, it would be up to me to fight. The residents, from the first to eighth grade, were either orphans, half-orphans or kids from broken homes. Predominantly mixed race children from Native American tribes in Arizona, New Mexico, Nevada and California, the blood of all races was represented. Most were from reservations, but there was a sprinkling of kids from the urban areas in California and Arizona. They were tough kids, battered by life, but I made some great friends. They had to test you, and if you faced up to it, regardless if you won or lost, they would accept you.

Our teacher was Sister Thomas Aquinas, she who loved the St. Louis Cardinals, hated sloth and dirt, and loved Jesus. She made my life hell for the first part of the sixth grade. But learn I did. She would not tolerate talking, horsing around, or goofing off when we were supposed to be studying. The only exception was when the Cardinals played in the World Series. She had a radio moved into our classroom. We listened during class time, but had to do our assignments afterwards. Sister Thomas thought big. She wouldn't use a ruler on you. Like my mother, she had a weight problem. She carried a yardstick. She could reach further with it, and quickly nail us youngsters with ease.

Our school day started at 8 a.m. and we had classes until noon. Then we all went to the big school dining room where we had lunch. The priests and sisters ate with us. After lunch we day students returned to the classroom to study until 2 p.m. when the parents would come to pick us up. The resident students had to work. And work they did, in the fields cultivating produce that was used in the dining hall and the dairy that provided milk, cottage cheese, ice cream and meat for the table. The resident kids worked hard. They had to clean up after themselves, make their own beds in the dormitories, do their school studies, and work at assigned tasks. The boys did all of the farm work and the girls worked in the kitchen, laundry and housekeeping. I felt guilt deep inside. I was in the classroom studying while they had to work outside in the hot sun. The inequality made an impression on me that has stayed with me all my life.

I hated math. My grades in arithmetic were average, but I had to work hard to get them. When Sister Thomas began forcing me to learn more about arithmetic fundamentals, life got worse. She was firm, but patient, and gradually I began to improve. Jack Calmus always did well in math. After one semester at St. Boniface the financial drain of transportation made our folks put us back in public school. That second semester of my 6th grade was great. I made an A in arithmetic, the only one I made in mathematics in all my school years. All due to the tyrannical, benevolent teaching of Sister Thomas.

Every year St. Boniface would hold its barbecue and fiesta. I think that it was the major fundraising activity that the priests and nuns sponsored. Hundreds of loyal patrons would drive up from the Los Angeles area for the event. The big meal, with beef from a pit barbecue, was the center-piece of the event. Chief Morongo from the nearby Morongo Indian Reservation was the head chef. He and his workers would dig a big pit, build a fire in it, and throw in great big rocks. After the rocks heated through, huge chunks of a whole beef, wrapped in burlap, were put in the pit. Then it was covered with earth and left to cook. After cooking all night, the beef would be ready for serving at noon on fiesta day. There was a lot going on beside the dinner. Mexican dancers and mariachis per-formed, carnival booths offered games, arts and crafts. I loved the music and the dancers. We had a lot of fiestas when I was growing up, and the Mexican dancers and musicians were always on the program. Grandpa and Grandma Smith, Lada and Uncle Louie usually visited from "down below" just so they could go to the St. Boniface barbecue.

My Grandpa Smith always had a car, and he successfully passed them on to my Dad. I think Dad was quietly resentful of that. He got the cars and had to pay a good price for them after Grandpa had just about ruined them. I remember we had the old Maxwell for a spell; then Dad, heretic that he was, went outside the family and bought a '26 Chevy roadster. Mom trashed it when she drove it through the garage on 88th Street. She never did learn to drive. She didn't drive; she aimed. Just before I went to

St. Boniface Dad bought Grandpa's Essex sedan. It was fine-looking automobile, with glass flower holders by the sides of the rear seat. Dad called the Essex "the Ass-ache." Mother tried to learn how to drive the Ass-ache, to no avail. After going with her on one trip from home to the gas plant to take Dad's dinner to him, I refused to ride with her any more. The Ass-ache was at the mechanic's being fixed more than it was parked in our garage. Then Grandpa Smith entered his Studebaker phase. He kept buying Studebakers until they went out of business. But Dad had learned his lesson. We never had a Studebaker.

No car? No problem. For most of the period in my youth we did not have a car. We walked everywhere. My Mother would even walk the one mile to mass on Sunday mornings. Most of the time we had a ride on Sundays. Having no car did not slow down my father when it came to community involvement. After only one term as a city councilman he decided not to run again. Some of the movers and shakers in town did not like my father's politics and they complained to his employer, the Southern California Gas Company. Dad said that his boss passed off the complaints, and said that as long as the council position did not interfere with his job, they had no problem with it.

J. Drew Funk, the leading real estate broker in town, was Dad's arch foe. They clashed over many issues confronting the community. Dad was Democrat, J. Drew Republican. We suspected that J. Drew was behind the effort to remove Dad from office. So Pete, Tony and I called a family war council. In our games J. Drew Funk became the hated enemy. Tony, who was just learning to talk, picked up on it. He would take a stick, holler "J. Drew Funk!" and slash at any object within his reach. One problem. His speech wasn't too clear, and he couldn't pronounce the "n." This was not a problem until Mom hosted a gathering of women for some sort of a social. They heard Tony in the bedroom beating on the bed with his stick and screaming, "J. Drew Fu'k, J. Drew Fu'k!"

Poor J. Drew was the target of many in Beaumont. His office downtown on the main street was a little box of a building. It was square, only one or two rooms, with a flat roof. One morning after Halloween everybody in town was laughing at the sight of J. Drew Funk's real estate office. Some creative pranksters had taken an old horse-drawn buggy apart, lifted it up to the roof, and re-assembled it there. The buggy sat on the top of the building for about a week, before J. Drew could hire someone to take it down. That insult was compounded the next year. The pranksters struck again the next Halloween when they installed an outdoor privy on top of J. Draw's office. The privy came down the next day.

Politics was always a big thing in our family. My first memory of politics came in 1928 when Al Smith and Herbert Hoover were running for president. Al Smith, the Democrat and a Catholic, lost. We were really cheering for old Al who, of course, lost the election. We were convinced that Smith lost because he was Catholic. My Dad was a moderate Democrat, and my Mom said she was a Democrat, until she became a Republican for Wilkie. The folks supported FDR in his efforts to rebuild the country and shore up its economic system, after the hated Herbert Hoover was defeated. Mother fell away from the fold when she supported Wendell Willie when he ran against Roosevelt. Dad grumbled about Mom canceling his vote. Grandma Smith was non-political, but Grandpa Smith was liberal with a vengeance. He hated what happened to the middle and lower classes during the Depression.

"To Hell with the banks, insurance companies and railroads!" he would shout whenever we began any political discussion. He was a devotee of odd-ball political-economic schemes-including the Townsend Plan and the Ham and Eggers-that would improve the lot of the working man

The financial houses had foreclosed on thousands of farmers in those bleak times, and Grandpa never forgot that. He even voted for Socialist candidate Norman Thomas once. Grandpa did not like the disparity between the haves and the have-nots. He maintained that for every $1 million made by a wealthy person, over 1,000 people became destitute. He believed that there was a finite limit to wealth, and that it had to be shared fairly. I call it the Frank Smith economic theory. My grandfather was a small businessman all of his life. He worked until he was in his late 80s. He finished his work career doing what he learned as a boy, a saddle and harness maker at Santa Anita and Hollywood Park tracks repairing saddles, bridles, harnesses, and leather jockey equipment. Grandpa owned and operated several saddle and harness shops, shoe sales and repair businesses. He maintained that people should be paid for their efforts and hard work, but there should be a limit on how much wealth an individual or company could acquire. He believed that no one should go to bed hungry, should not be denied medical care, and everyone should have the same opportunities. I don't think that he was a full-blown socialist, but he strongly believed in a controlled capitalistic society.

I grew up thinking that all good Catholics drank and smoked, voted Democrat, that we came from Ireland, France, Germany, and Mexico. If you went to college it was Notre Dame. Only Protestants were dry, voted Republican and went to USC.

Chapter 4

The Ranch

Business was in the grip of the Depression so Grandpa Smith decided to sell his shop and move to Beaumont. He and Grandma bought a 13-acre cherry orchard that was a mile west of town on the road through Jackrabbit Trail to the highway andRiverside. Later U.S. Highway 90 was punched through the hills and ran right in front of the grandfolks' place, grandly described as "The Ranch." Grandpa bought a team of horses, Charlie and Nellie, a cow, and a couple hundred barred rock chickens. The ranch did pretty well for a few years, producing great Tartarian, Bing and Royal Anne cherries. The Japanese fruit beetle infestation eventually killed the grove of cherry trees, and they were yanked out. The 13 acres was then turned into an alfalfa field. Grandpa had plenty of water. The well went down 1,500 feet and a huge Pomona lift pump could bring up 300 gallons of water a minute to a wood tank about 20 feet above the pump house. The pump was driven by a '26 Studebaker engine that drove a wheel and belt about 20 feet long to the pump. On the outside there was a gauge, actuated by an inside float, that showed how much water was in the 500-gallon tank. Pete, Tony and I liked to stand underneath the tower in the summer and get showered by the water seeping from the tank as it was being filled.

Grandpa Smith had a running feud with the cow, Old Bess. Grandpa said she was the Old Bitch. Grandma would scream in German at Grandpa and tell him to mind his language in front of us kids. Old Bess had Grandpa's number. Grandpa hated milking because Old Bess would smack him along side of the head with the end of her manure laden tail, kick the bucket over, or even worse, lift her back leg and step into the bucket of milk. One day she stepped in the bucket and Grandpa lost his temper. He grabbed the pitchfork and jabbed her hard in the rear. Bess did not take this kindly. She kicked out with both hind feet and hit the shaft of the pitchfork that went flying out of Grandpa's hands and stuck in the stack of baled hay behind him. Grandpa went white, saying not a word, turned and stomped out of the barn. I learned to milk and took over the twice-a-day chore when I was staying at the ranch. Both Old Bess and Grandpa Smith appreciated my visits.

Summer was a great time. And it would get hot! We were on the edge of the Colorado desert and the temperatures would climb above 100 degrees during most summer days. We discovered the joys of exploring and swimming. A favorite haunt of Beaumont youngsters was Owl's Bank. It was a hard sand formation south of town. The bank had holes high on the cliff-like formation. Swallows and owls nested there. We would dig into the sand at the bottom and make caves. It is a wonder none of them caved in and buried us. I shudder to think what could have happened. On these trips afield, we were always accompanied by Bozo, our dog. Bozo was a brindle, mixed breed with a white collar, a white tip on his tail and a white strip between his eyes. He looked a lot like some of the pit bulls you see today, but he was a gentle, tolerant pet. Except with Father Arthur. Father Arthur would park at the side of the house, get out of his car, and come flapping into the yard with his big brown robe. He would head straight for Bozo, flapping his skirts at him. Bozo would go crazy snapping at Father, barking and the hair rising on his back. Sometimes Bozo would catch the robe and Father would swing the dog around in a circle laughing like crazy, then dash into the house and slam the door before Bozo really got him. Father Arthur thought it great sport. Bozo thought it was a fight. We-Pete, Tony and I-thought Father Arthur was crazy.

The priests that we had following Father Arthur-Father Rupert and Father Phillip-paid for Father Arthur's playfulness with Bozo. Bozo wouldn't let a brown robe into the yard. They had to call ahead, and we would shut Bozo up in the cellar until they had left.

Bozo was our companion and champion. If Mom or Dad started to come at us in anger, threatening to punish us for something we had done, Bozo would quietly growl at them. I think he prevented our being punished at times.

Early every morning Dad would walk the mile or so, down across the tracks, to the gas plant. The huge tank, the holder, was the tallest structure in east Riverside County. When Dad made his morning walk to work, Bozo would go with him. Dad had to walk right next to the hobo jungle at the railroad tracks, and Bozo was good protection for him. Dad was confronted a few times, but with his big stick and Bozo he managed to stay out of trouble. Pete loved going down to the hobo jungle, and he made friends with some of the tramps there. At one time a couple of the hobos were building a shelter and a table out of some scrap wood. They complained that they didn't have any tools to work with so they could do a good job. Pete volunteered Dad's tools. So when Dad went looking for his hammer it wasn't there. He asked us where it was and Pete told him he lent his tools to some tramps to build a house. When Dad came down, he hollered at Pete to get his tools back. So Pete went down and asked the hobos if they were through with the tools, because his father wanted to use them. They were, Pete brought the tools home, and no one was more surprised than Dad to see them returned.

Neither Mom nor Dad spanked us very much. I can only remember one spanking that I got from my Dad, but Mom would use the flyswatter handle when we tried her patience too far. I remember one time when Mom was going to punish Pete for a misdeed, and she chased him through the house. Pete ran into our bedroom and dove under the bed. Mom got down on her hands and was striking at Pete with the flyswatter. Pete, like a monkey, had grasped the springs with his fingers and toes, and lifted himself up. Every time Mom would swipe at him, Pete would lift himself up. She never did get a clean hit on him. She gave up, promising that Pete would have to deal with Dad when he got home from work. The only spanking I remember was because Mom insisted that Dad punish me after some crazy thing I had done. I remembered a great suggestion made in one of the comic strips, "The Katzenjammer Kids." When the Captain was to spank the kids, the boys slipped a book or a pie plate into their pants.

I tried the same thing, but Dad read the same comic strip. I got my spanking anyway.

I think we three boys got a great liberal education. Dad would buy the out-of-state Sunday newspapers on Saturday night and bring them home. The Sunday editions of the *New York Post* and the *New York Mirror* tabloids were strewn about the living room floor as we read the news, features and comic strips. We loved those papers, the great comics, columnists and cartoonists. My favorite was Mark Hellinger and Damon Runyon and the side-splitting cartoons that went with their pieces. Great comic strips whetted our reading appetite-The Katzenjammer Kids, Mutt and Jeff, Rube Goldberg, Betty Boop, The Toonerville Trolley, Brenda Starr, Tarzan, Smilin' Jack and others. Then on Sunday morning we would get the *Los Angeles Times* and the *Examiner*. Reading was a big part of our lives. Mom started reading to us when we were very little. The two books I remember were *Black Beauty*, the story about the horse in England that was made into a contemporary motion picture, and *Beautiful Joe*, a story about a dog. Pete cried all of the way through *Beautiful Joe*. Once when I was home with one of the childhood illnesses, I think it was chicken pox,

Mom read "Hans Brinker and His Silver Skates" to me while I was sick in bed. Then she fixed me pea soup with cheese in it, and crackers. I remember there was something about pea soup in "Hans Brinker." Whenever she made pea soup she would always recite:

"Pea soup and johnny cake

"Make the Dutchman's belly ache."

We suffered all of the childhood illnesses prevalent at that time: chicken pox, measles, mumps and whooping cough. We got through all of them fine, except for one time when Pete really got sick. He came down with what was diagnosed as poliomyelitis, what was then called infantile paralysis, the same disease that struck Franklin Delano Roosevelt, and left him crippled. We were quarantined for two weeks. For a time it was very serious. Pete suffered some temporary paralysis on one side of his body. It took him years to recover the full use of some of his muscles. Mother and Dad massaged him, and did what they could, but treatment then was limited. It wasn't until 30 years later that a vaccine was developed and the disease effectively eliminated in the United State.

Pete was also laid out by a serious accident when he was a little boy. He was playing down at Bill and Margaret Duncan's house with Billy and Catherine Fay. They were jumping on sort of a hobby horse, made out of an old automobile spring buried in the ground. The spring had a handle on the end. The kids would straddle the spring, sit on the handle, and bounce up and down pretending that they were riding a bucking bronco. Pete had ended his ride, was getting off and somehow the spring was depressed and released suddenly. The handle shot up and ripped a terrible gash on the inside of one leg. I don't remember how he was rescued, but he ended up having about 60 stitches taken to close the wound. He was laid up the better part of one summer recuperating from the accident. Mom and Dad would read to him to keep him from getting bored during his recovery. Pete did recover from the effects of polio and his accident, and he led an active, energetic life with us.

Cherries were an important part of Beaumont culture. The orchards around town grew wonderful fruit, and every year there would be a Cherry Festival in early June, right after school let out for the summer. Cherry Festival time was wonderful. When we lived there it was really promoted by Guy Bogart, a developer who was touting to the world the healthful benefits of Beaumont's climate. There was even a Bogart Bowl established up in Cherry Valley. Bogart was great at planting pictures of girls in bathing suits up on ladders picking cherries. His efforts resulted in photos in main national magazines, including *Life*. One of his brainstorms was having a Cherry Festival royalty contest. For many years a Cherry King and Queen were chosen. Then he had the bright idea to have some Cherry Kids. Guess who had to run for that? Anyway, a little girl, I think it was Gretchen Coy, and I were chosen as Cherry Kids. Our families were proud of our pictures that ran in *The Los Angeles Times* publicizing the Cherry Festival. They great thing was that I got in free for all the rides at the carnival. I got on the Ferris wheel while I had to go to the bathroom. The operator thought he was doing me a great favor by giving me a long ride. My bladder was about to burst. I managed to hold it until the ride's end, but I barely made it the toilet before I embarrassed Guy Bogart and my town.

When the gypsies and medicine shows came to town, it was a chance to discover something new. I think that the 1930s saw the end of the traveling medicine shows. I can remember one that parked in a vacant lot down near Fierro's. It wasn't like the old horse-drawn wagon show; this one was enclosed in a truck and trailer. The trailer converted into a stage. The medicine show folks played different instruments, sang and danced and did some magic. My interest was sharply increased when the two girls, slightly older than I, appeared in scanty costumes and danced sexily on the stage. Then the principal guy brought out the bottles of medicine that were supposed to cure all kinds of ailments. I can remember being chosen to go up on the stage to help out with one of the magic tricks. The stunt involved a lot of coins and pie plates. The man would put the coins on the pie plates, shuffle them around and the coins would disappear. Then he would empty the pie plate by holding it over my cupped hands and the coins would miraculously pour into my hand. I spotted the trick, but didn't say anything. The man had hidden the coins between the pie plates, and the money had not really disappeared. 1 was disappointed, and felt dirty, because I was part of an act that deceived my friends and neighbors.

We were remarkably free of serious accidents considering all of the trouble we got into when playing at Owl's Bank, in the uppermost branches of a eucalyptus tree, sneaking into the carnival, or swimming at Wildwood Plunge. Every chance we got during the summer time we would hitchhike the five or six miles down to Calimesa to go swimming. Wildwood Plunge was a small pool, but it was the place where most Beaumont kids learned how to swim. I think it cost a nickel or dime to go swimming at Wildwood. Both Pete and I taught ourselves how to swim at that pool. We did it by watching the older kids who could float, swim and dive. Later it was sheer heaven when we would go on a special swimming party with our schools, the church or Scouts to the big municipal swimming pool in Redlands, 14 miles west of Beaumont.

About the time I was learning how to swim I joined the Boy Scouts. Harold "Had" Simpson was the scoutmaster, and a good friend of Dad's. They worked together at the gas company. I became a Tenderfoot in the Scouts when I was 12 years old and quickly went up through the ranks to First Class. Then I started working merit badges and eventually ended up with enough to make me Life Scout, a patrol leader, then Junior Assistant Scoutmaster. One of the merit badges had to do with electronics and radio, and I had to learn elementary Morse code. Had Simpson had a bunch of radio gear in his living room that he experimented with, and he taught us Morse code. I thought he was a magician. He could do all sorts of things with electricity, wires and electrical components. It wasn't until WWII when I was in the Marine Corps and sent to airborne radio operators school that I really learned Morse code and tried to grasp elementary electronics theory.

Had Simpson owned a 1937 Ford V-8, 60-horsepower sedan. He rigged up a device that he could turn on that would give a painful electric shock to any person daring to lay a hand on the nice blue finish of his new car. My dad bought that car from him when I was in high school. It was the first car my dad owned that had not been owned first by Grandpa Smith. Grandpa Smith scoffed at the deal.

"Fords are a heap of junk," he said. "Look at who made them."

Grandpa hated Henry Ford, who he thought of as a latter-day robber baron who stomped on the working man.

My most intense memories of being a Scout were hiking up to Snow Creek near Palm Springs and camping at Camp Emerson up at Idylwild in the San Jacinto Mountains. When we got up to Snow Creek I thought it was the most beautiful sight in the world-fresh, sparkling water cascading over the rocky creek bed with green foliage lining the bank. I was a dry land kid and that was the first time I had ever seen running water in a stream. We had plenty of dry washes, dry creek and riverbeds all over the place, but running water in a stream? I have never forgotten that first sight of a free-flowing stream. Up at Camp Emerson we went on a 12-mile hike that took us up to the summit of Tahquitz Peak, a mountaintop in the San Jacinto range. The views of the valleys below, looking down on the towns of Beaumont, Banning and Palm Springs have left an impression on my memory.

Life was pretty stable for us in Beaumont at that time. Dad's job provided us with all that we really needed. With his salary of $127.50 a month he had one of the best jobs in town. I remember when a new friend moved to town, David Ratke. His father was the purchasing agent for Wenzel and Hennock, the company that was drilling a tunnel through the San Jacinto foothills for the Colorado River aqueduct project. David's Dad made $200 a month, and they were rich. They had two cars, a Graham and supercharged, Auburn boat-tailed roadster, a real classy car. There were a lot of new faces in town when that project hired their crews, and it gave a boost to the town's economy. My folks were convinced that they could make a little money by renting our house in town, and moving out to the ranch to live with Grandpa and Grandma Smith.

The plan was for us to live in a small house across the lane from the grandparents' bigger house. So we left all our stuff in the place on Wellwood, we rented it furnished, and set up housekeeping in the tiny place on the ranch. We had no indoor plumbing. That meant that we had to use the outhouse out by the barn. Mom hated that outhouse. She was forever trying things to alleviate the stench. Lysol, other disinfectants, even perfume. Nothing worked. We were at the ranch for most of one year.

Pete and I had to take the bus to school from the ranch. I don't think Tony had started school yet. We had regular farm chores we had to do. One of the hated duties was pruning time in January and February. Grandpa trimmed back the branches of his cherry trees, and then we would gather them up and put them in a big pile behind the barn. We would hitch up Charlie and Nellie to a two-wheeled cart to haul the trimmings to the pile. I thought we were going to burn that pile. Grandpa had other ideas. It was up to Pete and me to cut all of those little bitty branches into firewood lengths. Grandma had both gas and wood-fired stoves in her kitchen. I think that by the time we moved back into town the pile had just about disappeared. The firewood pile was our torture rack. That and cleaning out the chicken coop. We were plagued by the chicken coops at the ranch and at our house in town.

Grandpa Smith treated his animals well. He was very particular about the horses' care. They had to be groomed every day, fed in the mornings and evening, and fresh water trickled into their tank continuously. I used to love to drive that team. Grandpa taught me how to harness them up and how to drive them. I learned how to ride horseback by myself, including how to fall off without getting hurt. One day, after tedious hours of picking up the pruned cherry wood, loading it in the wagon, and hauling it to the pile, I had an inspiration. Why not play Ben Hur? Grandpa had warned me about running the horses.

"Charlie and Nellie are work horses, not pleasure horses. They were bred to work, not run," he said. "Do not run them."

That warning was in the back of my mind, but Grandpa wasn't there. He had gone into town to buy stuff a short time before, and he would be gone for over an hour. I trotted the team back up to the far end of the orchard, stood up in the bed of the wagon, turned around, and prepared to race. I could hear the roar of the crowd in the Coliseum as the other chariots gained on me. I took the long ends of the reins, whacked Charlie and Nellie on the rumps, and we were away. I stood in the front of the two-wheeled wagon, the reins gripped tightly in my hands, and we rounded the north part of the orchard into the lane down to the barn. The old black Studebaker turned in from the highway when I pulled up to the stable. The horses, breathing heavily and sweating, rattled their harnesses like they wanted to take off again. I stood, shaking worse that the horses, expecting Grandpa to really tear into me. He got out of the car, walked over to the horses, stared hard into my eyes and didn't say a word. Grandpa walked into the stable, got the curry comb, brushes and a burlap sack, threw them at me and stomped into the house. I carefully took the harnesses and bridles off Charlie and Nellie, and led them out to the corral to walk and cool off. Then I brushed and curried them down. That hard-eyed glare from Grandpa was worse than any spanking I ever had.

When Grandpa was in a good mood he would let us ride Charlie and Nellie and we would proudly bounce along on their broad hard backs. Of course we rode bareback. Grandpa wasn't about to buy saddles. We had to use the work bridles with the blinders, and reins that were about 20 feet long. We would coil the reins up like lassos so the long leather straps would not drag on the ground. Riding a horse bareback with blinders into town wasn't the image that I wanted to project to my friends, particularly girls. I tried to get Grandpa to take the blinders off the bridles. He asked me why, and I told him how rustic we looked riding bareback with the blinders on the bridles. He muttered swear words under his breath, and walked off shaking his head.

We didn't have a cream separator, so Grandma Smith would take some of the milk and put it in big flat pans. After a while she would skim the cream off the top so she could make butter with it. The skimmed milk that was left over was mixed with grains and fed to the chickens. Grandma also made cottage cheese from the milk. She had a hand-cranked churn that we used to make butter. The churn apparatus screwed onto the top of a gallon-size glass jar. You would turn the crank and the paddles in the jar would go around and churn the milk. Grandma and Mom always had something they were making to use up the butter and milk-so we had a great supply of cookies, cakes and breads.

My Dad had bought an old Iver Johnson, single-barrel, 16-guage shotgun. The ejection lever had broken off, but Dad had made a new one out of some scrap metal, and it worked fine. Sometimes he would go rabbit hunting with his friends, but most of the time the shotgun sat unused in the corner of a closet. I talked my Dad into letting me have the gun. One night, when Mom and Dad were across the lane at Grandpa and Grandma's playing cards, I took up the shotgun to inspect it. I had cleaned it earlier in the day. Pete was asleep on the couch, and Tony was in his bed. I carefully inspected the shotgun, raised it up, aimed for the wall over the couch, and pulled the trigger. Blam! I had blown a hole about three inches wide through the wall. Pete and Tony didn't wake up, and I dashed out of the house, the shotgun still in my hand. The folks ran out to the lane, all white as sheets. I told them what happened. They were grateful that I had not shot one of my brothers. I told them I cleaned the gun earlier in the afternoon, and put it away, unloaded, in the corner. I maintained that I had not put a charge in the chamber. Pete insists that he did not even touch the gun, so he couldn't have placed a shell in it. Tony was too young to remember the incident. Some spy must have crept into our house, maybe a Republican, and loaded the gun? Dad didn't buy that argument. He and Grandpa lectured me at length on gun safety.

The shotgun became my daily companion as I went rabbit hunting down in the dry washes behind the ranch leading down to San Timoteo

Canyon. I became Daniel Boone, Davy Crocket, Buffalo Bill or an Indian scout. We had plenty of birds around the place including California quail and mourning doves. The day I knocked down my first dove was memorable. I brought it home to Grandma. She plucked it and cleaned it, then cooked it for me-praising me for being the grand hunter.

A big treat for Pete, Tony and I would be a trip for the day down to Haskell's Ranch, a 3,000-acre spread down in San Timoteo Canyon. Jim Haskell was a schoolmate, and all of his family, grandfolks, uncle and aunt, cousins and parents lived on the ranch. The Haskells were also parishioners at San Gorgonio. Jim would take us out to the ranch yard and we witnessed all sorts of new things. Our favorite activity was riding all of the farm animals: pigs, calves and horses. We had a pint-sized rodeo going all the time we were there. On one trip I saw how animals were butchered. They used a .22 pistol to shoot the pigs and steers in the head, then their throats would be cut to drain the blood out. The slaughtered pigs would be dunked in a great vat of hot water, then hauled up on a rack by their hind feet. The farm hands would then scrape the bristles off of them with scraping blades. Then the animals would be gutted and hung in a cold room.

I ran gagging from one scene. When the farm hands butchered a bull, and its throat was cut, one of the workers held a cup to catch the gushing blood. He raised the full cup and drank great gulps of it. I couldn't take it. Jim said the guy believed it would make him strong and potent like a bull. I was all in favor of potency, but I didn't want to drink bull's blood.

The Haskells had a complete dairy on the ranch, and our favorite treat was to get the paper cup of vanilla ice cream before going home. Nothing ever tasted better than that ice cream after a hard day of riding calves.

Chapter 5

Back home again

After moving back into our house on Wellwood Avenue, family life resumed its normal routine. Mom became much more happy, and she sang as she did her housework. She didn't have to use the perfumed privy at the ranch anymore. Her health was good, except for occasional times when she would go into coughing spasms. She was coughing up small traces of blood. The doctor again thought it might be tuberculosis, so she was ordered to undergo a full six months of bed rest. Dad set up a bed in the dining room for her. There was a lot of light coming in from the big windows, and it was a lot more cheery than the rather dark bedroom where Mom and Dad slept. My mother's day went something like this: she would take her pencil and pad and list the duties we were to do that day. Dad, Pete and I did most of the housework. Dad hired Juanita Fierro a few days during the week to help take care of Mom while he was at work, and Pete and I at school. Juanita would do the laundry, and ironing and some of the cooking, preparing a dinner that we would heat up after she left for home.

Again, and again, Mom would intone the litany, "I don't have any girls, so it is up to my boys to help out."

Mom would sit in her bed, like Catherine the Great, and dictate to us. She would tell us, step by step, how to use the vacuum cleaner, dusting procedures, and window washing hints. She had eyes like an eagle as far as her house was concerned. When I would use the vacuum cleaner and miss a few tiny pieces of white lint, she would store it in her memory until I was done.

"Go back there and pick up that *schnipsel*," she would say, pointing to something I could hardly see.

Schnipsel was one of those German words that peppered Mom's, Lada's and Grandma Smith's speech, expressions they learned from Great Grandma Whittliff.

This was the time I learned to cook. Mom would instruct Pete and me how to make the good solid entrees that were the standard in our town: meat loaf, macaroni and cheese and tuna casserole. I learned how to bake. My favorite was a red devil's food cake. I still haven't lost that touch, and now that I am retired I do all of the cooking in our house. So we learned to cook, wash and iron clothes and clean a house. I don't think Mom realized it then, but she was preparing us for the future. When I went into the Marine Corps in World War II, I made a nice little income ironing shirts and sewing on buttons, insignias and stripes for those who did not have those skills.

When Mom was in her invalid stage she did a lot of reading. That was not unusual. We all read a lot. On a typical winter evening before the good radio programs came on, and if Pete, Tony or I were not doing school work, we usually all had our noses in books. Mom would be reading her favorite novel by Faith Baldwin or Kathleen Norris, Dad had his poetry and biographies, and we three boys had own favorites, too. On Christmas Day 1936 Mom and Dad gave me *Minute Biographies*, by Samuel

Nisenson and Alfred Parker. The book, "intimate glimpses into the lives of 150 famous men and women," made history come alive for me. I read about Alexander the Great, King Arthur, Phineas T. Barnum, Napoleon, Bolivar, Luther Burbank, Arron Burr, Catherine the Great, and many more. Those short vignettes introduced me to the lives of people who made history, and their stories made them human. I think that book had much to do with me falling in love with the written word. I still have that book, tattered and ragged, but I treasure it.

Chapter 6

The Library

Good stories grabbed my attention. During the summer when I wasn't picking cherries, irrigating, baling hay, delivering papers or cleaning out the chicken coop I could be found at the Beaumont Public Library. We had a great librarian, Miss Helen Clapp. She presided over the checkout desk with iron-fisted authority, but would move mountains to get us books to read. After reading about lives of explorers in *Minute Biographies* I checked out travel books. I read about exotic, exciting places in the world. Then I became interested in the Edgar Rice Burroughs series about Tarzan, then moved on to adventure fiction. To a chosen few she would even give access to the restricted book section kept under lock and key.

One day in 1937, just before I started high school, I noticed a new book on the best sellers shelf. It was *Lust For Life*, by Irving Stone, the biography of Vincent Van Gogh. It hadn't been put on the restricted shelf yet, but it would be. I was enthralled and excited. The story was about the tumultuous life of the Dutch artist, his life in France, and relationships with Paul Gauguin, other artists, and the prostitute lover Rachel, "Le Pigeon," his "little pigeon." The explicit descriptions colors, emotions and sex really made sense to me and captured my interest. I was 13, and sex was the about the only thing that I could think of. I buried my face in the book, stumbled down the sidewalk to home, and continued reading. I never used a book mark, but would always remember the last page number I had read. The book was sitting on the dining room table, and my mother picked it up, opened it to page 385, and began reading:

"Rachel laughed loudly. She raised her glass to her lips. The joke struck her as funny again, and she giggled. A trickle of red wine spilled down her left breast, wound its way over the pigeon belly, and disappeared in the black triangle."

Mom screamed, slammed the book shut, and asked me why I was reading such filth? She started to cry, and said, "Just wait until your Dad gets home, I am going to let him take care of this."

I don't think she liked the part about "the black triangle."

Dad came home. Read the passage.

"You take this book back to the library, and I don't want to see anything like this in the house again," he raved.

I kept quiet. I didn't remind Dad that he had a stack of *Spicy Mystery*, *Spicy Adventure* and *Spicy Western* magazines hidden on the back porch. Dad used to buy those semi-erotic pulp magazines every month at DePeel's Drug Store. By today's standards those magazines are sissy stuff. The dialogues were sexy, but never explicit, and the line drawings revealed some bare breast and nipple, but never pubic hair.

So I took Vincent back to the library, and finished reading *Lust For Life*.

Sex, and the newly discovered, forever growing manhood, was giving me fits. I wanted to be a good boy, but the damn penis kept getting in the way. Early thoughts of becoming a priest vanished. I could more easily live on the moon that be celibate. The least little thing referring to sex would have our intense interest, even things that were not sexy. For instance: in school they would show us a movie about textile production, and we would find parts of that stale movie erotic. When the factory machines would show tools operating in a quick up and down motion-imitating what we thought was the copulating action-we would laugh so hard we would fall out of our chairs.

Life was an almost perpetual erection. Even church became painful. When I was serving mass, a good part of the time I was sort of hunched over. I didn't want my boner to stick out. All it would take would be to look a girl, spot cleavage while we were serving communion, or daydream in erotic fantasyland, and the pecker would rise. It had a mind of its own. I didn't worry about me, but I was afraid of what Mom, Grandma and Lada would think if they saw my cassock pushing out in front. One of the priests we had for a short time was Father Gerard. He was a German priest, with a very fair complexion, short and plump, with a bald head. A fringe of white hair ran around the sides of his head and the back. He would deliver very moralistic sermons, in both English and fractured Spanish, on modesty and behavior. The more excited he would get in decrying women's dress, the redder his face and head would get. He cried that women were wearing such low-cut dresses that even their scapulars could be seen. Scapulars were like fabric religious medals attached by brown, hairy cords that ran around your neck to your chest and back. The more he ranted the redder he got. I suspect Father Gerard suffered from the same affliction I had.

After I read *Lust For Life*, I started doing some research. Where do I find the great sexy books? I had heard that French authors were the best. They were always writing about illicit affairs, lovers and carnal things. So I started reading the short stories of Guy DeMaupassant. After my DeMaupassant phase I looked for more sex. So it was more French writers: Rabelais, Zola, Hugo, Balzac and Flaubert. My sex-driven reading was giving me a great literary education. When my life had progressed to the point that I was making a living writing, I had to admit that I became a writer because of my sex-obsessed youthful reading program.

During the *Lust for Life* incident Dad ran to his library to see if the book had been banned by the Church. The book was too new, I guess, because Dad couldn't find it listed. Dad was big on banned books. In my new-found independence I made it a point to read anything I could that was on the banned list. If my folks, teachers, priests or nuns said that I shouldn't read a certain book or article, I would do it. I don't think that I was doing it just to buck authority, but I wanted to find out why it was banned on my own. I wanted to decide for myself if it was a good or bad.

I think my attitude was fostered by the intellectual climate at home. When I was a kid I was included in discussions we would have at the dinner table about politics, current events and social issues. I learned how to develop ideas on my own and express them. Mom, Dad, Grandpa and Grandma Smith had created a problem child who was starting to question some precious family creeds.

Those *Spicy* pulp magazines got me into a fix with one of my classmates. I had smuggled a couple copies of them into my locker at high school. Tommy Coalson, David Ratke and I were on the steps leading from the hall in front of the music room. We slavered over the bare-bosomed drawings. Tommy told me not to hoard all the good stuff, and yanked the magazine out of my hand. The door burst open behind us and there was William Sewell, our esteemed principal.

"What have you got there behind your back, Thomas?"

"Nothing, Sir!"

"Give it to me."

Tommy handed over the magazine and old Bill Sewell turned red.

"I am ashamed of you, Thomas. You are a school leader, and someone the students look up to. Get to your classes!"

I don't know what Bill Sewell did with that *Spicy Adventure* magazine. Did he read it in secret like my father? I don't think that Dad missed the two magazines I sneaked out of his stash. If he did he never mentioned it.

Life in high school was much more exciting than grade school. I quickly became involved in many activities. My secret desire was to be a lineman on the football team. The only trouble was that I was only a little over five feet tall. After a big Sunday dinner I would weigh all of 115 pounds. Stuffing my desire, temporarily, to be a big, tough football hero, I became a cheerleader. Two of us, Nadine Julian and I, became the school yell leaders, an assignment we held with enthusiasm for three years.

Reading continued to be my favorite avocation, and I pursued the quest of more and more sexy books. Occasionally a rare gem, that had no sex in it, would sneak its way into my reading list. Dad always thought James Fenimore Cooper was a great author. He loved *The Leatherstocking Tales* and *The Last of the Mohicans.* He also loved Washington Irving, and Robert Burns, the Scottish poet, was his favorite. I came to share his interest in Washington Irving. Somewhere along the line I began to read poetry. I can't recall whether it was in grade school or high school, but one of our assignments was "Evangeline," and I remember Dad and I had a big discussion over this. He went on at length about his French Canadian heritage. "Evangeline" led me to Longfellow's other works, and I could recite "The Village Blacksmith" from memory.

I loved Mark Twain, and it wasn't until after my dad had died, when I was in my late 30s, that I found the parody Samuel Clemens had written on Cooper. My dad loved Twain, also, and I think he would have been deeply hurt if he had read that work.

If you would have called my father an educated man he would have laughed at you. Dad, with only half of a grade school education, was exceptionally well read. He prided himself as being "a working stiff all my life," and distrusted the bureaucracy of the public school system. He told stories of encountering arrogant, college-educated technicians in his work.

"Educated damn fools," he would growl. "They don't know about the real world of work, and practical application of engineering theories."

My folks encouraged us kids to read, and they provided an example. The Grandfolks did too. Grandpa Smith was great on westerns, and had read all of the Zane Grey books. When the cherry orchard died, Grandpa decided to go back into the shoe repair business. He opened a shop in the downtown area of Beaumont. When he wasn't busy working on shoes, saddles, harnesses and other leather products, you would find him reading.

Motion pictures played a big role in our understanding of the world. When Pete and I were younger, the closest movie theatre was in Banning, seven miles to the east. When we got to be 12 years old we were allowed to hitch hike over to Banning for the Saturday matinee. We got in for a dime. I never had any problem hitch hiking over to Banning, but Pete tells the tale of one old man trying to get in his pants. Pete jumped out of the car and outran him. Homosexuality was not something that was discussed, but it was understood, and a way, even accepted.

There was a guy who lived just a block north of us who drove around town in a roadster with the top down. He usually had some boy with him. One day the guy told me he had some pants given to him by a relative and they might fit me. I went over to his house to get the pants. He said he wanted to measure me to find out if the pants would fit. He had me stand on a table, took a tape measure and started to measure my inseam. The little finger of his hand holding the tape up into my crotch became very active. Always jumpy, I leaped up and angrily told him to stop it. He passed it off as if nothing happened, told me the pants wouldn't fit and held the door open for me. That afternoon when Dad got home from work I told him what happened.

"Stay to hell away from him," Dad said.

Later, David Ratke told me he used to make a dollar a session with the old guy after a visit. I didn't ask David what happened, but I could guess. The thoughts repelled me. I quit thinking about it. If I didn't I would have to explain to the priest in confession about my evil thoughts. Evil thoughts took up most of the time in my confessions. It was best not even to think about it. But how do you do that?

Chapter 7

High School, trying to grow up, and work

Up until the time I started high school, I was always looking for jobs to do so I could earn money. Money was tight, and I didn't like going to Dad and Mom for money when I knew they were so strapped financially. After selling papers on the street, I got on as a paper boy delivering papers on my bike. I carried *The Los Angeles Times*, the *San Bernardino Sun* and the *Riverside Enterprise*. My poor bike was loaded down, and I had to get up at 5 a.m. to get my papers, fold them, put them in the carrier and deliver them. It was always a treat to end my route downtown, and see Grandpa or Dad going into the café for breakfast, a roll, or a cup of coffee. I felt like I was a grown man, almost, when I would sit next to either of them in the morning, have a cup of coffee, and be treated to breakfast.

The newspaper distributor for Beaumont was Vincent Marcy. Occasionally I would go with Vince to help him on his car route to deliver papers out through Cherry Valley and the area around Beaumont. One day I opened the glove box in his car and a big cigar was in there. I pulled it out and stuck it in my mouth, wrapper and all. Vince dared me to smoke it. Grandpa was a cigar and pipe smoker so I knew all of the moves. I stripped off the wrapper, bit the end off and placed the cigar in my mouth. Vince held out his cigarette lighter, flicked it, and lit the cigar. I smoked about an inch of the cigar when my stomach began churning. Another half inch, Vince stopped the car, and I was on my hands and knees by the side of the road throwing up the soles of my feet. When I managed to climb back into the car I believed that my Grandpa Smith was one tough man. I had the paper routes throughout the year, but when summer came it was time to look for other work.

Vince branched out into other businesses. One of them was the Richfield Service Station on the corner of 5th Street and Beaumont Avenue. I started working in the station for him, and gave up my paper routes.

Between the service station and the Beaumont Women's Club was the Union Ice Company. I worked for one summer there, loading 25-pound blocks of ice into a vending machine. I had to cut up a big 300-pound block of ice and break it down into the 25-pound chunks. Then I would wrap hemp twine around the small blocks and tie them so they could be used as handles. I think customers would slip a nickel or a dime into the vending slot outside, and then a block of ice would drop down the chute to them. There was a good market for ice. Travelers and truckers headed for the desert stopped and loaded up with ice.

Ray Sampson, a contract hauler who was a friend of my Dad's and lived very close to us, made a weekly run from San Bernardino to Beaumont to supply the Union Ice Company plant with ice. He had a big truck with a flatbed trailer. The trailers was stacked high with the 300-pound blocks of ice. The load was wrapped with big canvas tarps to minimize the melting of the ice. I would help Mr. Sampson unload his truck, and store the big blocks in the ice house. There were long, slow periods between customers, and I had to sit and wait at a desk in the building. I amused myself by drawing pictures of naked women. More material for confession.

My next big job was at M&M Market. Bill and Rose McDaris were the owners. That was the store we traded at all of the time we were in Beaumont. I thought I was well paid. At least I got better money there that I had at any other job. Mrs. McDaris would give me $2 at the end of the day on Saturday. That was 25 cents an hour. With that money I could buy some of my own clothes for high school, take in a movie over at Banning, get a malt or two at Gray's Malt Shop, and buy a nickel cigar every Saturday.

The McDarises were originally from Oklahoma, but they had been in California for many years. Bill McDaris had done a lot of things, been a rancher, a cowboy, and a storeowner. Mrs. McDaris had taught school. Mrs. McDaris ruled the store with a steel hand in a velvet glove. My job was to stock shelves, mark prices, clean the produce, and wait on customers. About 80 percent of the business was done on credit. There was a big cabinet behind the counter that held all of the accounts. Each customer had a slot in the cabinet. I would write out the items and their prices on a pad of credit slips. There was the original and a copy of the credit slip. One went to the customer, and the other into the customer's slot in the accounts cabinet. The McDarises did not send out monthly statements, but put their trust in the customers. Every so often, a customer would come in and settle up a bill.

I remember that we had a grocery bill that would get to what I thought was pretty high. When it got up to over $100 I started to worry. I went to Dad and told him the bill was over $100, and would he ever have enough money to pay it? Dad told me not to worry, that the financial situation was under control. Sure enough, a couple of weeks later the bill was paid.

Bill McDaris was a Sooner. His family was in the 1889 land rush and horse race to claim unassigned lands in Oklahoma Indian Territory. He had an old "hawg leg," a .44-caliber, Frontier model Colt revolver stashed under the meat slicer at the cold cuts counter. It was loaded.

"I was robbed once, back in Oklahoma, but never again," he said.

Our customers were practically everybody in town, and the ranchers, orchardists and farmers from the surrounding area. We handled everything except fresh meat. McDonald's Meat Market was across the street, and if customers wanted meat we would get it for them, pay McDonald's, then bill the customer. Mom did all of her own meat shopping, but many people would take advantage of Mr. or Mrs. Mac's generosity. And in many instances customers would stiff them, move away and leave a big unpaid grocery bill.

Years later, I returned to visit Beaumont and spent some time with them.

"If we had all of those unpaid bills, we would have had a nice, comfortable retirement," Mr. Mac said. "I really respect your Mom and Dad, and your grandfolks. They always paid their bills. They were more than customers, they were loyal, good friends."

In the back room we had big sacks of chicken and rabbit feed, flour, sugar, rice and beans. People would save the feed and flour sacks because some came with colorful patterns printed on the fabric. Many would make clothes out of the flour sacks. I suspect that half of the kids in school at one time or another wore flour sack underwear.

Customers would phone in their orders, we would fill them, put their orders in wood boxes, and load them in the '28 Chevrolet pickup truck we used for deliveries. Twice a day, Mr. McDaris would make the grocery delivery run. When I got to be 16, and got my driver's license, I took over driving the delivery truck on Saturdays. I knew everybody, and everybody knew me. I was the delivery boy for M&M Market.

Mrs. McDaris, paid close attention to my school grades and my appearance. Before I went out to a dance on Saturday night, I had to drop by the market for inspection. My parents and grandparents were interested and involved with our many activities outside of the home. The neighbors, friends, merchants and farmers all seemed to take an interest in the town's kids and what they were doing. If I goofed up, Mom and Dad would know about it before I got home. The Beaumont desert telegraph, sort of an adult ESP network, would go to work and your misdeeds would flash eerily from a grown-up informant to the King household. If Pete, Tony or I would be a party to a prank, a forbidden activity, or a nasty deed then we could be sure Mom would be waiting for us at the back door with the fly swatter when we got home.

I experienced the effectiveness of the desert telegraph first hand. I was in my senior year at Beaumont High, a spotty, active, hormone-ridden young male who had not been laid. I was determined to lose my virginity before I graduated from high school. I was a sexual dullard, compared to my cohorts. So with a carefully crafted scenario I asked a girl out who I heard had "gone all the way." The evening with my date progressed satis-factorily, with much sweat, panting and groping in the back seat of a Model A sedan until the moment of truth. I call her Jane Doe because she is still alive. Jane D. grasped my hyperactive hand with a grip of steel.

"No more, Frank. I have my monthly visitor," she said.

I gracefully accepted the firm denial, almost crying at the cruel hand fate had dealt me.

Everything went well until noon the next day. I came home from school for lunch and Mom was hosting the Merry Janes, a sewing club that met every week at the members' homes. Dad called the Merry Janes the Coyote Club, because "they sit around on their asses and howl." As I walked into the house, the chattering women fell silent. Mom looked at me. Tears running down her cheeks, she ran into the bedroom. The women left. I knocked at the bedroom door. Mom came out.

"What were you doing out with Jane D. last night? You nasty, nasty boy!" she cried.

I assured her that I was pure, her still unblemished son. She went back in the bedroom. I went to the kitchen, reached under the kitchen sink for the bottle of sweet, cherry wine, took a slug and ran back to school. Walking up the hall came cries from my friends:

"Hey, how did you make out with Jane D.?"

"Heard you didn't score, Frankie!"

Down the hall to science class with Mr. Eberhard.

He greeted me, "Hey, I hear you went out with Jane D. last night,".

Then it was to church for Saturday afternoon confession.

"Bless me, Father, for I have sinned. It has been two weeks since my last confession," I muttered. "I took a girl out, tried to have sex with her, but it didn't work out."

"Yes, I know."

Not divine revelation, but the desert telegraph at its best.

Mrs. Mac said not a word, but she was very cool with me for about a week after the Jane D. incident.

I was an indifferent student. With the subjects I liked, I did pretty well. No A's, but getting B's was no problem. Mathematics began to rear its ugly head again. I took Algebra and Plane Geometry. I got a D- for two semesters of algebra and one semester of plane geometry. H. D. "Doc" Young, the algebra teacher, was a friend of my father's. They were both WWI veterans and were fellow members of the American Legion.

"I can't even give you a 'C' for charity," Doc Young said. "Your math skills really stink."

Science was okay, but I really liked biology. Spanish was okay, too. The first time I tried it I failed the class, but I took it over and passed it with no problem. Typing was also a problem. I got an F in that class, took it over and passed it. Little did I realize that using a keyboard for typing-teletype, then computers-would become a big part of my working life. English, history, geography and civics were great. I can remember my senior English class reading Dickens' *The Tale of Two Cities*. We would read out loud in class and we went through the whole book. I became totally engrossed in the story. Drama soon followed.

Beaumont High had an active drama program and I became a member of the Thespian Society. I think that I was in five plays in my Junior and Senior years.

Pete and I also played in the band. We had been taking music lessons while we were still in grade school from Mr. Thomas Jefferson Housekeeper. His son, Ben, or Benjamin Harrison Housekeeper, was three years ahead of me in school, and a great trombone player. Mr. Housekeeper lived just north of Wellwood School and we would go over to his place for lessons. Pete played the trumpet, and I started out on the baritone horn and tuba. I later played the trombone. Our high school music teacher was David Rosenthal, also known as Rosie, a USC graduate, and a marvelous clarinet player. I liked playing trombone, but hated the regimentation of written music. I never did learn how to read music well. Rosie despaired over my trombone artistry.

"You are the worse faker I have ever seen," he would say.

My hyperactivity bothered him, too. I couldn't keep from blowing my trombone, even if we were supposed to keep quiet.

"If you don't shut up, King, I am going to shove that horn down your throat," he would shout.

The ties between our class and Dave Rosenthal, and a math teacher who followed Doc Young, Mr. Bill Hawkinson, were very strong. When we had our school and class reunions in the 1990s, both showed up. It is amazing how well they aged. We kids thought they were ancient, but our teachers for the most part were very young. Most were in their early 20s, and Beaumont High was their first teaching job after getting out of college. They brought vitality, dedication and enthusiasm into our classrooms. It was hard to realize it then, as juniors and seniors, that our teachers were only about six to eight years older than we were.

I also took journalism and worked on Cougar Tales, the mimeographed newspaper the students published. The writing I was most proud of in high school was the calendar that I wrote for the yearbook in my senior year.

Mom and Dad were involved parents. They served as chaperones at many of our school dances, and during a typical day our house was filled with our visiting friends.

Looking back, I think that Pete, Tony and I received an excellent education in that small town. The school, the library, the M&M Market, the town characters, the dinner table discussions shaped my values.

I knew the difference between right and wrong, and sometimes you just had to do the wrong thing because it was fun. One Sunday my good friend Dolores Swearingen and her mother, Bernice, were visiting us. I asked Dad if Dolores and I could go for a ride. We had the Ford then and I had learned to drive. With the parents' permission, and a caution to be careful, Dolores and I set out on our adventure. Dolores, who we called DoDo, wanted to drive over to Hemet, about 20 miles away to see her current boyfriend. So off we went. We found the boyfriend and he wanted to set me up with a blind date, a Jean Easly, I think. We picked her up, and DoDo's boy friend bought some beer. We ended up on a necking party, drinking beer, until about 11 p.m. Then DoDo and I cut for home and the irate parents. We really got a chewing out, and I was grounded for some time.

DoDo and I became good friends. She was really supportive, and when I was chosen as the toastmaster for the Junior-Senior Banquet in 1940 at the Desert Inn in Palm Springs, she championed my candidacy. The banquet was great, and as I remember it I told funny jokes and kept everyone laughing but my date. I had been going around a little bit with Mildred Miller, who was my age but a year ahead of me. Mildred was my date. She had broken her ankle, and her lower leg was in a rigid cast. I bought her a corsage, a gardenia, I think, and everything went swimmingly until the banquet was over and the dancing was to start. Mildred walked up to me looking very sad.

"I am not having a very good time, Frankie," She said. "I won't be able to dance. Don Cox is having a miserable time, also, and he doesn't have a date. He is going home, and I would like to go back with him. O.K?"

What was I going to say? "No, you ungrateful wretch, you stay here until they play "Goodnight Sweetheart?"

"Sure, that's O.K. See you tomorrow."

On the drive home erotic daydreams of what I would do to Mildred who was marooned with me on a desert island filled my head. The damn cast had grown and kept me pure.

I made the 26-mile drive back to Beaumont solo.

Grandpa Smith taught me how to drive. He was a terrible driver, and I learned from his poor example. He would start the car, rev the engine until it almost jumped out of the frame, then start out with a jackrabbit leap. When coming up to a stop sign, he would throw in the clutch, let the engine idle, and use only the brakes to stop. I quickly learned how to use the engine, and to down shift, to help slow the car. Grandpa said that was unnecessary. His car had good brakes. One day, dust boiling, he skidded to a stop out at the side of our house. He stormed into the house and threw the car keys at me.

"Go on out and get the old lady," he growled. "We had a fight."

That was my solo drive. I proudly piloted the Studebaker out to the ranch. With care, concern and sympathy I helped Grandma into the car, and slowly made my way back into town. Tears were still in her eyes, and every once and awhile she would quietly wipe her cheeks.

"You are a good driver, Frankie," Grandma said.

As much as it made my Grandma sad, I always hoped for a fight, because Grandpa would roar into town, throw the keys at me, and tell me to bring Grandma in for shopping, an Altar Society meeting, or a card party.

After Dad bought the 1937 Ford V8-60, my social life improved. Part of my weekly salary from the M&M Market helped pay for the gas. Gasoline was only 10 to 15 cents per gallon, and all I needed was a gallon. We boys were always dreaming of owning our own cars. You could buy a Model T Ford for from $5 to $15, depending upon whether it was running or not. You could also buy an unbroken pony for $5 over at the Morongo Indian Reservation out beyond Banning. But you couldn't take a date, or score, on the back of an unbroken Indian pony, so the junker cars came first.

The cunning booze monster raised its ugly head in my senior year. Freddie Meyers, who had been one year ahead of us in school, came home from the Marine Corps to visit. He had completed boot camp and was in training at Camp Elliott, just outside of San Diego. One night Ralph Gonzalez and I were with him, and Freddie brought out a full, unopened fifth of whiskey. He started drinking it, and Ralph and I joined him. It was a great feeling, that warm glow in the pit of your stomach spreading through your body. I felt that I could do anything. It didn't matter that I was a shrimp; I felt like I was a 250-pound lineman and over six feet tall. I knew that I was brilliant, and a sparkling conversationalist. We ended up down at the Southern Pacific depot sitting on one of the loading docks. I knew it was time for me to get home when I couldn't feel my nose. I staggered off into the night. I remembered Dad's words:

"If you are ever out there drinking, and get drunk, come home so we can take care of you. I don't want you embarrassing the family."

I made it home, straightened myself up, walked in the house, past Mom and Dad who were sitting at the kitchen table. I don't know if they were waiting for me or not. I went into my bedroom and undressed. The bed was mobile. I caught it on its third orbit around the bedroom, and crawled in. As soon as I laid down, the stomach started the same orbit as the bed, and I lurched out. I staggered to bathroom and threw up, and threw up, and threw up. Dad came in and looked at me and I heard him tell Mom that I had been drinking and was sick.

"Mom! Come in here and hold my head," I whimpered.

No answer.

"Mom! Please hold my head!"

"You're drunk. I don't hold the heads of drunks!"

The next day Dad had another talk with me. He was grateful that I remembered his order to get home if I had too much to drink. He again told me the story of his father. Dad had an intuitive sense about alcoholism and heredity. He always feared that booze abuse might rear up in his sons. I told him that I would never drink again, that I had learned my lesson-another pledge I made that I would break many times over. My head hurt, I couldn't keep anything on my stomach, and Mom wouldn't talk to me, let alone hold my head. I didn't drink much until after I left home and was working at Douglas Aircraft Co. in Santa Monica. I would still sneak a slug from the cherry wine jug under the sink.

Many years later when we moved to Portland, Oregon, my mother, in her late 70s, was living with us. There was a Fred Meyer store, a big Oregon chain grocery and drug chain store, about a mile away from our house. My mother would not go into that store. Fred Meyer got me drunk and was to blame for all my problems. I tried to explain that it wasn't the same guy, but she couldn't be swayed. She never set foot in the store.

Drinking and sex were great topics for confession. The other five Deadly Sins were in the rumble seat of my Model A roadster of life. I think that my preoccupation with sex was beginning to affect my brothers. My little brother Tony, ten years younger than me, was a bright, inquisitive, adventurous kid, and usually in trouble. One day I was home while Mom was hosting a meeting of the Altar Society. I remember I was drinking a glass of milk in the kitchen. Mom was getting refreshments ready for the ladies. The screen door on the back porch burst open and an excited Billy Duncan ran in, red faced and sweating.

"Frank! Frank! Come quick! Tony and Jackie are screwing Catherine Fay," he cried.

I dropped the glass of milk. Mom started to scream, but remembering the ladies in the front room, bit her apron and choked.

I laughed. Mom hit me.

I went with Billy to see what the situation was with my precocious little brother, Catherine Fay Duncan, and Jackie Hirlbert. When I got down to the Duncan's house everyone had disappeared, and neither Mr. or Mrs. Duncan were there. But Mom was waiting for Tony when he got home-with the flyswatter. I don't remember the outcome, but I know that it was another situation for Dad when he got home from work.

I felt really bad about the whole thing. My little brother was eight years old and he had scored before I did. I would probably die a virgin. I might as well become a priest, but I didn't.

Graduation was a big deal. Traditionally we had what we called the Baccalaureate Service at the Community Church on a Sunday night just before graduation. There were 33 kids in my class, and 13 of us were Catholic. Those of us who were members of the CYO, the Catholic Youth Organization, had the idea of having an ecumenical service in the high school auditorium. During a class meeting we brought up the subject, and DoDo, a fiery leader, took our side. The class vote was to hold the service in the auditorium. We took our proposal to Bill Sewell.

"I don't think so. We have always held it at the Community Church," he said.

Then took it to the school board. We had a friend there. Louis Haskell was on the board and had served as chairman. His wife was Marie Haskell, a devout Catholic and a member of our parish. The board took a vote and our proposal was approved.

Activists that we were, we became more daring. We proposed that Father Phillip Baldonado, our priest, be allowed to deliver the baccalaureate address. That also was approved. I don't know when I was more proud. I thought Father Phillip was brilliant. He came from a humble Mexican-American family, and grew up in a barrio. We loved him. His speech was flawless, and his delivery brilliant. I can't remember what it was he talked about; all I know was that it had no parochial or theological overtones.

At the end of my junior year in high school year I became smitten with a girl from Banning. Beaumont and Banning were arch rivals, and you just didn't take up with a foreigner from that hated town six miles to the east. My friends called me a traitor. Mary Johnson, was a year ahead of me in school, and getting ready to go to Riverside J.C. We dated heavily in that summer between my junior and senior year. Her father was editor and publisher of the *Banning Register* weekly newspaper. On summer nights we would spend hours parked in the '37 Ford necking away in front of her house. We wouldn't want to say good night. After one of those necking sessions, I would come home tired, sweaty, and unrequited. The old *cojones* would really hurt. We used to call them "stone aches." I had heard that lifting heavy weights helped relieve the ache. So I would lift on the rear bumper of the Ford, trying to alleviate the turgid, achy feeling in my groin. One early morning my dad woke up and asked me what I was doing with his car. I told him I was testing the shocks. The lifting didn't help. Twenty years later I had a double hernia operation.

When she started junior college and I my senior year, the romance cooled off. I was all for continuing it, but Mary had found her a new "Sweetie" at Riverside J.C. My heart was broken for the first time, but not the last.

I had an English and drama teacher that I didn't get along with at all. Her name was Phyllis Hurst. Miss Hurst was a small, thin blond who walked like a duck. She had a high, lisping voice that made my teeth ache. She was a very nice person, a caring, talented teacher, and a strict taskmistress. I was sort of the class clown, and she didn't appreciate my sparkling wit and comments. She was the one who directed the school plays. As I remember it, we were in the process of coming up with a play, or we had already decided on doing one. The selected production-if I remember correctly was "It Can Happen To You." There was so much acrimony between the cast, production crew and Miss Hurst that she quit in tears. So we decided to put on our own productions. I think that Jack Calmus took over as director. The production scheme was simple, and the set minimal. It was a courtroom scene. The judge's bench would be stage center, and the lawyer's tables to each side. The audience in the auditorium were spectators to the murder trial. My good friend Jim Hawkins was the judge. O'Dell Gifford was the defense attorney, and I was the prosecuting attorney. O'Dell was defending a girl who was indicted for vehicular homicide in a hit-and-run accident. The defendant was my old friend DoDo. Dramatic conflict was provided by a previous romance that the defendant had with the prosecutor. It was pretty corny, but Beaumont loved high school theater and the production was a hit. I think we scored another first: the only all-student produced play in the history of Beaumont Union High.

With graduation approaching, and no girlfriend, I had a lot of time to think. My friends and I lived in the shadow of the dragon, the growing World War II. Our plans were all colored by what was happening in Europe. I remember a heated argument I had with Dad early in high school about Il Duce's invasion of Ethiopia. I maintained that Italy's imperialism was wrong. Dad argued that those good Italian boys would bring Catholicism to the heathen hordes in Ethiopia. I was outraged. My Dad would sometimes come up with off-the-wall political statements, but managed to come back to reality in a short time. I really think he took the opposite view of any argument just to get my dander up and get me to think. I came to know that he was violently anti-fascist and hated Hitler and Mussolini.

We were a family of huggers and kissers. Dad was always very affectionate, and Mom, too, but not as much as Dad. All mothers I knew loved and kissed their kids, but their fathers never did. My Dad was different. He would hug you and kiss you at the drop of a hat. He would do the same thing with your friends. He was a great user of affectionate terms. He would call Pete, Tony and me "Honey," "Sweetheart," "Darling Boy," or "Dear One."

I was with Dad out at Rowan's Service Station and he was playing the pinball machine with Howard Baker, his good friend and our milk man. Dad loved pinball. 'Honey," he said to me, "Go over and get me five nickels for this quarter." Howard teased him about his using such endearing terms for his sons, and asked him why he did it.

"Because I love them dearly," he said, throwing his arm around my neck and kissing me on the cheek. Howard's comments didn't bother Dad one damn bit. He, like my Grandpa Smith, marched to a different drummer in many respects. In others he was as straight as a Rotarian. My Dad was the one who could lift me out of the teen-age depressions I had. I was worried about the future, mostly the war and what I was going to do with my life. I would.be lying on my bed in a deep funk and he would jump on me, tell me funny stories, and get me smiling. It wasn't the stories that did it, but his caring and love that kept me sane in that insane teen time.

I knew that I probably would end up in the military. Lots of my school friends who were in classes ahead of me in school were joining the National Guard, the reserves and the regular military. This was the time of the CCC, the Civilian Conservation Corps. Many friends who graduated from high school could not get a job, and began service with the CCC. The CCC provided a great reservoir of manpower for the growing military. The uncertainty of the times and the war in Europe looming over us made me uneasy and unable to formulate a clear plan of what I wanted to do.

I had completed most of the course work I needed for graduation, so I only had two or three solid courses I had to complete in my final semester. I knew I wanted to go to college, even though I didn't have all of the math I needed. Junior college was probably the route I would take.

"I can't help you with money, but I sure hope you do," Dad said.

So I decided to work and go to school, if I could. My Uncle Frank and Uncle Jim, and their families, lived in Santa Monica and many of them worked at the Douglas Aircraft plant at Clover Field.

Two days after my high school graduation I left Beaumont for Santa Monica. I was to live with Uncle Frank and Aunt Elizabeth on Oak Street, just off the east-west runway of Clover Field. Uncle Frank and Aunt Elizabeth had four children: Neal, Agnes, Francis and Jim. Neal had been with Donald Douglas since the 1920s when Douglas formed his company. Agnes was married. Francis, or "Pinky," lived over on Pearl, was married and had a stepdaughter, Virginia. Uncle Frank was a guard at Douglas, Neal worked in a top production job, Pinky was in final inspection and

Jim worked in a tool crib. I roomed with my cousin Jimmy, who is two years older than me. After a week of looking for a job, I managed to get on as a carpenter's helper with a guy building a house. For a month I worked hammering nails, sawing wood, cleaning up the mess. Then Douglas hired me and I went to work at the beginning level in the cable department. Our job was to fabricate the control cables used in the airplanes being built at the Santa Monica plant: DC-3s, or C-47s (Army) or R4Ds (Navy), all the same aircraft, and A-20s, the attack bombers. I learned how to solder fittings on control cables using several techniques. I think my starting pay was about 63 cents an hour. That meant that I was making almost as much at my father did. Within two months I was making about $150 a month, and I felt bad. My father was much more capable, experienced and deserving than I. So I began sending Mom about $10 to $20 from my paycheck. It wasn't generosity, it was guilt.

I started working the day shift, and in September I asked to be put on swing. I wanted to take some classes at Santa Monica City College. Since my new shift would interfere with the household, with Uncle Frank and Jim both working days, I decided to move to a boarding house in Venice. A friend from Beaumont, Bruce Drummond, lived there. He also was a Douglas employee. I would get rides with him up to Beaumont about every two or three weeks. When I was living at Uncle Frank's and the Venice boarding house, the going rate for board and room was $40 a month.

I enrolled in city college and took two classes-journalism and sociology-that met in the morning on Monday, Wednesday and Friday. At that time there was no tuition. All you had to pay was a registration fee, books and materials. That great California educational system was to continue for many years-until Governor Ronald Reagan trashed it. A poor kid like me could go all the way from kindergarten to getting a bachelor's degree in a state university without paying a cent of tuition. I think we were what was described as the working poor. We were poor, but we didn't know it.

One of the things I enjoyed was visiting my cousin Pinky, his wife Mae, and their daughter, Virginia. Pinky would encourage me to put on the boxing gloves with him, and we would spar away. He had done some boxing during a hitch he had put in with the Navy in the 1930s. He taught me a lot about boxing, coaching that would help me in a few months.

Chapter 8

The War

On December 6, 1941, Bruce and I made our 90-mile trip up to Beaumont from Santa Monica. The next day, Sunday, I had gone to mass with the family. When we got home I turned on the old Admiral console radio in the living room, and was sitting on the floor tuning in a station. I got KFI Los Angeles tuned in. The news crackling from the speaker shocked us into silence. Pearl Harbor was under attack by Japanese forces. I was in a daze for the rest of day. I can remember the stunned expressions of my mother and father. Bruce and I drove back to Santa Monica and tried to keep our minds on our jobs. I decided to move back in with Uncle Frank and Aunt Elizabeth until I decided to enlist in the military. They seemed happy to have me back on Oak Street.

The next two months were a jumpy time for me. Blackouts were imposed on all the coastal cities, and there were many bomb scares. Rumors could fly further than Japanese planes, and there was always word of an impending attack. A few futile shells were lobbed shoreward by Japanese submarines, but we didn't learn of these until after the war. When we grew really frustrated, Jim and I would buy a bottle of whiskey, and go down to the beach, drink it, and wonder what was going to happen.

In early February I made my move. I drove the Ford over to March Field to enlist in the Army Air Force flying cadet program. The folks there took my application, and I had to pass the Army General Classification test. And I did. Next came the physical exam. I passed it. The doctor asked me some questions like: "Have you ever had cancer, diabetes, tuberculosis, etc.?" "Have you any allergies, or asthma?" I truthfully told him that I had had asthma when I was very young, but didn't suffer from it anymore. He looked at me, and told me that I had failed the physical because of the asthma history. I was crushed.

So I immediately drove down to Los Angeles and enlisted in the U.S. Marine Corps. I would show that damn Army Air Corps. I went home, sat Mom and Dad down, and told them what I had done. Dad jumped up, his face turning red.

"What the hell are you thinking of," he shouted. "Do you want to go off and get yourself killed?"

He started to cry, and Mom did, too. Dad recalled how many injured, blinded, gassed Marines, many of them childhood friends, his ship had carried from France back to the U.S. in World War I.

I can't remember how I got down to Los Angeles to leave for boot camp in San Diego, but I do remember all the assorted sizes and shapes of men and boys herded aboard the Southern Pacific for the 100-mile trip to the south. The train pulled into the station at San Diego, and the drill instructor, or DI, was waiting for us. He lined us up in four ranks, screamed in our faces, and called us shit heads. Then to Marine Corps Recruit Depot, San Diego. We were shorn, shaved, and stuck. Sea bags, clothes, equipment, and our rifle were thrown at us. To the dispensary we marched to be probed, prodded, and pierced by needles in our arms and asses. Finally to a tent with from six to eight cots in it with mattress pads on them. That was to be our home for the next two months. We were ordered to get up, to shave, to bathe, to chow, to drill, to work, to play, to pray, to bed. The first days were spent marching from place to place to get what we needed for our new life in the Corps. We marched in close-order drill for about six hours a day. That first week we ran into each other a lot, and we were screamed at. Our DIs were Sgt. R. E. Meister, Corp. H. Tedrow, and Corp. J.H. Pope. I think they were all from the South.

"Y'awl are a bunch of shit heads!"

When we stripped to shower, our tonsured pates gleamed dead white above sunburned faces. I thought: "Did Grandpa Smith have anything to do with this?" We were a motley crew of 60 from every corner of the U.S., but no African Americans, no Hispanics, no Asians, nor Pacific Islanders. That was the way it was in early 1942, and I wouldn't see minority and women Marines until 1943. We hardened, we toughened, became leaner and more confident. The Marines had a simple philosophy: Grind you down to nothing, then build you into something. That grinding down came in many forms. You would be drilled, run and exercised until you thought you couldn't do one more thing ordered of you. Your clothes had to be folded and stored in military precision, the blankets on your cot-otherwise known as your rack, fart sack or just sack for short-had to be so taut that you could bounce a coin off the wooly surface, and your rifle-or your piece, but *never* your gun-had to be spotless. A gun was a cannon. Your rifle became your brother, your best friend, your boon companion. We were told our rifle was the most important thing in our life, outside of following orders. If one of us was unfortunate or careless enough to drop our rifle on the ground-the deck-it was a disaster. If the DI spotted this misdeed you had to sleep with your rifle. That's right, the piece had to be between the sheets cuddled up next to you. Not a fitting bed companion.

The *pro forma* lexicon of the Marine is studded with salty, sea-going terms. We learned that the ground is the deck, that left is port, that right is starboard, that stairs are a ladder, upstairs is topside, downstairs is below, a hospital is a dispensary, that an officer up to a colonel is addressed as

"Mr." A medic is a Corpsman. I guess that comes from the Navy Medical Corps. To mess is not to foul your pants, but to eat. Gunny is not a sack, but a gunnery sergeant, a minor god. Our drill instructors were prophets sans beards, and they told us that to become a sea-going Marine was a sure way to Heaven. Select members of each recruit platoon were selected for Sea School. That was an academy unto itself. By select I mean that they had to be over six feet tall, be slim, athletic, good looking. Sort of male Barbie dolls. We gnome-like creatures who would only reach six feet if we were standing on a chair had no chance.

I was one of the feather merchants in the 232nd Platoon of 1942. Feather merchants were the ones in the front of a column of four ranks, the shortest Marines of the bunch. My best friend in this time was Chuck Ferrerro, who was on the other end. He was over six feet, blond, handsome, a college football player, a halfback from San Jose State. All the things that I wasn't. Chuck came up with some nicknames for me. He called me Duck Butt and Grunt Legs. The names stuck. Being in the front row of a four-rank column puts you right in the eye scope of the drill instructors. If you had a pimple out of place, they would see it. With our short legs, we strove mightily for the right step length. The big guys in the back would kind of shorten up their steps and mutter about it. Then we would do an about face, go the other way, and the feather merchants would split their trousers reaching out with monster steps to stay in step.

The drill instructors would mete out what they called correctional steps, but to us it was torture. We did not refer to our rifle, or piece, as a gun. If we did, this was the punishment. We had to stand at attention, lift our rifle up to shoulder height, and cry:

"This is my rifle!"-lower rifle.

"This is my gun!"-grasp your crotch with your right hand, and release.

"This is for shooting!"-raise and lower rifle.

"This is for fun!"-grasp crotch with right hand again, and release.

This little ditty had to be repeated 50, 75, or 100 times.

Cleanliness was another credo. Your piece, person, gear, bedding, surroundings had to be spotless. Any infraction was dealt with swiftly. A favorite DI trick was to have you use your toothbrush to scrub the deck in your tent, or the duck boards on the walks outside. When unable to find any appropriate punishment for a recalcitrant recruit the DI would always fall back on the old stand by having you stand on the parade ground with a bucket over your head and shouting 50, 75 or 100 times:

"I am a shit head!"

It was not only humiliating, but painful. The DI would hit the bucket with his swagger stick, and yell, "Louder!" When you got through, your ears would be ringing, and you couldn't hear anything for hours.

Cleanliness in boot camp was a lot like cleanliness at home. One day my Dad suffered horribly because of my Mom, the clean freak. My mother hated dirt, dust, lint, *schnipsles,* and bad odors. She thought that Lysol was God's gift to man. Every week she would scrub the bathroom, and douse everything with Lysol. Mom scrubbed the toilet as usual, poured a great amount of Lysol in the bowl, and was called to the phone. She usually brushed and rinsed the bowl. Dad had to go, came in, sat down, lit a cigarette, and began reading. He called the can the library. Ten minutes later he cried out in pain. The end of his tally whacker had encountered the caustic Lysol. Mom told me about the incident when I got home on my first liberty. She urged Dad to show me his wound. He would not. Dad went the doctor, got an ointment that he used to ease the burning pain. He walked spraddle-legged for two weeks. Mom said he had no lasting scar, thank heavens.

Life was spartan. We got no liberty, and were confined to the base. We could receive, write and mail letters, but phone calls and visits were limited to family. My folks came down to see me once while I was in boot camp, and they were good about writing to me. Home was only 100 miles away, but it seemed much further. Entertainers from town would come every week and we were marched into an outdoor arena where amateur actors, singers and dancers would perform. One I really disliked was a pair of tap dancers from San Diego. A boy and a girl, " Little Bobbie and Bonnie," in their late teens like me, would tap dance to "Tea For Two." I think I had to suffer through that performance six times in boot camp. It was as bad as hollering "I am a shit head," 100 times with a bucket over your head. I have not been able to stand listening to "Tea For Two" up until this day. I don't like tap dancers. Ronald Reagan was a great tap dancer.

Professional athletes would come in as visiting coaches and we received excellent instruction in boxing, wrestling and hand-to-hand combat. As we ended the final phase of boot camp we had to go on forced marches, and trained in extended order drill, the basic infantry techniques. We traveled about five miles up the coast to the rifle range every day for about two weeks. There we learned how to shoot our beloved .30 caliber rifles, the '06 Springfield. I wasn't a distinguished marksman. The DI's mission in life was to get us qualified at least as marksmen. There were three categories: marksman, sharpshooter and expert. Experts were considered bearers of the Holy Grail; sharpshooters, members of royalty; marksmen, respected arms bearers; and those who did not qualify on the rifle, dung carriers. I was a dung carrier.

During practice, I reached marks that were promising, and I thought I would qualify, despite my battle with marksmanship. I was still 5-feet-5 and ¾ths of an inch tall, and 135 pounds, wringing wet. That damn rifle would discharge and push me all over the place. My right shoulder was black and blue. When I fired in the prone position, the recoil would push me back six inches. Firing from sitting and kneeling positions, I would get knocked over backwards. When I fired in the standing, or off-hand position, I would sway like a poplar tree in a hurricane. I was one of the two or three pariahs who did not qualify

I redeemed myself, somewhat, by shooting the highest score in the platoon with the .45 caliber Colt automatic pistol. It seemed as if that handgun was an extension of my right hand. All I had to do was point it, squeeze with my entire hand, and the bullet would go where I aimed. Every time I fired, the slide would shoot back, the spent shell ejected, and a new charge rammed into the chamber. The slide would graze the pad of muscle on my right hand between the base of the thumb and forefinger. The area was worn raw, and would bleed a little when I fired for an extended time. I considered the tiny wound a mark of honor. So I shot for record and won the Pistol Expert badge that I wore proudly on my uniform.

After the firing range we marched in a Saturday graduation inspection and review. Then most of us were sent across the bay to the North Island Naval Air Station. Half of us were assigned to a month of guard duty, and half to mess duty. Wouldn't you know it, I got mess duty. We washed the dishes, scrubbed pots and pans, and were mess cooks. Mess cooks had the enviable duty of serving food on the mess line to hungry sailors and marines. Navy and marine cooks were our bosses. I think that every marine group that went through the North Island mess hall had heard the story of the sailor that had been court marshaled because he was boiling his dirty socks in the coffee urn. I didn't like coffee that much, so I switched to milk and water.

It was at North Island we learned that we were being assigned to Marine aviation units. We didn't have anything to say about it. The only good things about mess duty were that we were out of boot camp, we got liberty, and there was a Marine slop chute. The slop chute was sort of a military beer garden-with no garden. You could drink pitchers of beer with a 3.2-percent alcohol content. It didn't take much to make us real happy. Every marine got to drink beer in the slop chute. It didn't matter how old you were. We had some kids who had lied about their age to get in, and their parents went along with it. Some were as young as 15. The slop chute and liberty passes were sheer heaven. Just to be able to walk the streets and do as you pleased for a few hours was like being in paradise. We couldn't do too much. Our pay was only $21 a month. There was a small passenger ferry that ran between North Island and the Broadway Street landing in San Diego. The Nickel Snatcher would make its run about every 30 minutes. The fare was five cents each way. There was a big sign on the landing that read: **Do Not Jump to Catch the Ferry!** Nobody paid any attention to the sign. You always waited until the ferry was pulling out before you tried to catch it. It wasn't an athletic event; you just wanted to be on liberty as long as possible. On Saturday nights the townspeople would sit on the benches and watch drunk sailors and marines trying to leap aboard the ferry when it was pulling out. It was the best show in town. The townies would make bets on who would make it. A crewman on the Nickel Snatcher had a long boat hook he would use to snag dripping sailors, and haul them aboard for the trip to North Island.

Then came the day that we had been waiting for. Our assignments to the service schools had been posted on the bulletin board. I was scheduled to leave within two weeks for aviation ordinance school at the University of Oklahoma. I thought that over. Some of my friends got assignments to radio school, and I thought that was better. Getting radio experience seemed wise, because the job opportunities after the war would be better. Becoming an ordinance expert, fixing guns, wouldn't be a very good occupation, unless I wanted to move to Chicago. I didn't. So I went to the sergeant major of the marine detachment and asked him if I could switch to radio school. He reviewed my records, found my test scores were good enough, and he reassigned me to the airborne radio operator school at Texas A&M. A week later I was on a Southern Pacific troop train to College Station, Texas.

Texas and California were sure different. We got to A&M the first of May, and the weather was pretty nice. We considered our quarters palatial. We were housed in brick barracks, with two to a double-bunked room. A typical college dormitory. The food was great. We ate in a mess hall that had white tablecloths, nice flatware and we were served by Aggies who were working their way through college. Some things were hard to take, grits and stewed okra. Okra looked like slugs, snails without the houses on their backs.

We went to classes from 8 a.m. to noon, and from 1 p.m. to 4 p.m. We studied electronics, typing and radio operation. A good part of the time was involved in learning to send and receive Morse code. I think that when we graduated we could send and receive about 15 words per minute Morse code.

Every Saturday we had inspection. We had to turn out in freshly ironed khakis, stand in the hot sun for an hour, then break for town for liberty. Liberty was usually in Bryan, but the guys with money would go to Houston and Dallas. In a south central Texas July and August freshly starched uniforms become wet and wrinkled in minutes. We would stand on chairs to put our pants on so we didn't break the creases and wrinkle the uniform. Stiff legged we walked to inspection. After "fall out" we dashed for the buses and freedom. Freedom usually meant the USO club, a movie, or a dance. If you were lucky you hooked up with girl who lived in town. I met a lovely young lady, a school teacher, who even took me home to a Sunday dinner. Just the two of us. I had met her at mass. I was doing great, until a red-headed Irishman, a former student at Boston College, started to beat my time. I thought I had the inside track, until one day I had to stand guard duty. This consisted of staying in the duty station and answering the phone. I was only supposed to stand a four-hour watch, from the end of inspection until 4 p.m. Then I had a date with the school teacher. 4 p.m. came and no relief. 8 p.m. came and no relief. At about 9 p.m. some relief showed up. By then I was drunk as seven owls. Guys coming back in from town, with booze, stopped off at the duty shack, would commiserate with me, and give me a drink.

I staggered back to our barracks, climbed the stairs towards my room singing, "The Eyes of Texas Are Upon You." Mike, a friend who was on duty as CQ, Charge of Quarters, told me to pipe down, I was waking everybody up.

"Oh yeah! Make me! Beside that you don't have your duty belt on. I don't have to take orders from you unless you have a duty belt on."

"Just wait, you son of a bitch. I'll get the damn belt; then you go to the brig."

`Discretion, the better part of valor, prevailed. I ran to the top floor, hid in someone's room, on the top bunk. I could hear Mike thrashing around the building trying to find me. I went to sleep. Then woke up because the bed was wet. I liked to think that I sweated a lot that hot night.

Then next morning, through my headache, Mike chewed me out. I apologized. Mike said his bad night started with me coming in drunk, and ended a little while ago when a guy complained that some asshole had peed in his bed. I learned that my red-headed friend from Boston had met my stood-up girlfriend while I was stranded on guard duty getting drunk.

That was when I decided I wasn't going to drink anymore. I made my pledge to my roommate, Private Arley J. Stone, aka Rocky. Rocky and I went through boot camp at the same time, but we were in different platoons. He was nice kid, just about the same size as me, but a wonderful athlete. He went to Huntington Park High School in Los Angeles and was a football star. He was an outstanding running back, at only 140 pounds, and made the All-City team. Rocky was a stable kid, was saving all of his money because he wanted to get married. We were only making $21 a month, so we decided to economize as much as we could. I wrote home and got Dad to send me his cigarette rolling machine. So Rocky and I would roll our own out of Bugler and Target cigarette tobacco. Then, wonders of wonders, Congress upped our pay. We went from $21 a month to $50 a month. Life was definitely getting better. In boot camp and radio school we closely followed the war. We heard about the disasters in the Far East, the fall of the Philippines, Wake Island being overrun, and Douglas MacArthur's flight to Australia. Then came the Battle of Midway, the Doolittle raid on Tokyo, and out first offensive in the Pacific, the Marine landing on the Solomon Islands in August.

We were through with radio school the last of August and the Marine Corps sent us to the Miramar Marine Corps Air Station, just outside of San Diego. I was assigned to VMF-112, a Marine fighter squadron. I was really disappointed. My friends from Texas A&M got billets as radio-gunners in dive bomber and torpedo bomber squadrons. Some even went with transport outfits, and those flying multi-engine bombers. So I went to the slop chute. I didn't drink as much as I did when I got drunk in Texas, just enough to take the edge off my disappointment.

We piled aboard the *Lurline*, a Matson liner, in San Diego. We made a quick dash, unaccompanied by a convoy, across the Pacific. One day out of Dago the weather became rough. We were stacked like sardines below decks in troop compartments. The bunks were stacked about four to six high. If the guy on the top bunk got seasick, he would throw up on those below, and soon the whole compartment reeked of vomit. I did not get seasick, but the smell below decks really got to me. So I spent most of my time at sea on that trip topside. I ran into an old schoolmate on the trip. David Ratke was working as a merchant mariner in the mess room of the Lurline. We had a nice reunion.

Ten days after leaving San Diego we landed at Noumea, New Caledonia. We learned that our destination was Cactus, the code word for Guadalcanal. We didn't do much in the way of training, but we had regular assigned tasks to do. Mine was to help out on the garbage run from the mess hall to the dump. We would load the truck with the big garbage cans, drive down through Noumea to the nickel docks on the harbor. New Caledonia mined a tremendous amount of the mineral, and nickel ore was shipped down to the docks for transport to refineries. We would dump the garbage, and women and their families would throng to the dump and go through the trash we had emptied on the pile. There were huge tenements next to the nickel docks road. The cubicles were occupied by Oriental people from Southeast Asia. They were the nickel workers.

One night I woke up to hear quiet, musical chanting and beating on some sort of percussion instrument. I went out of the tent, and the camp, down to beach where I saw a campfire. Four big native New Caledonians with dark skins and fuzzy red hair were beating on a log-like instrument with sticks. They were singing and swaying in time to the beat. They looked up at me and smiled, and never missed a beat. I must have sat for an hour listening to them before I went back to my tent. Beaumont was sure a long way off.

We got liberty in Noumea. Three Cajuns from Louisiana who could speak French became very popular. Two of them were named Herbert and Hebert. We would go to the sidewalk cafes and have lunch. I remember the great French bread. We would get Herbert or Hebert to translate for us, and try and pick up girls. I don't know of any in my outfit that managed a date with a French civilian girl. They were polite and friendly, but that was all.

I came down with a bad case of bronchitis in New Caledonia. I was running a fever and not able to get out of my sack, when they took me to the dispensary. I was in the dispensary for five days, and while I was there my outfit was shipped north to Guadalcanal. They packed up my gear, except for my rifle, and my sea bag with me in the dispensary. When I was well enough to travel, I was transported to an airfield in the highlands of central New Caledonia. I, along with an Army colonel, were the only passengers in the Navy R4D, a converted civilian DC-3. It was my first flight in an airplane. We climbed up to about 12,000 feet en route to the Solomons. I had no proper clothes for the cold flight. The temperature was at freezing. My breath came out in cloudy puffs, and froze on the metal bulkhead of the plan. The damn colonel had blankets and an overcoat, and he didn't offer me any. It was then I developed a hate for some commissioned officers. Those bastards got the nurses, the booze and the blankets. We drank beer, went woman-less, and were out in the cold.

We landed on Henderson Field. I was taken to our squadron headquarters on Fighter One, a fighter strip about two miles from Henderson Field. We landed just after the last big shelling of the island struck. The Japanese fleet had come down the slot and lobbed the big shells around the fields. I got there on November 13, my little brother Tony's ninth birthday. We lived in tents, with lots of mosquito netting draped around us. Latrines were dug so we could relieve ourselves, and Lister bags that held chlorinated water hung from the trees. When we bathed, it was from our helmets. We didn't have showers. We only ate two meals a day. For over a month our rations were sort of a soup made from corned beef; canned tomatoes, corn and peas. We had that in the morning and the afternoon. We had a squadron of about 20 fighter planes, Grumman F4Fs. VMF-112 had most of the fighter planes on Guadalcanal then. I had heard that we only had about 45 planes we could put in the air from our island against the whole Japanese air forces.

We had two daily aggravations. Pistol Pete, a Japanese howitzer, would lob shells all around the area occupied by Marine forces. His aim wasn't very good, but occasionally he would hit a gasoline drum, a latrine, or a chow line. Maytag Charlie was worse. It was some sort of Japanese patrol craft that would make a nightly sortie over the island, haphazardly dropping his small bombs. Our anti-aircraft weapons made much more noise than the bombs.

Conditions were primitive, but much better than the marines fighting on the front lines only 1,500 yards away from our fields. For three nights we were called out to set up a perimeter line around the strip. The Japanese were on an offensive. We took our rifles and field packs and went into the foxholes. It made me remember that all marines are basically riflemen. On Christmas Eve 1942 Condition Red was sounded at twilight. I don't know why they call it twilight in the tropics. It goes from daylight to dark in a flash. So when it went dark we went into the big foxholes we had dug for bomb protection. The cannons roared, the bombs fell, and blasted away. We sang "Holy Night," and "Oh Little Town of Bethlehem." I missed my family, I missed the girlfriend I didn't have, and I was scared. And I never felt closer to a God that I didn't understand. I truly believed the adage: "There are no atheists in fox holes."

We had rigged up receivers so that we could monitor the tactical radio frequencies on which our pilots transmitted. We could hear their cries of "Tallyho" when they spotted Japanese planes. We were glued to the radios during the dog fights, and we could hear when our pilots were bailing out, and waiting for the PBYs to pick them up.

I was a regular at mass on Guadalcanal, and I took up where I left off from Beaumont. I became a server. One memory is vivid. After we had been sent over to a new strip, Fighter Two, closer to the front lines, I went to mass at a CB, a Naval Construction Battalion chapel. Another man and I were the only ones at mass. He was a Solomon Islander. A big, shiny black man, with muscles like Charles Atlas, he had a bone necklace, and a huge mane-like head of red hair. He wore a stark-white cast on his left leg that reached from hip to ankle. He couldn't kneel, just stand and sit. We recited the Latin mass responses together.

My work in the fighter squadron consisted of working on radios, something I knew nothing about. I would take transmitters and receivers out of the planes to the shop, where they were worked on, then reinstall them in the aircraft. Working in the belly of a fighter plane, in 100-degree tropical heat, is a sure way to lose weight. When we moved to Fighter Two conditions improved. The food got better, we had better tents, and an outdoor shower. The water temperature was always the same, about 85 degrees Fahrenheit. The Japanese tried one more big push while we were there. One night there was a tremendous amount of shelling. We had 105mm and 155mm howitzers parked all over the airfield. When they would cut loose at night, when I was in the sack, the explosions would suck in the mosquito netting over my bed, then blow it back out. We had one of those big howitzers about 50 feet away from our tent. When it would go off, it would almost knock you out of the sack. The morning after the big shelling, we found a curious sight on the strip. Japanese infiltrators had sneaked in and planted charges on the motor mounts of some of the aircraft, We had some Army planes next to ours and those are the ones that were hit. The P-40 Tomahawks and the P-39 Airicobras had their engines drooping with the propeller hubs on the ground. The sabotaged aircraft were but 200 yards away from us.

We had our radio shack up on the side of a hill next to the strip. We had dug a latrine close by. We put a box over it and made a nice comfortable seat for the radio crew to sit on. The line chief, a tech sergeant, kept coming up the hill and using our head. We told him to cease and desist. He told us to go shit in our fists. We rigged up a magneto from a field telephone and attached it to nails driven flush in the contoured, comfortable seat. We ran the leads from the head up to our workbench in the radio shack. The old nasty tech sergeant came hurrying up the hill, got to our head, dropped his trousers, and we could hear his audible sigh as he relieved himself. I grabbed the magneto crank, turned it like I was churning butter for Grandma, the electricity sped down the lines, and the tech sergeant flew straight in the air. He was in the middle of his business, and he made quite a mess all over himself and our nice new head. When he hit the ground, he reached for his trousers and belt, snatched his pistol from the holster and shot a round over our heads into the tent. The radiomen dropped like stones. Swearing, the tech sergeant came for the radio tent. The crew ran over the hill to squadron headquarters a lot faster than he did. He didn't have his pants on all the way. We got a reprimand. The tech sergeant got restricted to quarters-that meant he couldn't go to the movies for a week. We hosed down our new head, and nobody else used it but the radio crew.

While I was on Guadalcanal I got my third stripe. I became a Sergeant Frank W. King, USMCR. At one time a buck sergeant in the Marine Corps was God, but with the war promotions were coming a lot easier. February 1943 came and we were put on a United Fruit Company banana boat and taken down to the New Hebrides. Our pilots were pooped out from combat stress, primitive living conditions, and ready for a time to rest in Australia. I think that the place were we were sent was the Turtle Bay fighter strip. It was also the headquarters for Marine Air Group (MAG) 11. One of my regular duties was to stand a radio watch in the operations shack, a Quonset hut next to the air field. I usually pulled the watch at night, monitoring the frequency on which a military net operated. As I remember it, Pappy Boyington was the operations officer. He was just organizing the Black Sheep Squadron. I remember when the first F4Us, the new Corsairs, came. They were brought in by carrier hauled to our airstrip where we had the assignment to un-pickle them. That mean getting rid of all the anti-weathering materials, and getting the aircraft ready for combat. We worked hard at the task. One other task we had was to unload 50-gallon drums of gasoline from a freighter in the harbor onto landing craft so they could be hauled to our base. I spent a lot of time on the ocean. First going from one place to another, and then in duties like unloading stuff from ships. Anytime we went places by ship, we did not have a gangplank to walk down, except of we were coming home to San Francisco or San Diego. The only way on and off the ship was by a landing net over the side. You had to climb down the rope netting, with a full pack and your rifle, into the landing craft. Or it was from the landing craft, climbing up the rope ladder to the ship's deck. No wonder I was in such good shape. When we were in boot camp we had to train for that. One thing we had to do was learn to swim, which I already had accomplished. In order to graduate, we had to jump off of a high tower, into a swimming pool, with equipment on, get rid of it, and swim out of trouble. I didn't have any trouble with that.

In letters from Mom, Dad and Tony I had learned that my younger brother Pete had joined the Navy and gone to radio school as I had, only he went to the University of Wisconsin at Madison. Pete was assigned to the Navy Amphibious Service and was a radioman with a landing party. He had been in on the invasion of North Africa and his ship was torpedoed off of Iran in the Mediterranean. Pete had gone over the side, uninjured except for his feet being burned on the scalding decks, had been plucked out of the sea, and was safe. I could imagine what Mom and Dad were going through with both of us overseas in combat zones.

Life on Turtle Bay was nice. Bubbles Hawkins, whose real name was Barbara, began writing to me. She was a sweet girl, the younger sister of my good high school friend Jim Hawkins. She sent me a picture. We wrote nice, sort of mushy letters back and forth. Letters from Mom, Dad, Tony, Lada, Uncle Louie, who had joined the Navy CBs, and Bubbles kept me sane. I can't describe the elation you would experience when you got a fist full of letters at mail call, or the dark depression that would hit when you walked away empty handed. When no letters would come I would delve into the small stash of beer that I had. We would get beer occasionally and it was a very popular item. At Turtle Bay we even had an ice machine, and that was a luxury.

We lived in Dallas huts, pre-fabricated units made from plywood. We had cleaned up our area that used to be a copra plantation. We lived near a grove of coconut trees right next to a beautiful little harbor with a rough, coral beach, an Eden I would trade for Beaumont any day. We had cleaned up all of the old palm fronds that had littered the place, and gathered every grounded coconut, put it all in big pile and burned it. That reduced the number of land crabs that came in to feed off the coconuts that dropped off the trees. The land crabs were terrible creatures with huge claws that could inflict a very painful bite. We kept the grass trimmed down with machetes. We had a still. Into the still went anything that would ferment, sugar, coconut meat, raisins, cornmeal we would steal from the mess hall, etc. After a short fermentation period we would distill it. We made a still out of some five-gallon gasoline tins and copper tubing from a wrecked airplane. The stuff smelled bad and tasted worse, but when mixed with grapefruit juice it was potable. We called it torpedo juice. Real torpedo juice was the 200-proof alcohol used in Navy torpedoes.

My first experience with our torpedo juice was not pleasant. We renamed it Kickapoo Joy Juice, from the Li'l Abner comic strip. I took my cup from my mess kit. It was all black inside from drinking that horrible marine coffee. I put about two inches of torpedo juice in the cup, and another two inches of grapefruit juice on top. We went to the movies. We had made little stools, like milking stools to sit on. We did that because the land crabs couldn't bite you on the butt. The last thing I remember was falling off my milking stool. Everybody hilariously reminded me what an ass I had made of myself. After I fell off the milking stool, I sang "The Eyes of Texas Are Upon You." I was thrown out of the movie. My bunk-mates led me back to the hut, put me to bed, only to see me rise up, go outside, pee, and climb about 15 feet up the trunk of a coconut tree. I clasped the tree like it was my lover and wouldn't let go. They had to pry me from the tree, and I passed out, again. The next morning even the white coating on my tongue hurt. That black-from-coffee canteen cup? It was bright and shiny on the inside. Again I resolved not to drink anymore.

Food was a problem on New Hebrides. Maybe it wasn't the food, but my appetite was disappearing. Marine cooks could take good food and turn it into something that was inedible. We began to get supplies from New Zealand and Australia, some of which was butter and mutton. The butter was wonderful. It came in huge tubs and reminded me of the butter we churned with Grandma Smith. The mutton was something else. The day they cooked the mutton the smell pervaded every corner of the island. Marines stayed away in droves. We finally hit on a solution to part of our hunger problem. We decided to make potato soup. We would get dehydrated potatoes, onions, seasoning and milk, put in a little butter and a lot of water and mix it up. Our cooking container was an empty five-gallon gasoline tin. We would take four gasoline-fired, blow torches, light them, and place them around the tin. The soup would come to a boil, and we would shut down three of the torches, cut down the flame on the last torch and simmer the batch for about an hour. It was good soup. On the side we would take loaves of fresh bread we swiped from the bakery, with that good New Zealand butter, and it was a meal made in heaven. I have to give the marine cooks' credit; they baked great bread, particularly when it was fresh, right out of the oven.

In late June 1943 and I had to go in for a physical. The corpsman gave me an exam and referred me to a doctor. He rechecked my weight, and told me it was time for me to go back to the states. I wasn't sick, but my weight had plummeted. I was down to about 120 pounds. By that time there were only about 20 of us left of the original VMF-112 Squadron out of 250 people Many had been sent to Australia and New Zealand hospitals, and a few back to the states. The pilots had their rests and were assigned to other squadrons or sent back home. Tropical diseases were a real problem. Many of the men had malaria, some dengue fever, and a few, elephantiasis. Skin diseases broke out on many. Jungle rot was a generic term that covered almost anything, and I suspect there were a lot of allergies and infections involved. I had a reaction to mosquito bites. I would get big white welts where they bit me, then I would scratch them, then the bites would get infected. My arms from just below my shoulders to just above my wrists were covered with infected sores that had to be treated every day. My back broke out in lesions, and I suspect that the sores on my back were infections from the coral dust that was forever blowing around the airstrip. All we had on were shorts because of the intense heat.

So I was a sorry, skinny, scabby sight when I climbed up the landing net aboard a President liner to return to the United States. Sacked out in a comfortable bunk, clean sheets and cool air from the blower was heaven. We stood in line for breakfast, and a civilian cook would take our order: "How do you want your eggs?" I hadn't had a fresh egg for 10 months. I had my first drink of fresh milk in 10 months. The voyage lasted 10 days, and we took the great circle route back. That meant we would be going through the central Pacific on our way back. I drew the assignment of gun captain of the number two gun tub on the bow of the ship. We had a battery of four 20-mm, anti-aircraft machine guns. Nothing unusual happened on the voyage home, except we went through a big Pacific storm. The huge swells were 25- to 30-feet high. We secured watches on the gun tubs, because the bow of the ship would dip down into the trough between the waves, scoop up tons of salt water, and fling it back over the bridge, like Charlie tossing his head at flies. The seven-day sea voyage agreed with me. I put on about five pounds. When I weighed in stateside I tipped the scales at an impressive 128 pounds.

We sailed under the Golden Gate Bridge at San Francisco and tied up at Treasure Island. As we were waiting to get off the ship, this time with a gangplank, I saw two women on the dock dressed in marine green. An old grizzled gunny next to me growled, "They are signing up Negroes, we have German shepherd combat dogs, and now they even letting in women." I thought they, the women marines, looked pretty nice. The gunny called them BAMS, broad-ass marines.

Piling off the ship, we were taken to the Southern Pacific depot and put aboard the train for San Diego, then the truck ride to Miramar. I was on my 30-day leave in July. I would be going to a new home.

Dad, Mom and Tony had moved from Beaumont to Santa Monica. Dad had got a nice job with Douglas as a maintenance plumber and pipe fitter. He had been with the Southern California Gas Co. for more than 19 years, but the company would not increase Dad's wages. He was still making $127.50 a month when he resigned. He was making twice that in his job at Douglas. They had bought a beautiful little California Spanish type of bungalow on Ashland Street in Santa Monica near Ocean Park. The house was on a roomy lot, had two bedrooms, stucco over frame construction, a red-tiled roof, and a little walled patio in front with a banana tree. They paid $4,500 for it, and they sold the old homestead in Beaumont. I eagerly began visiting all of the relatives, the uncles and aunts in Santa Monica, Grandpa and Grandma Smith, Lada and Louie, then the friends I knew in the Los Angeles-Santa Monica area.

In addition to Mom, Dad and Tony, there was sort of a mass exodus of family and friends from Beaumont. Most were drawn to the Los Angeles metro area because of the booming wartime economy and the great job opportunities. Grandpa and Grandma Smith had sold the shop and the ranch in Beaumont and had moved to San Gabriel Valley. Grandpa had opened another shoe repair shop in Monrovia and was doing a great business. The Hawkins family had also moved and was living close to Inglewood, in south-central Los Angeles. Being home with Mom, Dad and Tony was something I had dreamed of nightly for the past 10 months. I had been home a week and I dated Margaret Ann Powell, a girl from Beaumont whose family had moved down near the folks. I don't remember where I got the car, but I borrowed it from someone and I picked her up, resplendent in my dress blues with my campaign ribbons. We went to the Aragon Ballroom on the Ocean Park Pier. Some name band was playing and we were having a great time, when suddenly I felt very ill. We went outside and Margaret Ann felt my forehead, and said that I was burning with fever. She got me out to the car, and she drove me back to my folks' house. Dad took Margaret Ann home and Mom put me into the bed that Tony and I had been sharing in his bedroom. Tony slept on the couch that night. I remember vivid dreams, and not being able to get comfortable in the bed. Dad woke the next morning and asked me if I remember what had happened. I said "no" and he recounted my actions. I had gone to bed, wandered into their bedroom, stark naked, raving about the bombers about to strike. He put me back to bed, and watched me until dawn. That morning I began chills and fever again, shaking uncontrollably, and unable to get warm. Mom piled blankets on top of me and I still shivered. Dad called the U.S. Navy Dispensary at Lilac Terrace in L.A. and told them about my sickness. The duty corpsman said it sounded like I had come down with malaria, and they would send someone to pick me up. Within an hour an ambulance, with red lights flashing, pulled into our driveway. The corpsmen came in the house with a stretcher, put me on it, and put me in the ambulance. As we pulled away, I could look out the back window and see Mom, Dad and Tony in front of the house waving goodbye. Mom was wiping at her eyes with her apron.

I was in misery for the first week in the Long Beach Naval Hospital. The malaria attacks kept coming-chills and fever, chills and fever-and they wouldn't give me anything to stop them. The corpsmen had drawn blood from me, but the tests did not come back positive for malaria. So they waited until I was at the height of an attack, and the again took blood from me. That did it. They got a positive smear, and they began dosing me with quinine immediately. The quinine did the trick and the malaria attacks subsided. The doctors also began treating the sores on my arms and back that had stayed with me since Guadalcanal. They tried everything, including X-ray treatments. The nasty infections stayed with me, but not as bad as before. I was not to get out of the Long Beach hospital until November.

I was much better in three week and began going on liberty. One of the first places I hit was the Hawkins home, to date Bubbles. We went out a few times, and after I would take her home I would hit the bars. I quit seeing her, because I thought that I really wasn't worthy of her. About this same time a Navy lieutenant with the Navy Industrial Incentive outfit came by the hospital looking for bodies to take on War Bond drives. He selected me as one of the returning heroes to go with him to the plants manufacturing equipment for the war effort. He chose guys who had been in combat in the Pacific. We were put up in the Lankershim Hotel in downtown Los Angeles, given food chits, and a little spending money. It was like turning the fox loose in a hen house. We really lived it up. We would go out mainly to the aircraft plants like Douglas, Lockheed, Northrup and North American. Girls would slip us notes with their telephone numbers.

There was a man shortage, and women were everywhere. I was still unbred. One night I ended up in a bar just south of downtown, became friendly with the waitress, and I stayed until closing. I asked her to go back to the hotel with me. She said okay, and I managed to sneak her past the desk clerk, up the stairs to my room. I found out that she was married to a Navy chief petty officer who was in Hawaii. I asked her if she felt guilty about being with me.

She said, "Hell, no. He is doing the same thing in Hawaii."

She was a nice, friendly, easygoing person, who came from one of the farm states like Iowa or Nebraska. I drove her back to her place where she lived on Washington Blvd. Then I began looking for a Navy first aid station. Flashbacks of those nasty venereal disease movies they made us watch flickered through my brain. Horrible genital scars, brain damage, crippled and spastic muscles. With my luck I would come down with them all. All I wanted was to get that initial treatment for venereal. I had heard it was painful. They injected a fluid into your penis and it burned and stung for hours. I couldn't find the prophylactic station. They said you had to get treatment within 12 hours after intercourse or it was no good. So I prayed. I prayed to God the Father, God the Son, God the Holy Ghost, to Mary His Mother, John the Baptist, St. Francis, St. Joseph and all the saints in heaven. I carefully inspected my penis every time I went to the bathroom. Two weeks passed. Nothing happened so I thought I was home free.

I was getting better so I was to take a test to see if I had any more malaria in my system. They would give you a Wasserman or Kahn test. It was the same test they used to test for venereal disease. My first test came back positive. My God! I've got syphilis. I am going to become a drooling, brain-dead idiot, living out my life at the poor farm. I took an oath to not have any more sexual intercourse, to stop drinking, again.

The docs assured me that I did not have a venereal disease, that the positive test results meant that the malaria bug was still in my system. So it was back on the road again, talking plant workers into buying more War Bonds. My story was getting stale, at least it was to me. So I began to embellish my experiences, borrowing tales told by my friends who had gone through boot camp and radio school with me. One day I would be a radio-gunner in dive bombers, and the next day something else. Guilt has always been my loving companion, and he began to sit on my shoulders with a huge leaden weight. I was a drunk, a fornicator, a liar and a phony. I was no good to myself or anyone else.

About this time I met Donna Miller. She was working for Lada in the office at Mandel's. Mandel's was a shoe chain, owned by Maurice Mandel, with stores all over Southern California. Lada was the office manager and the accountant. Donna and I began dating, and soon we were getting serious about each other. November came, I got a negative test on malaria and I was all set to return to active duty, after nearly five months in the hospital.

My orders were to report to Miramar from the hospital. I reported in and the sergeant major told me that his records showed me as being AWOL. I gave him my papers that indicated I had been in the hospital, but somehow the word never got back to my unit at Miramar. After they straightened that out, they asked me what my military specialty was. My service and medical records had been lost or destroyed between New Hebrides and the states. I had been telling everyone that I was a radioman-gunner, including my folks, friends, the bar flies, and the war plant workers. So I automatically told the sergeant major that I had gone to radio school and was a radioman-gunner. The next day I was on my way to El Toro Marine Corps Air Station and assigned to VMSB-132, a dive bomber squadron. Upon arriving I was taken to the supply sergeant, outfitted with flying gear, and assigned to quarters. The day after that I went on the second airplane flight of my life.

My pilot was Lt. Boatright. I climbed into the back seat of the SBD, the Douglas Dauntless dive bomber. I had my helmet on, found the connection for the headphones and microphone, twiddled with the radio, found the intercom system working with Mr. Boatright. We took off.

I sat facing front, but I quickly learned how to turn around in the seat. The SBD had a scarf ring that ran around the top of the cockpit in the rear seat. On that scarf ring were twin .30-caliber machine guns. I knew how to operate the machine guns. I had learned that in boot camp. You would pull the twin .30s up and out from a section in which they were stored in the aft fuselage. You had to be careful when firing the guns. You could cut your airplane's tail off if you weren't careful. I think that is the only mistake I didn't make. We joined up with two other aircraft. Mr. Boatright was flying as a wingman on the port side of the leader. We had another three airplanes, in the same formation, right behind and beneath us. We climbed out west of El Toro to a bombing range. According to my altimeter we were at 12,000 feet when the leader went into a descent, wobbled his wings, peeled off over the starboard wingman, and went into a steep dive, then the starboard aircraft did the same maneuver. We were next, peeling off, swooping down in a vertical dive, and I was facing backwards with my guns out. The microphone went flying out of its holder, things were rattling, and I about shit my pants. I had never been so scared in all my life, but the worse was yet to come. When we went into the dive, Mr. Boatright had cracked open the dive flaps, the perforated sheets of metal on the trailing edge of the wing. The slowed the plane down, and made it more stable so the pilot could aim his bomb. I opened my eyes and there they were. Three SBDs right behind us, pointed right at our tail.

One of them was gaining on us fast, and went swooping by, only feet away. It seemed that two hours had passed since we started the dive, but it was only seconds before Mr. Boatright dropped the dummy bomb and pulled out about 500 feet above the ground. The G forces forced my head down into my neck, my neck into my crotch, my crotch down around my ankles. I had encountered alcoholic blackouts, but nothing like this. We leveled off, went back to base, landed and taxied in. My legs were shaking so badly I could hardly climb down out of the cockpit.

Why didn't I keep my big mouth shut? Me and my grandiose bragging about being a valiant air crewman. Hell! I could have had a billet some place as a ground radio operator if I had shut up. I wondered if there was an opening for cooks and bakers school

The dive bombing and aerial gunnery hops continued. I had come down with a nasty cold and we went on a flight up to the Mojave Desert for dive bombing practice. This time we went up to about 14,000 feet, with no oxygen, and I could feel that I was getting sicker. By the time we landed I was in the throes of a full-blown malaria attack. Off to the dispensary at El Toro for three days, more quinine, and I recovered. The only trouble is that I developed a horrible itch after I was discharged. The docs said that it was scabies. So back into the dispensary and out came the tincture of green soap, sulfur salve and three showers a day. I would shower, scrub with a brush loaded with the tincture of green soap, dry off, and rub myself down with the sulfur salve. The scabies went away, and amazingly so did the lesions on my arms and back.

VMSB-132 was ordered overseas, and because I had so many malaria attacks I was kept stateside and put in another squadron. They were flying SB2Cs, the Curtis Helldivers. I hated those aircraft. Then we got the TBMs, the Avengers. The Avenger was then the largest single-engine airplane in the world. It carried a crew of three: the pilot, the turret gunner, and the radio-radar operator. The turret gunner was seated in a compartment topside behind the pilot. My office was in the belly of the beast. I had a small door to crawl through to get to my station, two tiny windows on each side of the fuselage, and a plexiglass enclosed .30-caliber machine gun, a stinger sticking out below the tail. I had all sorts of new equipment to learn how to operate, and I loved it. My new pilot's name was Jerome P. Barnier, who came from Morgan Hill, California. He was a little younger than I, and had been going to San Jose State College, and was another football player. He was a huge guy. His nickname was "Big Barn Smell," again borrowed from Al Capp's Li'l Abner comic strip.

Donna and I had been dating for over a year, and in January 1944 we were married at Blessed Sacrament Church on Sunset Blvd. in Hollywood. Our marriage night was a disaster. I got drunk, and the night is a blur. We went to a motel in West Los Angeles right after the wedding dinner. My new bride was so upset the next morning that she demanded we return to her mother's house. We went back there and spent the rest our honeymoon nights in Donna's room, with all the mementos of her childhood. I was a day late in getting back to the base, and the old man, our commanding officer, restricted me to barracks for a week. I couldn't get back into town to see my new bride.

Donna and her mother lived in Hollywood. I would hitchhike into Hollywood from El Toro. Much of the time I would have Lada's 1940 DeSoto sedan. Getting gasoline wasn't too much of a problem. We had gasoline rationing stamps Lada would get for me, and much of the time I would fill the DeSoto up with aviation gasoline. The aviation gas pumps were an easy mark for us, and we stole a lot of it to put in our own tanks. That 100-octane gas sure made the old DeSoto go fast.

On liberties I would dash up to Hollywood and stay with Donna and her mother at the little house on Lexington Avenue in Hollywood. We did a lot of partying, going out to night clubs, and drinking. One weekend I was hitching a ride from the base to Hollywood after a party at El Toro. I had just been paid and was half drunk. The couple who gave me a ride dropped me off in downtown L.A. I reached into my pocket for streetcar fare, and my wallet was gone. My booze-driven imagination shifted into overdrive. I would tell Donna that I had been mugged by some thugs who had tried to knife me. I took some broken glass and slashed the sleeve of my jacket. I would tell her that the guys struck at me and missed. I got a ride home. Walked in the door and told the tale of my attack. Donna, and her mother, Tibby, led me to the couch and consoled me. Brought me a drink, and made me lie down on the couch. We sat down for dinner, and the doorbell rang. It was the couple who had given me a ride. They had found my address in the wallet I had dropped on the back seat of their car. I thanked them profusely, offered them a reward, and they declined. They left.

"Who were those people, Frank?" Donna asked.

The truth came out, and there was no crack in the floor small enough for me to crawl through. Our relationship cooled rapidly. Things did not get better a few days later when a Western Union messenger rang the doorbell. I answered it, signed for the telegram from the War Department, and took it to Donna and her mother. They opened it. Donna's oldest brother, Joe, a navigator in the Army Air Force, had been killed at Bari, Italy, in the crash of a B-24 bomber. Donna was never the same after that. One night in a spasm of grief she cried, "Why did it happen to Joe? Why not you?" I was crushed. My world was falling apart. Every time I climbed into my airplane her words haunted me.

After anti-submarine school our squadron was assigned overseas. I wasn't looking forward to another trip into a combat zone, and leaving Donna and her grief was really hard. We took the train up to San Francisco to Treasure Island, climbed on a new troop transport and headed overseas in early 1944. After a week we anchored at Ulithi Atoll where there were thousands of Allied ships, all gathered for the great invasion of the Japanese homeland. At Ulithi we climbed aboard an LCI, landing craft-infantry that took us to the Carolines. We were stationed on Peleliu (now Beleliu) in the Palau group of islands, about 200 miles southeast of the Philippines. Our job was to do anti-submarine patrols around all of the islands in the chain. Peleliu had been the site of a terrific battle between the Marines and Japanese forces in the previous year. Other islands in the chain, including the main one of Babelthaup, with the capital city of

Korror, were still occupied by the Japanese. Our patrols took us just off-shore and we were continually looking for Japanese activity.

On one patrol I spotted a small boat, a Japanese Type A landing craft, with a small boat tied to it. The landing craft it was about 50-feet long, and looked as if it were stranded on a coral reef on the west coast of Babelthaup. We strafed with our machine guns. I could see the wood splinters flying into the air from the impact of our bullets. It looked as if there was no life aboard, and no returning fire. It was the first time we had fired our guns against the enemy, and we were excited. Excitement was welcome.

We monitored the short wave radios every night, listening to news broadcasts and the baseball games. Word came about the German surrender and VE Day, and the wonderful celebrations that were taking place all over the U.S. We were happy because that meant more troops to help us end the war in the Pacific.

We suffered the enervating boredom, and worked at finding things to occupy our time. I read a lot. I told Mr. Barnier that I would like to learn navigation. He eagerly accepted the challenge. Each of the pilots had a plotting board for dead reckoning navigation. They would take them into the briefings, get the coordinates of the courses we were to fly, and lay out our patrol patterns. Mr. Barnier taught me how to lay out a course, draw a wind triangles, and account for magnetic variation a compass deviation.

The day came when I was to take over the navigation. We walked out to the airplane. I carried the plotting board.

"Aren't you going to give the board to Mr. Barnier?" Bray, the turret gunner asked.

"No. I am doing the navigation on this trip."

"No way am I flying in that plane with you navigating!"

"Get in the airplane, and shut up," said Mr. Barnier.

We flew two triangular patterns in the two-hour hop. I would call out the headings, and time to change course, on all of the legs. When base ops called and told us to terminate, another aircraft was on its way out to relieve us, Mr. Barnier asked for a heading to the point at which we were supposed to get back on the island before landing. I gave him the heading, and anxiously waited until I got word from him on how good my plotting was. We flew over the coastline.

"How did we do?" I asked.

"Look down below."

There, just passing underneath us a little to starboard, was the white triangle marking the point of entry. Bray, who was above me in the turret, didn't say anything. He had been monitoring our conversation on his headset. I hit him on the foot. He looked down at me. I stuck up the middle finger of my right hand at him. From that time on, I did all of the navigating on our hops at Peleliu and later on Okinawa.

After a short time in the Pallaus we got a new assignment to VMTB-131 on Okinawa. We flew by Curtis C-46 from Pelelieu to Guam. We had an overnight stay on Guam, and I managed to get in touch with Uncle Louie. He was a chaplain's assistant with the Navy CB's; we had a nice visit. We then climbed aboard a C-54, a new Douglas 4-engine transport that took us from Guam to Okinawa. VMTB-131 was stationed on Ie Shima, a small island off the coast of Okinawa. It was the place where war correspondent Ernie Pyle had been killed. One of the first things we did was visit the site where they had put up his monument. We had plenty of excitement on Ie Shima. Shortly after we got there we had a three-day condition red. The Japanese were sending down all the airplanes they had left in a big raid. Many of them were kamikazes. On our field we also had Army B-24s, a P-47 Thunderbolt squadron, a Marine fighter squadron. During the battle a Japanese Zero plummeted down through the overcast and dashed right through our traffic pattern. It was trailing smoke and headed out to sea. Two Marine Corsairs that were in the traffic pattern spotted the plane, tucked up their landing gear and took after him. They caught the Zero in seconds, raked him with fire, and we stood on shore cheering like at a football game as the Japanese plane splashed into the sea.

We had arrived on Ie Shima as the last fighting on the island was raging on the south end of Okinawa. After a few weeks we were reassigned to another small airfield, right next to Buckner Bay, on the east side of the island. There were plenty of alerts, and the ships anchored in Buckner Bay were frequently being attacked by Kamikaze pilots. We did a lot of traveling around the island, exploring caves where the Japanese had holed up in resisting our invasion. Living conditions were luxurious compared to what we had on Guadalcanal and the New Hebrides in 1942-43. We continued our almost daily antisubmarine patrols around Okinawa, and were also ordered to fly bombing runs on outlying Japanese-occupied islands that were still putting up some resistance.

Mr. Barnier was an excellent boss. He took good care of Bray and me. He was a generous, considerate, honest commander. He gave us booze. That made him a hero in my book. The officers had a liquor allowance and were allowed to buy so much booze every month, when it was available. Barn Smell would buy the bourbon and Scotch for himself, but he would also get rum, gin, any oddball stuff with alcohol in it and give it to Bray and me. I asked him if we could pay him for it, because I knew that it came out of his pocket, but he said it was his gift to us. Big Barn Smell could do no wrong in my book.

The island was declared secure on June 21, but the mop up continued until July 2.

The next month the first atomic bomb was dropped on Hiroshima. We heard the news on short-wave broadcasts from the states. The A Bomb was euphemistically referred to as a "super weapon bomb," but we had no idea what it really was. Then the second one was dropped on Nagasaki on August 9, 1945. Then the rumors began to circulate that Japan was surrendering. A night or two later, news swept over us that the war had ended, and that Japan was surrendering. The ships fired rockets, shells and parachute flares. We grabbed our sidearms, ran outside and started firing in the air. It was the biggest fireworks display I had ever seen. Our officers ran out and hollered at us to quit shooting. We ran off where they couldn't see us, and shot again. Then the news came: the war was not over and the Japanese had not surrendered. On August 15, we received word that the Japanese had accepted the surrender terms. There was another big firing display that night, but not as big as the false surrender. We had got it out of our system, and we knew for sure, at last, that Japan's days as a foe were numbered.

We were hit with two typhoons while I was on Okinawa. Mr. Barnier had been sent up to Japan with our airplane to fly light freight and courier missions after the armistice and before the last big typhoon. I didn't go with him, because I had enough points to return home, and I was to stand by for transportation to the states. Mr. Barnier had wiped out the airplane on a takeoff in Japan, and came back to Okinawa before the second typhoon hit. The first one didn't do too much damage, but the second was a monster. I can remember huddling anywhere we could to get out of the wind. Sheet metal peeled off the Quonset huts, went flying across our area like scythes lopping off trees. The shore around Buckner Bay was littered with flying boats, destroyers, tankers and many different types of ships. My last flight as a Marine radioman-gunner was with Mr. Barnier. We were one of the first airplanes in the air after the runway was cleared. It was my job to take aerial photos of the destruction. I had the old K20 aerial camera that I used for the photography. We removed the side entry door into my compartment so that I could stick the camera out and take the photos.

Then it was time for me to ship back home. On November 9, 1945, I loaded my gear aboard a ship that carried about 200 sailors and marines. The rest of the passengers were civilians who had been interned in Japanese prison camps during the war. We headed home taking the great circle route, and in a few days it began getting cold. The Marines on board, me included, were assigned guard duty. We were posted at the entries between the military personnel area and the civilians. The ship's skipper wanted to keep the raunchy sailors and marines away from the civilian women. Marine guards became the most hated people on the ship. I didn't care. We were going home. We suddenly took a southerly heading. We learned that we were headed for Hawaii to disembark some of the civilians. After tying up at Pearl Harbor, we were allowed to go down on the dock, but not into town. Oh, how I wanted that trip into Honolulu. I settled for a phone booth, but it had a line a block long and I couldn't place a call. It was back on the ship, and within hours we were back at sea. We sailed under the Golden Gate Bridge with the horn blasting, and signal flags flying. Immediately after we landed I called my Dad in Santa Monica, told him I was home, and asked him to call Donna and tell her. That was a mistake. I should have called Donna first. We had to get back on the ship and take it down to San Diego, a one-day trip. They hurried us to Miramar, and I was discharged on November 19, ten days after I left Okinawa.

I got into Los Angeles, took a taxi to the house on Lexington, greeted my mother-in-law and waited for Donna to get home from work. She arrived, I got a cool kiss, and a perfunctory hug. Mother-in-law left the room. Donna lit into me, crying and asking me why I hadn't called her first when I got to San Francisco? I told her I wanted to check with Dad first, because he was finding out about a job I was interested in. That seemed to placate her a little. She was all for me getting a job soon and earning money so we could share the rent with her mother. I had asked Dad to look into a job I had heard about that was being offered by the U.S. Civilian Aeronautics Administration. They were hiring and training aircraft communicators, air traffic controllers, radio and radar technicians. I was a trained radioman and I was wondering if I would qualify for one of the jobs. The second or third day after I had returned, I went out to Santa Monica to visit Mom, Dad and Tony, and I went to the Western Region Office of the CAA. Their offices were in Santa Monica. I was interviewed by Harry Helmus. About two or three weeks later I was notified that my application had been approved and I would be getting an assignment within six weeks to two months.

Donna frowned upon me sitting around the house, so I looked around for a job that I could do during the waiting period for the CAA. I tried the

Hollywood Market, but I hated stocking shelves. After three days I quit. Donna's frown became deeper. I went to work for Muller Brothers Service Station on the southwest corner of Sunset and Vine in Hollywood. I really enjoyed that work. Donna didn't. She said she hadn't married me because I enjoyed being a grease monkey. I was put on graveyard shift, from midnight to 8 a.m. I saw a lot of crazy things, and enjoyed myself. The tips were good, too. A lot of actors, actresses, directors and producers would come in and many were generous people.

Donna, her mother and I were invited out to my grandparents place in El Monte for some sort of celebration. I was working graveyard, and I wouldn't get home until about the time they were to leave. Lada and Uncle Louie picked up Donna and her mother for the trip to El Monte. I had just got home, and I was going to take a bath, get cleaned up and take the streetcar and bus out to the grandfolks' house. I had been drinking while working that night, and when I got home I wasn't feeling any pain. After Donna and her mother left I had a few more drinks, then climbed into the tub. That's the last I remember until I heard until Uncle Louie shaking me awake. The water in the tub was ice cold. I hadn't showed up at the party, they tried calling me on the phone, no answer. After a couple hours Louie drove back into Hollywood, climbed in the bathroom window. He stepped down into a tub of cold water, jumped out, and angrily shook me awake. I was sober by the time I got out to El Monte, but the reception was colder than that damn bath water.

Chapter 9

Needles

I took the long Greyhound Bus ride from Los Angeles to Needles, California, to start my new career. Needles has a reputation as being one of the hottest places on the North American continent. It is a railroad town, right on the Colorado River that is the border between California and Arizona. I reported into my station chief, Peter Joseph Clark. Pete was a retired Navy radioman who was a career man with the CAA. He laid out what I would be doing as a trainee aircraft communicator. We had to pass a written exam very similar to a commercial pilot exam in navigation, meteorology, air traffic control and communications procedures, and civil air regulations. Then we had to pass a Morse code test and demonstrate radio voice communications procedures. The training period would take about three months of intensive work. Pete was a demanding chief, but a fair boss. One Saturday I was downtown buying a ticket at the theater before going to a movie. Pete and Olive, his wife, were driving by in their car. Pete slammed on the brakes and called me over. He wanted to know why I wasn't home studying for my navigation exam that was scheduled for Monday. Olive hit him on the arm and told him to take it easy. He just frowned at me and drove away.

Pete was a good teacher. Surprisingly, navigation was tough even though I had learned a lot about it under Big Barn Smell's tutelage. After he had left the Navy, Pete had worked with a tuna fishing fleet in the Pacific as a radioman and a navigator. He had taught himself celestial navigation, and could write a book on dead reckoning. He taught me again on drawing wind triangles, setting a course, doing radius of action, and radius of action with a moving base problems. I became expert in using the E6B aerial computer, and had to learn math and formulas. Sister Thomas Aquinas would have been proud of me. I earned a 98 percent on my navigation final, and Pete was really mad at me. I should have scored 100 percent. I passed meteorology and U.S Weather Bureau observer exams, and was all set for promotion. When I started out as a CAF5 I think I was making $1,590 a year, and that jumped up to about $2,450 when I got my CAF-7.

Meanwhile, I had been hitchhiking, begging rides, or taking the bus every other week so I could get back to Los Angeles and see Donna. After I got my promotion we took some of the money she had saved from the allotment while I was on Okinawa, and bought a used 1937 Chevrolet sedan. That meant I could drive the 600-mile round trip every other week on my days off. I urged Donna to quit her job at Mandel's and to set up housekeeping in Needles. She firmly declined. I had been living in a public war housing project, in a one-bedroom apartment. I decided to move into a rooming house in Needles.

Mrs. Bland owned the place, and had about two renters. One moved out when her son Frank and his new bride returned home from the Marine Corps. His name was Frank also. Years later he would become the sheriff of San Bernardino County. So Frank Bland and his new wife moved in down the hall from me. I was working day shift and it was the middle of the summer. I had the swamp cooler on in my room blowing right on me. I had been working graveyard and I tried to sleep as much as I could during the day. At night I would take a nap before driving out to the airport to get there about 11:30 p.m. It seemed that every time I went to bed, the Blands were in their room down the hall. Sounds of their love-making, the thumping bedstead, moans and cries; drove me crazy.

I could hardly wait to get back to L.A. and get Donna in bed, except she didn't want to go to bed. When we did go to bed she ordered me to "take precautions. "I didn't want to "take precautions" because it was a mortal sin. I caved in. When I went to confession, the priest refused to grant me absolution because I was using a condom in relations with my wife. We had a pretty good fight, and Donna let me know in no uncertain terms that she did not want to have any children. Before we had married, Donna and I had taken instructions from a priest at Blessed Sacrament in Hollywood, and we were told about the church's stand on birth control and family. I reminded her of this, and then the silent treatment started. My marriage was going to hell, and I thought if I wasn't so far away it would ease things. So I resigned my job with the CAA in Needles, and moved back to LA.

It didn't help and things quickly became worse. I loved Donna, and didn't know what to do. After one confrontation I told her that I thought she and her mother would get along better if I wasn't there-the wrong thing to say. She agreed. So I packed up my things, and tearfully moved out. She didn't cry. I went to the priest who had married us at Blessed Sacrament and unloaded my tale of woe. I asked him what I could do about getting an annulment. The priest's face turned red and he yelled at me to get back to my wife and work things out, that I didn't have any grounds for an annulment. I was in trouble with the church, my family, my wife, and it seemed that everything I was doing in my life was turning to shit. One other thing bothered me. Donna and her mother didn't like my father. I couldn't understand that, everyone liked, or loved, Dad. She wouldn't come with me when I went out to Santa Monica to see Mom,

Dad and Tony. Dad would ask, "Why doesn't she come? Why does she hate us?" I don't think it was the folks, I believe that our marriage was failing, and the relationship with my folks was just another bone to have a dog fight over. Donna's attitude towards the rest of my family also changed, including Grandpa and Grandma Smith, Lada and Uncle Louie.

At some time during this period a family legend was born. Richard Milhouse Nixon was running for the congressional seat that he would win. He was campaigning in San Gabriel Valley, and strolled into my Grandpa Smith's shoe repair shop. He started to put up one of his campaign posters in Grandpa's window.

"And what the hell do you think you are doing?" Grandpa shouted.

"I am putting up my poster in your window."

"It'll be a cold wave in hell the day I let a Republican asshole like you put your ugly face up in my shop. Get the hell out of here."

Nixon started to argue, and Grandpa went after him with his shoe hammer, and chased him out the front door.

"The last I saw of him he was looking back over his shoulder, still talking, and not saying much," Grandpa said. The whole incident made me feel good. Donna and her mother were Republicans.

I had been working at Pacific Freight Lines in the billing department. I had tried several jobs, one of which I liked very much as a trainee underwriter with Aero Insurance Underwriters. After about four months they decided to cut back and several of us were terminated. So in 1947 I was really looking for something to do. I landed a job as an assembler with Technical Products Inc. That was O.K.. for awhile, but I really wanted a job that I was adapted for, that I could do, and stay interested in for the rest of my life. The Veterans Administration had a counseling service for vets and I decided to take advantage of that. I went out to Sawtelle to take the exams. After two days of tests and interviews I was called in to see the counselor. He told me that the aptitude, intelligence and interest tests indicated that my primary interest and potential skills were in writing. The proper occupation for me would be a newspaper journalist or a magazine writer. He said that I should try to get a trainee job with a newspaper or magazine, or go back to school for training. I heard about a cub reporter job opening with the daily newspaper in Las Vegas, Nevada, so I drove up there and applied for the job. After a week's wait I was told I did not get the job.

When I was working at the trucking company I met Don and Ann LoPresti, and they became very good friends. One night I was out at their place with my '37 Chevy when I got drunk. They wanted me to spend the night, but I was determined to get back to Santa Monica where I was staying near the folks. Somewhere in south Los Angeles I went to sleep driving the car. I woke up when I was smashed into the rear of a parked Model A sedan. I wasn't hurt, and ran away from the scene. I looked at the street signs so I could remember where I was and started walking. I ended up sleeping for about an hour in the back of a car on a used car lot. I made my way downtown, to the bus line, and got a bus home. Later the next morning Uncle Louie drove me to the area where I crashed my car. The Model A sat there, its rear all crushed in, but my car was gone. Next day was Monday so I went downtown to the LA Police Department and told them what happened. They turned me over to a plainclothes cop who interviewed me. I told him that the night of the accident I left the party because I was feeling sick. I told him I had malaria and that I was having a chills and fever attack when I piled into the ass end of the Model A. I had been drinking, and I knew that if the cops showed up I would have been arrested, but I was sick so I took off to get home. He stared at me, tore up the citation, and told me to get to the VA Hospital. He also released my impounded wrecked car. I had insurance on it, and even got it fixed up so I could sell it. Once again I knew booze was getting to be a problem in my life, so I cut back on my drinking. That meant I didn't get drunk every weekend.

I enrolled again at Santa Monica City College, started on the GI Bill, and carried a full load. I worked nights at Marquardt Aviation in Ocean Park as night watchman and janitor. Working nights I had a lot of time to study, and my grades were good.

To make some extra money, I joined the Marine Corps Reserve. There was a detachment of the 13th Marine Infantry Battalion in Santa Monica. I signed up, and as a sergeant I was given a squad leader's job in a machine gun platoon. In the summer we would go on two-weeks training at Camp Pendleton. Little brother Tony was about 14 years old, and he and two of his friends also joined the Marine Reserves. They lied about their ages to get in, and they really enjoyed getting paid for the drills they had to attend. It was better than any allowance their folks could give them. Later the Marine Corps discovered their true ages and they were discharged. Just in time too, just before the Korean conflict broke out. I stayed in the Marine Reserves until early 1950, when I resigned. The men who I served with for almost two years in Santa Monica were called back in for Korea, shipped to Pendleton for a little training, then went overseas into combat.

On drill nights at Marine Reserve we would end up at Gus and Charlie's, a bar and grill in the Arcade Building in downtown Santa Monica. We would sing, and most of the other customers left. Our raunchy songs such as "Roll Me Over in the Clover" offended the sensibilities of the dignified civilian customers. They finally put us in a back room where we could sing and our lyrical offerings not offend. One of the guys in our chorale was George Temple, Shirley Temple Black's older brother. He was a professional wrestler.

I managed to complete three semesters at Santa Monica, and I had started my fourth, when things got pretty bad with the family. I had been on my own, and visiting Mom, Dad and Tony frequently. They had sold the house on Ashland, and were working as live-in domestics for Virginia Bruce, the movie actress. Mom was an excellent cook, and my dad worked at the Pacific Palisades estate as a handy man. Then Dad came down with some heart trouble, and mother's physical condition deteriorated quickly. I went back to the CAA to see if I could get my job back, and that effort was successful. The plan called for me to get back on as an aircraft communicator, and then bring Tony up with me until Dad and Mom could get back on their feet.

One of the important things that I did was get a civil divorce from Donna. Some time in early 1948 I filed the documents in Santa Monica, and after a court hearing the divorce was granted, with an interlocutory decree. The divorce would become final after one year. I was very sad after the hearing. I should have become a priest. I was doomed to celibacy, whether I liked it or not. Not that I was getting very much when I was married to Donna-once a week, two times if I was lucky or a very good boy. We had a schedule for sex. Either Friday or Saturday night because she didn't have to work the next morning. Sex exhausted her.

So in early February 1949 I got on the Greyhound again for the 18-hour trip up to Ogden, Utah, where I would go into training again. I was told that I had been away from the CAA too long, and I would have to start at the bottom of the training ladder again. The pay wasn't very good as a GS-5, about $2,900 a year, but I could live on it.

Chapter 10

Ogden and June

The further north the bus was from California and Nevada, the deeper the snow was piled. By the time the Greyhound bus pulled into the station in Ogden, Utah, there was over two feet of snow on the ground. I had arrived in the middle of the worst winter that the Intermountain West had recorded. It was the time of the Snow Lift when Air Force transports were drafted into duty as aerial hay wagon. They would fly out to places where ranchers could not get to their stock because of the snow, and drop bales of hay. It was a disaster for many ranchers. Thousands of cattle died of exposure and starvation in the deep snow. I put up at the Ben Lomond Hotel and reported in to the CAA communications station. My new chief was Larry Jones. He told me of a rooming house where I could live, and because I didn't have a car, I arranged to have the guys who I was working with pick me up. They were a great bunch. I was down to my last $10 when I got to Ogden. A Mrs. Settlemeyer was the rooming house owner, and she let me move in without paying in advance. I didn't have kitchen privileges at the rooming house, but I could heat up soup and other canned stuff out at the station. I ate a lot of canned soup that first month. I would only eat once or twice a day and I lost about 10 pounds. It wasn't a diet that I liked, but I knew that I could hang on for a little while. The first payday came, and I didn't have a check yet. The mysterious ways of U.S. government demanded that I wait at least six weeks until I got a partial paycheck. I was down to nothing, and I couldn't call on the folks because they were in such bad shape. My chief, Larry Jones, gave me $50. "Pay me back when you can," he said.

With $50 in my pocket I finally got a great meal downtown and things looked rosier. Right after my first paycheck arrived, I got a phone call at the station from Dad and Mom. Mom was in real bad shape. She had a nervous breakdown. Over the phone Mom told me that the doctors recommended that she enter a mental institution for treatment. She was scheduled to go up to Carmarillo State Hospital. Dad was looking around for work, and hadn't found anything yet. I told them I could have Tony come up and stay with me, and go to school in Ogden until things got better in California. I mailed the folks the money to have Tony come up to live with me. There would be two of us living in the rooming house. I can remember going to St. Joseph's, getting on my knees and praying that Mom would be get well. I think that was about the lowest time in my life. I had lost my wife, would never have a family of my own, my Dad was out of work and sick, Mom was going to the nut house, and I had to take care of my baby brother, now 15, and I was almost broke.

I progressed through the training steps at the station, and was soon qualified to operate all of the positions, but in 1949 there were few openings for journeymen communicators. I had to wait until an opening came up at some station so I could get my GS-7 rating back. I had been on the station for about two months, Tony had arrived, was in school, and we were eating regularly. We even managed to get to the movies now and then, and life was getting a little better. We would get letters from Dad saying that Mom was getting along fine with her treatments and that he was looking for work. Then I met June.

I was outside the station taking a weather observation. It was raining and I was smoking my pipe. I had my pipe upside down, with the bowl down, so the rain wouldn't extinguish the burning tobacco. A red Dodge sedan drove up and a fine-looking girl climbed out of the car. She smiled, nodded at me and I could tell she was choking back a laugh. I wondered what was the matter with her. She thought I was a crazy man who smoked his pipe upside down. I was working with Tommy Martin and he told me that the girl was June VanDeGraaff, the airport manager's secretary. I didn't think anything about it until a couple of day later, my fried Emil Henich, who worked in the control tower at the airport, said June was asking about me, who I was, where I came from, and stuff like that. He said I ought to date her. I don't remember exactly how we became acquainted, but I know that I was invited over to her house for dinner at Easter.

June thought that most of the guys at the communications station were an odd lot.probably because of Art Adamson. He was really odd. One freezing night his car wouldn't start. The engine wouldn't turn over it was so cold. So he grabbed a huge armful of used teletype paper and stuffed it under the crankcase of his car. They he lit the paper. The oil on his engine started to burn. He ran with a bucket of water and doused the fire. He didn't get the car started, and spent the night at the station. His oddness was confirmed when Hank, the airport's night watchman, investigated strange lights coming from the little water reservoir just east of our station. A light was flashing in an odd pattern. When Hank looked over the concrete side of the tank he saw Art. He was ice skating, and singing. It didn't matter that he had to make weather broadcasts at 15 and 45 minutes past the hour, and take weather observations on the hour and 30 past the hour. Art was bored on the graveyard shift and he needed his recreation. He was not a drunk like me. Art was just crazy.

I walked over to June's place met her father, John, and all of her brothers and sisters. June was the oldest and there were ten more brothers and sisters: Bud, Wayne, Ellen, Luciele, Sherma, John, Fred, Kent, Merrill and David. June was 24, and David was five. Bud was a year younger than June, an Army veteran who was with the 101st Airborne and had gone through the Battle of the Bulge. June's mother, Ellen Louisa Jackson Van De Graaff, had died of cancer about four years before. Her dad, John, had remarried a woman named Ethyl Maxwell, and she had four kids at the house. June was living with her grandmother, Anna Van De Graaff, a block away. She and Ethyl did not get along. There were all of these little guys giggling and pointing at me, shouting at June that her boyfriend was there, and lot of teasing. June quieted them with a look and I sat down to a great meal. June had done the whole thing; roast turkey, all the trimmings, pies, the works. At first it was hard for me to identify that polished, sleek, office professional with the glowing kitchen commander that ruled with a firm hand over a household of loud, unruly kids. She served, patted heads, kissed cheeks, kept everyone talking, and our eyes met often over the full table. I thought, "Man! This is one great, funny, bright, lovely woman. If she can cook like this, care for her brothers and sisters, and hold a good job, you are missing a great bet if you don't make a move." I couldn't take my eyes off June. Thoughts of celibacy receded. Only one problem, she was Mormon and I was Catholic. I decided to face that the next day, or whenever.

I still had to pass a test that I didn't know about. June invited me to a family hike up Waterfall Canyon on the face of the steep Wasatch Range that formed a backdrop for the city of Ogden. The foothills and the mountains soared into the sky just east of where the Van De Graaffs lived. We walked up the trail to the falls, which were beautiful. After a short breather we started down. Little David was having a tough time with his short legs and began to complain. I hoisted him up on my shoulders, and we strolled down the mountain. It reminded me of how I used to pack Tony around on my shoulders when he was David's age. We got back down to the house, we rested and had something to drink. We were sitting on the lawn and June nestled up to me and became pretty affectionate. I couldn't wait until dark until we could really kiss out of sight of the kids. That night June told me I passed the test that I didn't know about. If she were to get serious with anyone, that person had to love the outdoors, be able to hike, and get along with her family. She had been in love with a man by the name of Larry Usher, a promoter and salesman. She took him on the Waterfall hike, and he failed. She said one reason she quit going with him was that he drank too much, that she thought he was an alcoholic. I felt a little guilty.

June and I began seeing each other in every spare moment. Our interests meshed. On one of our first dates, June took me to a night class she was enrolled in at Weber College. She had graduated from Weber two years before, but was enrolled in all of the writing classes they offered. We shared a deep interest in writing. Her teacher was a Mr. Perrins, a staffer with the daily *Ogden Standard Examiner*. June was continually writing something, a journal, articles and poetry. Some of her poetry and pieces had been published in Utah newspapers. Writing and books drew us closer together. It was as if we had been searching for each other all our lives, and that wasn't very long; I was 26 and June was 24.

June was continually writing little notes, letters, poems and articles. Our courtship was punctuated with almost daily verses and notes that she would send to me. One of my favorites that I can share is a poem she wrote on June 7, 1949.

> Now that I have learned the heights
> To which a heart can reach
> I stand, soul drenched in tears at
> The littleness of speech.
>
> Precious, precious love of mine,
> This thing has struck me dumb.
> I reach back through all my life
> For words that just won't come.

I am filled with melody –
Carillon chimes and birds –
But I must ache in silence.
I fail to find the words

And so, I hold you very close,
And hope you'll find a way
To learn the secrets of my lips
Find words too small to say.

I'll always love you,

June

We walked everywhere, except when we could use her Dad's milk
truck. Her father had a large milk sales and delivery business. He sold and
delivered dairy products to stores, restaurants and homes in Ogden. June
and I would be together most evenings and I would walk her home. Many
times she would take her Dad's truck then drive me home after I walked
her home. It was the most crazy, wonderful time of my life.

In early May we were standing beneath a blossoming apple tree behind
her grandmother's house holding each other while a thunderstorm raged
overhead. Lightening flashed, thunder shook the ground, rain and hail
pelted us and we held each other, fierce as the storm, and cried out our
love for each other. June asked if were going to marry. I said yes, if she
wanted to, but I couldn't feel more married to her than I did at that
moment. I didn't need a piece of paper, or a minister, to say we were married. I had already made a commitment to myself to spend the rest of my
life with her, if she would have me.

I knew that religion would be an issue. After I left Donna, my folks had
contacted Uncle Steve, Grandma Smith's brother, who was a priest in
Detroit. Rev. Stephen Wittliff wrote to me and told me of the steps I could
take in the long process of getting an annulment. I rationalized that I was

entitled to an annulment, and I knew that God felt the same way about it, so why go through the Church's bureaucratic dance just for appearance's sake? If I was right I was right. If I was wrong, I was wrong, and I had to take the consequences. Uncle Steve later wrote to my folks and told them how disappointed he was that I hadn't gone ahead with the annulment process. I was in love with June, and we were going to be married.

Little brother Tony was doing well in school, and he had become really good friends with June's younger sister Lucielle, and her boyfriend Ralph Rackham. When June and I began going together, it really took the heat off Lucielle and Ralph. June was always checking the driveway at night to see if they were necking in Ralph's 1938 Ford convertible. She would sneak up on the car, try to see through the steamed up windows, bang on the roof, chase Ralph away, and drag Lucielle into the house to do her school homework. June's pressure on them really eased when I showed up.

June was determined to go to California and meet Dad, Mom, and the family. So she packed up, made me promise to stay away from blossoming apple trees until she got back, and with Laurel Hinckley, her best friend, she set out for a week of getting to know the Kings. The first day she sent me five postcards. She loved Dad the moment she saw him, visited Mom in the hospital at Camarillo, and lunched with Pete. She met the Lada and the grandparents. Went out to see Uncle Frank and Aunt Elizabeth. She passed the tests with flying colors. Her letters were loving, newsy and sensitive. She told of meeting Dad and their instant rapport, of her talks with Mom in the hospital, and the doctors' encouraging prognosis. For the first time I had a clear picture of what my mother went through in being treated for mental illness. June's letters were triumphant. She was accepted. She wrote every day, sometimes two and three times. I did the same, and had a letter waiting for her when she got to Los Angeles. In a post card she wrote: "Dearest Frank...Having a wonderful wish. Time you were here. I love you...June."

Dad had been after me to make sure that my divorce was final, and about that time the letter from the lawyer came with the final decree. We were all set to get married.

When June stepped off the bus I was there to gather her up in my arms. We were married on her birthday, June 22, 1949. We had had our first date in April. The wedding was at Uncle Svend and Aunt Mathilda Mogensen's house. Aunt Till was June's aunt, her dad's sister. June wore a simple, lovely, blue dress with black eyelets. The dress brought out the color of her eyes. Gold-red highlights in her chestnut hair gleamed in the sunlight. She was radiant, and I had never seen a more beautiful woman. We exchanged vows before Bishop Compton, from June's home Mormon ward. Emil Henich was my best man. Aunt Till's place was packed with June's relatives and friends.

I don't remember much about the ceremony and reception after, but I do recall what happened next. I was overpowered by Bud, he was a huge guy; Wayne; little brother Tony; and a few more stalwart males. They threw me in the back of Pop's milk truck, and three of them guarded me. We took off, and they told me to change clothes. They stripped me, dressed me in jeans and a flannel shirt. I kept shouting, asking where was June, and where were they taking me? Thoughts of a beautiful wedding night vanished. After 30 minutes of driving, we stopped. I could tell we had driven up Ogden Canyon and were somewhere up near Huntsville, up in the mountains. They let me out. Emil and his soon-to-be wife Gloy drove up. They had kidnapped June. We were at a place called Wolf Creek, out in the wilds east of Ogden in the mountains, right next to the stream. The kidnappers threw out two sleeping bags, a gallon of milk, a half-gallon of wine, and drove off in a cloud of dust.

June and I stood looking at each other. She was laughing and crying, at the same time. I think I was, too. It was dark and we tried to organize things, gathered some twigs and wood. We tried zipping the two sleeping bags together, but that didn't work. So we decided to use one as a mattress pad, and both of us would climb into one sleeping bag. The guys were nice enough to put a book of matches in my jeans, and we got a fire going, but it was getting cold. We were up at about 7,000 feet, and it cools off quick after sundown. We got out of our clothes, wriggled into the sleeping bag, and I zipped it up behind me. The ice-cold zipper touched my bottom, and the reflex made me thrust forward.

"My! Aren't we eager?" June whispered in my ear.

"No, that damn cold zipper is in my butt."

She tried to hit me, but we were squeezed together so tightly she couldn't get a good swing. Little wet drops kept falling on our exposed faces. We could see the stars, so we knew it wasn't rain. We snuggled down in the sleeping back trying to keep our faces dry. We slept. Some. We were up at sunrise. The drops of water were tiny little worms, or grubs, that had been dropping from the tree. We danced around naked, brushing the worms from our bodies, the sleeping bag and our clothes that were damp from the dew. We put them on, knowing the sun would soon dry them. We rolled up the sleeping bags. Drank our breakfast, mostly milk with a little wine, gathered up our stuff, and began walking down the road towards civilization. Ralph and Lucielle drove up in a dust cloud, and took us back to Ogden. I was in love. Sex didn't exhaust June. She thrived on it.

We had rented an apartment at 3043 Jefferson Ave. Our next night was in our comfortable, new bed. June had borrowed one of her boss's cars, a maroon 1946 Dodge sedan. Art Mortensen, her boss, was the Ogden airport manager. He also had the Piper Aircraft distributorship, Utah Pacific Airways. He had been a pilot since the 1920s, an old barnstormer, and had a flying school training military pilots during the war. He treated June like a favorite daughter, but I always suspected he was secretly in love with her. He didn't like me too much. I was the "California prune picker" who was going to steal June away from him. He was always very cool in his dealings with me.

We drove south for our honeymoon. First stop was Bryce Canyon where we had rented a cabin for the night. There were twin beds. June said she would take the one by the door. Laughing hard, she fell back on the bed.

"I wish you could see your face! Come here," she said.

We only used one bed. We were pretty skinny, and in real good shape. We hiked the trails of Bryce Canyon and Cedar Breaks, and drove to other places that June knew about. She gave me great lessons on Utah, and how to fall in love with a Mormon girl.

Back in Ogden we set up housekeeping at the new apartment. Dad was in the process of getting back with Douglas, and Mom was due to be released from the hospital. Dad and Tony decided that he should move back to California. I hated to see Tony go, but he had been a great companion for me, and he fit right in with June's family and their friends. Tony went to live with Pete and Nona while Dad was getting settled in his new job with Douglas at Long Beach. Mom was released from the hospital and she and Dad found a small place on Signal Hill at Long Beach. Tony stayed with Pete and Nona until he enlisted in the U.S. Air Force in January of 1950.

June continued working, and transportation was beginning to be a problem. Some of the time I was filling in on odd shifts when somebody was sick, or if annual leave left a watch open. We needed a car. June talked to Jack Olson, who owned Chevy dealerships in Morgan and Layton, Utah. Jack had a nice 1940 Chevrolet sedan, and we could afford the cost. We paid $575, $586.50 with sales tax, for the car. We put $230 down, and Jack carried the balance. We made our first payment in October and paid it off in January 1950.

Jack was included in a bunch of friends who were close to Art Mortensen. They all owned, or had owned, airplanes and that was their common bond. Art was a member of the QBs, or Quiet Birdmen. It was an aviation community that included most of the famous and near famous of the time. They would fly off to spots like Jackson Hole, Wyoming; Elko, Nevada or Sun Valley, Idaho, for their meetings. It was mostly a social organization, but the membership requirements were tough, and you had to be voted in by the members. Their meetings were one big party. That involved much two-fisted drinking. When Art's bosom buddies, Willard (Bill) Eccles and Heber (Hebe) Scowcroft would come out to Art's office to visit, they usually brought a bottle of whiskey with them. They tried to get June involved in the party, but she and I had been trying to cut down on our drinking. For one thing we couldn't afford it, and we had other important things that occupied our time.

I had started taking flying lessons at a small strip, the Ogden Airpark, between the Ogden Municipal Airport and Hill Air Force Base. In November I got my license. Art Mortensen was the examiner on my flight test. After I passed my private pilot's exam and flight check, Art became more friendly.

June was worried about her father's drinking. Pop would knock back a gallon of wine almost every day. Several years before he had an accident in which his back was severely injured. He had to work on the milk route every day, and the pain became bad at times. He said he drank to ease the pain. I think that was true, not only physical pain, but emotional pain as well. Pop never got over the death of June's mother. When I helped him out on the milk route he would tell of their life together, and how she was the love of his life, and how much he missed her.

Much of our life centered around June's family. Pop gave us a piece of land to grow a garden. So when the next spring came along we planted tomatoes, peppers, peas, beans, corn and squash. I became a truck gardener, and loved it. The garden really produced and June and I preserved a lot of it. Canning time was a big event at the VanDeGraaffs. We would have a fire in an outdoor fireplace, fill a huge galvanized tub with water and get it boiling. We could can about 24 bottles of peaches or pears in one batch.

Whenever we went on vacation, or a trip, or a picnic, her younger brothers were always invited to come along. We took off on one trip, before we had the Chevy, with Art's Dodge. We were going to Yellowstone National Park. I had never been there, and June wanted to show it to me. In addition to June and I, there was John, Kent, Merrill, David, and Leslie, one of Ethyl's boys. June and I had saved $40 for the trip. We had crammed sleeping bags, cooking gear, food, clothes and supplies into and on top of the car. We were a fine-looking company. The first night we camped by an irrigation ditch on the Indian reservation between Pocatello and Idaho Falls. The next day we went through the Grand Canyon and the Snake to Jackson Hole, then up to Yellowstone. The boys still talk about that trip. I know I had a great time. June and I still managed to get into one sleeping bag. When we pulled into Ogden to take the boys home we still had $5 left in our pockets.

A few months after we were married, Grandpa Smith paid us a visit. He was on a train trip from Los Angeles to Port Huron. He stopped off in Ogden and we picked him up for a two-day visit with us. Grandpa wanted to buy us a wedding present, and we told him we would like a rocking chair. We went to Deseret Industries, the Mormon Church thrift store, and found a great oak, wingback rocking chair that had just been refinished. It only cost Grandpa $5 and he thought he got a great bargain. He stayed overnight with us, then resumed his journey to Michigan.

When Saturdays rolled around, and June and I both had the day off, it was a chance to really celebrate. We'd go down to the Bamboo Noodle Parlor, have noodles and go to the movies. There were two good theaters in the downtown area of Ogden, and when there were good shows playing at both we would see two double features in a day, a movie-going orgy. We would top that off with more noodles, then rush back to the apartment to make love.

Our first Christmas was a great celebration. On Christmas Eve June took her Bible and asked me to read St. Luke's passage on the Nativity. I was very moved, my lips quivering as I read the words. I remembered Christmases as a child, Christmas Eve on Guadalcanal, and I was so grateful for the Christmas I was having. However, something was missing. I wanted to go to midnight mass. I didn't say anything, because I didn't want to spoil that moment June and I were having. She was active in her religion, The Church of Christ of Latter Day Saints, popularly called Mormons. She would frequently attend services, and loved her religion.

Surprisingly, religion never became an issue in our marriage. We talked openly about how we had been taught about religion as children, the theology of our churches and the religious practices. We never had an argument over religion. I felt that, technically, I was excommunicated, because I had divorced and remarried. I was on the outside of the Catholic Church, but inside were the Catholic values that shaped my belief, ethics and personality. My belief had become like a banked fire, a coal burning under ashes waiting for the time to flame up. There would be a little spurt of fire at Christmas and Easter. Anytime I would go into a Catholic Church I could feel the tears start to come. Then I would become angry with myself, order myself to grow up, and get on with my life. Most of the time it worked.

June and I wanted a family. After eight months she went to Dr. Clark Rich, her family doctor, to find out why she hadn't got pregnant. Dr. Rich said the first thing was to have me tested. The sperm count was normal then June had to undergo some tests. Her fallopian tubes were blocked and she had to have some uterine cysts removed. The treatment worked and June would become pregnant with our first child in about 15 months.

A big event in our lives came about in this period. Ralph Rackham and Lucielle were married. This came about just before I was to get a new job assignment. Ralph and Luciele's wedding was held at their older brother Wayne's house in Ogden. Bud and I were determined that Ralph and Lucielle would get a great wedding celebration. I had helped June with arrangements for the ceremony. June decorated the house with flowers we picked up at her Dad's place. We also picked a bushel of Russian olive blooms. The blooming branches were covered with little yellow flowers, and the perfume from them permeated the house. It was payback time for what June and I had to go through on our wedding night.

The wedding went off without a hitch, and the reception provided enough booze for me to get well oiled. We put Ralph and Lucielle in different cars and proceeded to parade through the City of Ogden with lights flashing and horns blaring. We terminated the procession at the Ben

Lomond Hotel where we had reserved a room for the newly married couple. We marched Ralph and Luciele up to the registration desk. Bud and I were right behind them carrying our shotguns that had huge white ribbon bows tied to the barrels. After they signed in we went to the elevator, and a couple that was waiting to ride upstairs took one look at Bud and me with our shotguns, and they sidled around the elevator cage, out the door, rushed away, casting glances back at us. We left them when they locked the door in our faces at their room.

Chapter 11

Hanksville

I had been bidding on jobs that would get me a promotion. That meant that I could be assigned to an Airways Communications Station at any place in the western United States. June wasn't enthusiastic about leaving Ogden, but she realized that for me to make more money, I had to get the promotion, and a move was more than likely. In June 1950 I received a teletype message that told me I had been promoted to a GS-7 and assigned to Hanksville, Utah. The Hanksville station was located on an emergency airfield on the old Red 6 Airway between Bryce Canyon, Utah, and Grand Junction, Colorado. There was federal government housing on the airport, seven two-bedroom houses. We were assigned one of the houses. The closest town was Hanksville, with a population of 80. Hanksville is in south central Utah between Green River and the Capitol Reef National Monument. To get there you had to drive on 50 miles of dirt road from Green River, or if you came in from Loa, Bicknell and

Torrey through Capitol Reef, it was 50 miles of dirt road that way also. The town of Hanksville did not have any commercial electric or telephone companies. There were a couple of small engine-driven generators in houses, and the store had one also that powered a single light bulb, the freezer and refrigerator. Ekker's Store was the cultural, social and economic core of Hanksville. They had a single gasoline pump out in front, the kind with a glass tank on top, a hand pump that you worked to get the gasoline from the underground tank up into the glass part. The gas flowed by gravity down the hose, through the nozzle into your tank. The glass tank would hold ten gallons.

Out at the airport we had all of the amenities of a small city. We had three 75KVA diesel generators that provided all the electricity we needed for the communications station, our electronic navigation aids, radios-and power for the houses. Each house had a fuel oil furnace, an evaporative air conditioner, electric range and refrigerator. It was up to June and I to provide the rest of the furnishings. Water was a problem. We had a well and pump on the airport, but you couldn't drink the water. It was so alkaline and nasty tasting you couldn't even make coffee with it. We did use the well water to bathe, wash clothes and dishes. Water we used for drinking and cooking was hauled in weekly from Hanksville. We had five-gallon containers we would fill once or twice a day at the tank truck.

There were no commercial communications facilities so we had to provide our own. The Hanksville station had a point-to-point radio telegraph and radio telephone circuit with Bryce Canyon and Grand Junction airways communications stations. We would take weather observations on the hour and send the report to Grand Junction. Grand Junction would take that report and relay it on a teletype circuit. All of our communications-flight plans, flight movement and position reports and administrative messages-were handled the same way. If we couldn't contact Grand Junction on the radio, we would try Bryce Canyon. About 60 percent of the messages we handled were with voice communications. The other 40 percent were with Morse code. The CAA had a requirement that the communicators at Hanksville-as well as those in overseas communications stations-had to be able to transmit and receive 30 words per minute in Morse code. I began the hard task of building up my code speed.

Life in Hanksville was exciting, which amazed us. June and I became rock hounds. We would explore places around the airport looking for agate, jasper and petrified wood. We picked up a lot of gem quality material for our collection, and I became interested in mineral prospecting. Just off the west end of the airport runway we discovered a place where there were many arrowheads, spear points, chips from tools made by Indians many years ago. On my days off we would explore places such as Robber's Roost, where Butch Cassidy, the Sundance Kid and their gang hid out. Every week one of the crew would take the Dodge four-wheel drive, military surplus truck and drive into Green River for groceries. Every family on the airport had a charge account at the Green River Store. June and I made the run whenever we could. The families would make grocery orders that would be filled while we waited. There wasn't much to do in Green River, not even a movie. If you wanted a movie, a doctor or a dentist you had to drive 120 miles to Price, Utah, or Grand Junction, Colorado. One weekend June and I drove over to Grand Junction just to taste the fruits of city life-eat in a restaurant, go shopping in a dime store, and sit through two movies.

A great trip was over to Richfield. We had to drive through the Capitol Reef National Monument, and the Capitol Reef Gorge. The red rock gorge was only wide enough for one car to get through at a time. At its center, it was almost as if you could reach out and touch the wall with your outstretched arms. Indian pictographs were carved into the rock. Explorer John Wesley Powell and pioneers had also written their names and the dates on the rough walls. Signs at both ends of the gorge warned people not to enter if it was about to rain. Old timers told stories of how people were caught in gully-washers resulting from the driving rain and hail in thunderstorms. We carefully scanned the skies, read the weather reports, and paid attention to the forecasts when we traveled. We never got into trouble because of the weather, because we were alert, careful and prepared. The dirt roads ruined tires in short order. We were in Hanksville just short of a year, and I had to buy about one new tire a month.

Our social life in Hanksville was mostly visiting or playing cards. We had all of June's brothers and sisters come down and spend some time with us. Little David spent almost a month with us. Merrill, Kent and Fred thought we lived in a wonderful place. On one hike, Fred found an arrowhead. June said he was so excited, and his hands shook so much, that he could hardly hold his prize as he showed it to her.

We became friends with several families in Hanksville. The Ekkers were the predominant family in the area, and they were famous for their big, tough sons. They were very large men, and their personalities ranged from serene to volatile when drunk. One Saturday night, one of the younger sons in his early 20s came banging on our door out at the airport. He was drunk, had run out of beer, knew that I always had some sort of booze on hand, and he wanted some. He was too big to argue with. So June and I invited him in, but he wanted to party. I think I had a little whiskey left, so I gave it to him. I told him that I would drive him back into town. I took my car, because June didn't think it wise for the young Ekker to drive. I left him off in town, went back to the airport and into bed. He had to get a ride out to our place, badly hung over, to get his truck the next morning.

Every month, on a Saturday night, there would be a dance at the Mormon church. We went two times. The three-piece orchestra could only play three songs, one of which was "Bonaparte's Retreat." They would go through their set of three pieces, start over again, then rest for five minutes. We had great fun. It's the only Mormon church that I know of where they would clean up the beer bottles from the lawn early Sunday morning before services started.

Sunset in Hanksville was a symphony of color. The land would change its costume in different hues as the sun went down over the western horizon. The turquoise sky was a backdrop for the accents of lavender, violet, deep blue, and muted rose painted on the buttes, hills and mountains. This was 1950 and 1951. There was no television. We depended on the radio for communications with the outside world. During the day we could get one commercial station, KSL in Salt Lake City. At night stations from all over the western U.S. and Canada would boom in. My favorite program was "Gunsmoke." William Conrad was Matt Dillon. June and I had invested in a Silvertone radio phonograph that we bought on time from Sears and Roebuck. It was a neat little console that provided us with hours of entertainment. We had started a record collection that included the Ink Spots, Mills Brothers, and many of the big bands. We also had a few classics.

June loved classical music, particularly Italian opera. Every Saturday morning she listened to the Texaco Metropolitan Opera program. She was joined by Debbie Carmona. Her husband Al was one of the communicators, we worked together, and he and I became pretty good friends. Debbie and June would listen to the opera and do their ironing at the same time. Life can grate on one's nerves in a small community, and Debbie and June encountered that when some of the women made barbed comments about the "two high-class ladies who listen to opera." It bothered Debbie, but June didn't care. "We are pearls before swine," she said, paraphrasing Dorothy Parker.

Al Carmona was an amateur radio operator. He had bought an ARC5 at some war surplus outlet. That was the first little transmitter and receiver that I had worked on when I was with VMF-112 on Guadalcanal. Al let me fiddle with his rig, and I sent some Morse code with it, but never got an answer. It wouldn't be until some 43 years later that I would become interested in ham radio.

The Hanksville CAA communications station also provided emergency communications for the folks down in town. If anyone had to go to the doctor, hospital or other emergency we could relay messages for them. We had two airplanes, one down in town owned by the Mormon bishop who was also the state roads maintenance man. He had a dirt strip next to the town. He would taxi through town to and from the strip to land and take off. We had a Piper Cub Coupe at the airport. It was a two-place aircraft powered by a 65-horsepower engine. We used it to make emergency trips when anyone became ill. The only transient airplanes we had land at our airport were prospectors, those making emergency landings and CAA inspection aircraft. We had two runways, both 5,000 feet long and 500 feet wide.

June caused a minor crisis in the community life at the airport. It was sort of a tradition that all of the families would get together for the Thanksgiving dinner. They would go in together on the cost of the turkey, and each wife would bring a dish. June said no thank you, that Thanksgiving was a family affair and she and I would be spending it alone. The other families went ahead with their Thanksgiving plans. I came home from working days-I only had to walk about 50 yards from the station to the house-and I had a beautiful Thanksgiving dinner awaiting me. June had moved the kitchen table into the front room, had it covered with a beautiful tablecloth, set with our best china, crystal, silverware and an autumn leaves centerpiece. She served the dinner, with a nice white wine, and we were having our dessert-apple and pumpkin pie, when Debbie Carmona rushed in the back door. The community dinner was going to hell. The women cooking their turkey had got drunk, and forgot to turn the oven on. The families were hungry, getting testy, and the grownups were getting drunker by the minute. Debbie cried that she wished she had put her foot down and done the same as June. After Thanksgiving, things got back to normal, and as I remember it, every one of the families had their own individual Christmas celebrations that year.

Rumors could fly pretty fast in our little enclave-who's pregnant, who had a fight, who said what, and who did what to whom. Some of the wives visited back and forth, but the main gathering place was the laundry. We had a laundry house with washing machines in it located in the center of our cluster of houses. There were no dryers, but good clotheslines had been installed on stout posts. Hanksville was in the center of the dry desert of south central Utah. After Christmas I was helping June with the washing and it was a very cold day. The sun was shining brightly, and not a breath of wind was blowing. We were working with light sweaters on. We would hang the clothes on the lines, and they would freeze stiff as a board in an instant. I thought that they would never dry. June said that we would come out in a couple of hours and all of the ice would have been evaporated from the clothes. She was right. We went out and took them off the line. The clothes were cold, but as light and fluffy as if they had been hung out to dry in the middle of the hot summer. I checked the weather observation at the station, and it was minus 21 degrees Fahrenheit when we had hung the clothes out.

I was having trouble getting up to the 30 words per minute Morse code, sending and receiving. I had been at Hanksville for ten months. I was supposed to pass the code speed test in six months, so I had to get an extension. I managed to record 28 words per minute receiving, and 32 words per minute sending. I argued with the station chief Clarence Trahan, that 28 and 32 averaged 30 so it could be said that I had completed the requirement. He said no, that I had to do a minimum of 30 words per minute receiving and sending. If I didn't pass the code test the CAA would assign me to any vacancy that was available, and that could mean a station that was really undesirable. There was an opening for a trainee air traffic controller in the Salt Lake City Airport Traffic Control Tower. It was a GS-7 position so I would not be losing a grade, or pay, if I was to get it. I bid on the job, and I got it.

Chapter 12

Salt Lake City

There was only one moving company, Sugarhouse Transfer and Moving, that would come down to Hanksville and move us. They came down and hauled our stuff up to Salt Lake and put it in temporary storage. We found a house to rent in Clearfield, Utah, just outside of Ogden, and 35 miles from the Salt Lake City airport.

It was good being closer to June's family. We were only in Clearfield for a few months, but while we were there Grandpa and Grandma Smith, Lada and my mother came up to visit us. They stayed at our house for a couple of nights, and I could see first-hand how much my mother had changed. She was not the same person who carefully nurtured me and my brothers through our childhood. Mom would have periods when she would become demanding, almost childlike in her behavior. On their last night before going back to California we were sitting down to dinner and Mom demanded that she be served a hot pork sandwich. I forget what

June had fixed, but conversation came to dead silence. Grandpa and Lada tried to talk Mom out of it, but she only became more strident and disruptive. I told her to calm down and I would get her what she wanted. I went down to the neighborhood restaurant, had them fix a hot pork sandwich to go, and brought it back to the house. Mom said, "My Frankie knows what's good for me." She ate her dinner. We ate ours and silence reigned. I think Grandpa and Lada were upset that I had succumbed to Mom's demands. I didn't care. I just wanted everyone to get along, no arguments or bickering. June took the situation in stride, but she was peeved, much less than the folks, with Mom's behavior. It was hard for me to explain my feelings to her, but I tried. I told her that Mom wasn't always like this. When we were growing up she was the most kind, forgiving and tolerant mother I knew. My friends thought so, too. She was a favorite with all of the kids. Mom also became a midwife, delivering and helping deliver many babies in Beaumont when I was growing up. It tore me apart to see the change in her.

While we were at Clearfield I told June I would like to start taking some college classes. I had about two years of college credit, but I needed some science and humanities to complete my lower division work. I signed up for a biology and lab course, along with music appreciation, at Weber College, June's alma mater. The biology professor was Dr. Young, and he ran a tight ship. He graded strictly on the curve, only one A and one F, a handful of B's and D's, and a bunch of C's in every course. I was told that he was a devout Mormon and if he ever saw you smoking your grade came down one point. I was sitting in the car studying before class, smoking my pipe, and Dr. Young appeared at my window. We greeted each other, passed the time of day, and he moved on. I didn't think anything about it until class time, then I thought my grade would go in the toilet. I studied very hard, much of it at work at the tower during the slow time of a graveyard shift. I knew I aced the final exam. I had received a B-plus with my term paper on compulsory sterilization. I really thought I would get a B in the class. When I got my grade at the end of the term I rushed home. I told

June I was in heaven-I got the only A in biology and scored anther A in music appreciation. Those were the first A's I had every scored in my life. I had broken the sound barrier. Things would be different.

I was happy. Work at the control tower was demanding, challenging and satisfying. New things had to be learned: air traffic control procedures, phraseology, and operating new equipment. When a controller was assigned to a station, he or she had to pass an area examination. We had to know all of the terrain, airways, minimum en-route altitudes, instrument approach and departure procedures, and emergency operations. In addition we had to demonstrate that we could operate each position of operation in the tower: local control, ground control, flight data, approach control and departure control. At that time it took about four years to progress through the training program before you became a journeyman air traffic controller. It was at Salt Lake Tower that I witnessed my first civilian air crash. I had seen others when I was in the Marine Corps during the war, but that one crash really upset me. It was just before Thanksgiving. A pilot called for take-off instructions. He was flying from Salt Lake to Pocatello, and said that he was going up to spend the holiday with his wife and children. We gave him take-off clearance, wished him a good flight and Happy Thanksgiving. He took off to the south, made a climbing right turn and was northbound out west of the airport.

"I can't control this thing," he shouted. "I am going in!"

The Luscombe Silvair, after wobbling erratically, went into an abrupt dive and smashed into the swampy ground west of the airport. When he took off there was a small amount of wet snow on the runway. Later, the aviation safety inspectors theorized that his control surfaces might have been affected by the freezing slush. We went out to the crash site, and debris was flung in a wide circle. There was a muddy turkey, and groceries for the Thanksgiving meal.

I remembered our Thanksgiving in Hanksville, and how much it meant to me. That night I toasted my unknown pilot friend with an extra drink, the extra drink that helped me sleep.

We decided to move from Clearfield to Salt Lake City so I could be nearer my work. We could save on car expenses. We managed to get into Air Base Village, a war housing project located on the Salt Lake City Municipal Airport. We got a one-bedroom apartment, and I think we only had to pay $40 a month rent. The move meant that we could save money, because our family was growing.

June became pregnant, and our first daughter, Rosanne, was born December 8, 1952, at Dee Hospital in Ogden. Luciele's and Ralph's first-born, a son, Michael, had come into the world about 11 months before. Lucille had been regaling June with stories about how she suffered during her labor with Mike. "It was like trying to shove a watermelon through a keyhole," Lucille said. June did take Luciele's advice on one thing, choosing Dr. Lindsay Curtis of Ogden to be her obstetrician, the same doctor who had delivered Mike. December 8 was a stormy day, and Rosanne was born while huge white flakes of snow fell outside. I felt that my life was complete with a wonderful marriage and a beautiful child. Secretly, I was glad that we had a baby girl. I was afraid it was going to be like it was with Mom and Dad, all boys.

Now we were the same as the other families at Airbase Village. We had a child. The men in the housing project were all veterans, and many were going to college and trade schools on the GI Bill. The village was never quiet. Children would be crying, shouting or playing noisily most of the day. In good weather the kids were a lot more active outdoors, but we seemed to be oblivious to the noise. When we had visitors they would ask how we slept in such an environment. It didn't bother us, and I managed to get enough sleep working the crazy shifts assigned to me at the tower. Our neighbors became good friends, particularly Roy and Elfie Hutchinson and their children who lived in the apartment next door to us. The walls were like paper, and we could hear each other's scraps, joy and domestic disasters. Sister-in-law Luciele reminded me that she and June, at first, thought that Elfie was a very tacky person. Elfie did not iron her pillowcases. Such intimate details did not go unnoticed in our elbow-to-elbow conditions. Despite the crowding, June and Elfie became great friends. They would swap horror stories about their husbands and how crabby they were when working graveyard shifts. Roy was working for Standard Oil refinery and he had to put in the same sort of erratic and demanding shifts as I.

Tony had joined the U.S Air Force and had served in Japan, Korea, and England during the Korean conflict. Shortly after Rosanne was born I was reading copy of the *Los Angeles Mirror* and got a big surprise. There on the front page was a big photo of one of Tony's childhood buddies, Ernie De La Cruz clinging to the top of the huge Southern California Gas Company natural gas holder that towered over Ocean Park, California. Ernie was drunk, and swore that he "was going to conquer the Iron Man," the name he gave to the gigantic gas tank. After the incident he spent another term in jail.

In mid-2000, Tony got a call from Ernie, after a 30 year silence. Ernie had been sober and off of drugs, off and on, for the 30 years.

"We talked, scatted 'Way Beyond the Blue Horizon,' talked a lot of jive. I can still understand him. That's scary," Tony said.

Tony spent a lot of time at Tyndall AFB in Florida. There he met Edna, and they were married. While they were in England their first child was born, Dolores Theresa. After Tony and his family got back to the states they visited us in Airbase Village. I could tell that Tony was a lot different than the little brother I had known all my life. I didn't know it then, but he was hooked on booze, also, but he had another monkey on his back. In Korea he started using drugs. He kicked that habit, but the craving for alcohol stayed with him. The King curse of boozing had skipped a generation, and Tony and I were carrying on the tradition.

I progressed through the training program at the tower, and was becoming qualified on all of the operating positions. After a couple of years, Salt Lake Tower was one of the facilities due to get the new ASR 2 surveillance radar. After the installation was complete, we had to learn a completely new method of controlling traffic. The radar was great. We had a two-dimensional picture, direction and distance, of what was going on in our control zone. We could vector, or guide, aircraft to our instrument landing system, monitor their approaches and departures, give them headings to fly to keep them separated from other aircraft, and speed up arrivals and departures.

Unlike today we had no way of actually marking the blips, or targets, with information like aircraft identification, altitude and airspeed on the scope. All we had were the little green blips on the screen that we had to keep track of. Technology would later catch up and controllers would have all of the information they needed right on the screen next to the targets. We also had no means of determining the altitude of aircraft other than the reports that we would get from the pilots. Traffic would become very heavy during the fall, winter and spring at Salt Lake City. Working aircraft on Instrument Flight Rules (IFR), mostly air carriers, was demanding enough, but when marginal weather came in we had an added burden. In good weather, most of the smaller private and corporate aircraft, or general aviation, flew under Visual Flight Rules (VFR). When we had fog and reduced visibility we could operate under Special VFR conditions when the visibility was one mile or greater. The catch was that we had to provide IFR separation between all of the Special VFR traffic and the IFR traffic. We could be working up to 10 or 12 airplanes IFR on departures and arrivals, and have at least that many on special VFR in the control zone. It was a demanding, nerve-racking job that sometimes left you weak and wringing wet with sweat after an eight-hour watch. We would swap positions periodically, and would switch from the radar room up to the tower cab, and vice versa. It was a demanding job that at time would leave you weak with fatigue and nervous tension after a busy watch.

When I got to Salt Lake, the Utah National Guard fighter squadron was flying F-51 Mustang fighters. They would later switch over to the F-86D jet fighters. The Mustang was a difficult airplane to master for some of the National Guard pilots. One particular pilot had many minor accidents and brushes with disaster in flying the F-51. His last flight in the airplane was one that left white hairs on my head. He was taking off to the south. He gunned the engine and raced down the runway. The engine torque forced him to the left, because he didn't use enough rudder to offset the force. His left wing dipped down as he was climbing and he headed straight for the terminal building and the control tower. He zoomed past us, eye-to-eye, only 50 feet away from our windows. I was too scared to hit the deck, but two of the controllers working with me were halfway down the stairs when the frantic pilot hummed by.

During the winter months we would get fogs that were a big safety hazard to pilots. Norm and I were working the day watch when a pilot called in an emergency and said that he was in the fog, could see the ground but had no forward visibility. Norm asked him to describe landmarks he was flying over. After determining where he was, Norm gave him a heading to fly to the airport, but the pilot couldn't get lined up with any runway. I ran out on the roof of the terminal building, just in back of the tower, and listened for the plane. Finally I could hear him west of the airport. I pointed toward the sound and Norm gave him headings to fly to try and up with the runway. I pointed out his progress and he flew around the field.

"I see it! I see the runway," he shouted.

Norm and I claimed we invented a new air navigation approach system-GSA, or ground-sound approach.

June did her best to take the strain off of me, because she knew how demanding the job was. We did a lot of things on my time off. When it was good weather we spent a lot of time in the mountains and going on outings. One of our favorite things to do when I was working a swing shift was to have breakfast at one of the nearby campgrounds in the Wasatch Mountains that formed a backdrop for the Salt Lake Valley. I would pack up our Coleman camp stove, the grub box and food and we would head for the hills. I enjoyed those breakfasts in the cool pine forests more than any other meals I have had.

June's Uncle Joe Jackson, Aunt Catherine and cousins Carol and Marie lived in Salt Lake City, and we visited them frequently. June said that

Carol and Marie were her double cousins. Joe was a brother to June's mother, and Aunt Catherine was her father's sister. I had been going hunting with Pop, Bud, Ralph and the boys every October since June and I had been married. I shot my first deer, and Bud showed me how to clean it. At first I used an old Winchester Model 93 carbine with a long octagonal barrel. I used it until I got my own rifle. That rifle I bought for $5 from the National Rifle Association. It was my old nemesis, the Springfield 30.06 that I fired for record with the Marine Corps. Uncle Joe was an amateur gunsmith, and he re-loaded all of his own ammunition. I took the war-surplus rifle apart, and Joe showed me how to buff all of the parts down to the bare metal. Then I took it to a gunsmith and had the bluing surface applied. With a new stock, my rifle looked like something out of a sporting magazine. Bud gave me a Weaver K2.5 scope to mount on it, and I had a dream rifle. I even bought a military surplus leather sling that I used to carry and steady the rifle when I was hunting. That rifle shot true, and I never failed to bring home a deer. Some of the shots I made amazed even me. I was beginning to realize that I was a slow learner on some things like guns, radios and women. Later, I would add alcohol to the list.

After Rosanne was born I began to get horrible stomachaches, usually after I ate a big meal. It was in September or October and we were over to Uncle Joe's on one of our visits. I wasn't feeling good, because I was having one of those off and on stomachaches. I was in the front room by myself, Joe was working, Aunt Catherine and June were in the kitchen. The World Series was on, and I was watching the televised game. We didn't have a television, so we'd go over to Uncle Joe and Aunt Catherine's for big events like the World Series. I was sitting in a big overstuffed chair, holding my stomach when Willie Mays made that great catch against the center field wall. I jumped up off the couch, and bellowed out a loud cheer. June and Aunt Catherine ran into the living room. They thought I was having one of my bad attacks.

The post-World War II housing boom was reaching its peak. Hoffman Construction Co. was building a new development at Kearns, a suburb of

Salt Lake City about six miles south of the airport. We went out to look at the Hoffman homes and found one we really liked. They were of concrete block construction, on concrete slab foundations, with a carport and three bedrooms. The model home looked like a palace to us, and the price was about $7,900, which seemed like an astronomical number. We could get into the house with a VA loan, and our payments would be about $60 a month, on a 30-year mortgage, with payments of slightly more that $60 a month. Most important, we didn't have to pay anything down, only minor closing costs. We signed up and in late 1953 we moved into our new home. We put in a lawn, landscaped the lot, and decorated the new house.

Mom and Dad came up to Utah for a visit. It was great being able to show them all of the natural wonders of my new home state. We took a long day trip up through the Uintah mountains with the folks. It was mid-summer. We had a cold front move through and there were a lot of thunderheads in the sky. When we arrived at a lake for lunch it began to rain and then snow. Dad was really impressed, "Imagine, snow in July." When we got home the thunderstorms continued to march in over the Great Salt Lake desert. A ferocious storm hit with thunder, lightning, hail and a driving rain squall. I was sick. All of my hard work in seeding a new lawn was probably going for naught. Forever the optimist, Dad said, "That rain is just driving the seed into the ground." I had my doubts, but the lawn came up fine and I only had to re-seed a few spots that washed out.

Late in 1954 I received word that I had been chosen for an assignment in Albuquerque, New Mexico. That meant that I would be getting a two-grade promotion, from a GS-7 to a GS-9, with a substantial raise in pay. June and I talked it over, and decided to accept the new job. She wasn't too happy, because she would be leaving our new house, Utah and her family behind. I promised that I would get back to Utah as soon as the right job opportunity appeared. We managed to sell the house with no loss. We had a little bit of money saved. We had managed to save quite a bit, according to our standards, when we were in Hanksville, and that money was still in the bank.

Chapter 13

Albuquerque

Just before Christmas in 1954 we set out for our new home in New Mexico. We arrived two days before Christmas and checked into a motel. The next day, Christmas Eve, we rented a duplex in the southeast section of town. I went out to get a Christmas tree, and got one free because the lots were all closed and the vendors were giving away the trees that were left. The mover had dumped off our stuff at the new place and the first thing we did was put up the Christmas tree. After Rosanne was in bed we put out all of the presents from Santa Claus. Rosanne was afraid that Santa wouldn't be able to find us in New Mexico. We had all of our things unpacked and the house cleaned and decorated on Christmas Day.

Life in Albuquerque was strange at first, but we adapted quickly. We discovered the great Mexican food of New Mexico. Our favorite place was the La Cocina in Old Town on the plaza. There, for the first time, I tasted sopapillas, and I have never found another restaurant that could make them like they did at that restaurant. Sopapillas are a fried bread that looks like an apple turnover. The texture on the outside is like that of a fine croissant, and the inside is soft and puffy. The sopapillas were served with butter and honey. My mouth is watering as I write this. The quacamole, enchiladas, tamales and chili rellenos were outstanding. Our gastronomic adventures usually resulted in me having a bad stomachache. June insisted that I go to the doctor and find out what was giving me such pain.

Our resources were limited, and we didn't want to incur a lot of medical bills, so I decided to take advantage of the medical entitlements offered to veterans. I checked into the Veterans Administration Hospital for some tests. After X-rays, and an extensive physical examination, the doctors said that I had gallstones, and I should have my gall bladder removed. I was in the hospital for three days, and when I was discharged I called June to come pick me up. I waited and waited. She was about an hour late. I phoned the house and there was no answer.

Finally June and Rosanne drove up to the entrance to pick me up. Right away I jumped on her.

"How come you're so damn late? I've been standing here for over an hour!"

"Don't give me any trouble, Frank. This has been a morning from hell!"

June slid over so I could climb into the car. I was still steaming, but I calmed down when I saw she was about to cry. She held Rosanne on her lap, and told me the story.

She had packed up Rosanne, gone out to the garage where our car was parked, lifted the garage door and climbed into the car. June began backing up and was just about out of the garage.

"Mommy, I need a hanky," Rosanne said.

She had been picking her nose, and had a long stringy line of snot from her nose to her outreached finger pointed at her mother. June let go of the steering wheel, grabbed for a tissue to wipe Rosanne's nose. The car came to an abrupt stop. The right front bumper had hung up in the large spring by the side of the door-the spring that opened and closed the door. June tried going forward, backing up, but she couldn't get the bumper loose from the spring. June was not only beautiful, smart and creative, she had a great mechanical sense, too. She saw how she could get the car loose from the spring. She dived into the trunk, lifted out the jack and its handle. She put the car in gear, set the emergency brake and placed the jack stand under the bumper near the caught spring. She jacked up the front of the car, and the spring began to spread. June gingerly opened the driver's side door, let the car out of gear and released the emergency brake. She then rocked the car gently back and forth and finally pushed in backwards. The car released from the spring, fell off the jack and began rolling backwards. June jumped in the car, set the brake and closed the garage door. When she picked me up she had grease on her face, her hands were dirty, dress rumpled, and she looked like the tears would flow any moment.

"I had Rosanne fixed up so pretty, and I put on my nice outfit, just to welcome you home. Now look at us!" she cried.

Ashamed, my anger dissolved. I grabbed her, put my arms around her and told her how pretty she looked, dirty nose and all.

Things mechanical did not intimidate June. She had learned so much about aircraft engines; electrical, mechanical and hydraulic systems by working with Art at the airport. I had been having trouble with the car when we were at Hanksville. I was too lazy to do anything about it. I found June dressed in some of my work clothes out at the car with its hood up. She had disconnected the battery, cleaned off the anode and cathode stumps, and taken a wire brush to the ground and positive connector cables. She had washed off the battery, put the cables back on, and put baking soda, to neutralize the battery acid, around the posts. We let the car sit for awhile. When she turned on the ignition key, the battery cranked the starter over without any trouble, and the car started right up. We didn't have any trouble with it after than. She would check the oil, the coolant in the radiator, the air pressure in the tires every two or three weeks. It was like having a service station attendant on tap all the time.

June taught me a lot about women. Not just sex. I quickly learned that if I was going to live with her, I had to accept her as an equal. She was not aggressive, even assertive, but her intelligence and logic shined brightly when she confronted me when discussing subjects such as politics, equality, and tolerance. I found out in short order that she was brainy, always exploring new things, loved travel, staying at home, and hated Las Vegas and Reno-"I can't stand a place where they don't turn the lights out at night."

One of her heroes was Joe Louis. June detested what Germany had done to the Jews in the 1930s and 40s, and the Third Reich's bullying tactics with the rest of the civilized world. She and younger brother Bud closely followed Joe Louis and his climb to fame as the picture-perfect boxer-fighter. She was devastated when Joe was knocked out by Max Schmeling in their first fight. She rejoiced mightily when Louis floored Schmeling in the first round in their second bout, and went on to the World Heavyweight Championship. She despaired when Louis fought beyond his prime. When he was defeated by Ezzard Charles, June sat by the radio with tears running down her cheeks, feeling the pain that Louis must have felt that terrible night. Her hero had gone down, and the world was a much bleaker place. The great Joe Louis had been beat. To June he was the embodiment of triumph over a cruel, inhumane despot. She could never talk about Joe Louis after that without her eyes welling with tears. This great affection for a black fighter was in dramatic contrast with her gentle and sensitive nature. But she saw poetry, grace and beauty in Joe Louis's athleticism. June was fiercely loyal. Don't say anything bad about her loved ones, her family or Joe Louis, or you would be in deep trouble.

I soon discovered that my job at the Albuquerque airport was going to be a lot different that anything I had encountered before. We were civilian air traffic controllers, on a military base, but employed by the Civil Aeronautics Administration. We operated a facility on a joint-use airport. It was both the Albuquerque International Airport and Kirtland Air Force Base. The mix of air traffic, and the amount that we handled was impressive. We had one long east-west runway, almost two miles long, and a shorter diagonal runway from northeast to southwest in operation. The north-south runway was closed for major work for the year that I was at Albuquerque. The traffic we directed included most of the Air Force and Navy fighters, bombers and transports, airliners, commuter planes, private and corporate aircraft-everything from huge six-engine B-36s to Piper Cubs. This was the time that the United States was experimenting with the atomic bomb blasts in the Pacific and at Jackass Flats in Nevada. Los Alamos was only a short hop to the north, and the Sandia Corporation, the contract developer of strange and exotic weapons for the U.S., was headquartered only a short distance from the field. The Navy had its Special Weapons Command represented at Kirtland, as did its Air Force counterpart. Every conceivable type of military aircraft was used in the tests, and it was our job to safely expedite air traffic, and keep the airplanes from running into each other. Albuquerque was rated in the top 10 busiest airports in the United States at that time. Only airports like Chicago O'Hare, Los Angeles, Atlanta, LaGuardia, Washington National and Atlanta had higher traffic counts.

When I would come home after a busy eight-hour shift, particularly the day watch, I would have to unwind by drinking at least two bottles of beer. Then the nerves would begin to settle, and I could talk about the day. I would be really bad after an accident, and we had plenty of those. One day when I was working the local control position, I cleared a Navy fighter for takeoff. He began rolling down the runway, lifted off, then rolled off to the left, his wingtip catching the ground, and he rolled up into a fiery ball that flamed down the line of runway lights. After a day like that I would drink more than two beers, and end up drunk before going to bed. A nice thing about our new home in Albuquerque was that there was a liquor store less that a block away from us.

I found that air traffic control was a lot like flying in combat-a lot of boring, waiting time punctuated by short periods of frightening action.

Our low activity time was filled with training, learning new procedures and telling stories. We had several characters at Albuquerque Tower and the most colorful was Jack Sturges. Jack was in his early 40s, a Texan, an avid golfer, and a reader of dictionaries. He followed a regimen of learning a new word every day. His only problem was that he fractured the King's English.

For example, our tower chief was hospitalized with a painful case of hemorrhoids. Jack visited him after his operation and reported to us on the swing shift that night.

"That poor chief. He is in such pain. Do you know what those goddam doctors did to him? They catheterized his piles."

He meant cauterized.

The other favorite Jack story was about his ability to verbalize in any situation. Jack was working the local control position and he had two airplanes ready for departure. An Air Force fighter was waiting for departure on the east-west runway. He would be taking off to the west. A Navy fighter was holding in take-off position on the northeast-southwest runway. He would be taking off to the southwest. Jack cleared the Air Force for takeoff. The Navy was supposed to hold in position until he got take-off clearance, but he started to roll the same time as the Air Force fighter. Jack was facing south, and his eyes were on the departing Air Force aircraft. He looked over his left shoulder, and there was the Navy fighter barreling down the runway. Both aircraft were closing fast on the common intersection they would cross. Jack could see an imminent collision was possible. The planes were going too fast to stop, so he couldn't hold either of them.

"Jump him Navy!" Jack screamed.

The airplanes did not collide, but Jack's "jump-him-Navy" phrase became our battle cry when we were confronted with a knotty control problem.

The tower was isolated from other buildings. It was an old structure that had been built in WWII. We had no way of trotting downstairs for any kind of a break, or to buy lunch or dinner at an airport restaurant. We had to bring our lunches with us. June was confronted with the problem of coming up with different kinds of sandwiches for me. Once I complained about the boring contents of my sandwiches. That was the wrong thing to do. The next day I had a beautiful lunch, a sandwich masterpiece-medium sharp cheddar nested between two slices of sour rye bread. The bread had been gently spread with herbed mayonnaise, and a bright slice of red onion promised extra flavor. With gusto I bit into the sandwich, chewed, and found something between my teeth. It was a small piece of paper. On it June had penciled a note:

"I hope you enjoy your damn cheese sandwich!"

I never complained about my lunches again. The best way to get a tower colleague into trouble was to say to his wife:

"I traded sandwiches with your husband, and you pack a great lunch."

When we were about to leave Kearns for Albuquerque, June realized that she was pregnant. As winter changed into spring, we knew that we had to make a decision as to where the baby was going to be born. I was all in favor of June having the baby in Albuquerque, but she was determined that the child would call Utah its birthplace. So we made arrangements for June to go up and stay with Ralph and Lucile in Ogden. Dr. Curtis would deliver the baby again at Dee Hospital. We drove up to Ogden, and I hated to leave June and Rosanne but I had to get back to work at Kirtland AFB. This was about the first of May, and we wrote letters back and forth every day. I was surprised at how much I missed June and Rosanne. It was hard filling the hours away from work, so I spent a lot of time at the tower working at jobs like revising training manuals. About mid-May I drove up to Ogden for the birth of our second child. Jeanine Nell King was born May 21, 1955. A spring baby, she began life in when the lilacs were in bloom, a favorite flower. The song, "Jeanine I Dream of You In Lilac Time," was a decided influence in picking her name. Her middle name was in honor of June's beloved mother, Nell. One week after Jeanine was born we were on our way back to Albuquerque. June insisted we visit some of the pueblos on our way home. Despite the discomfort of having just given birth, she wanted to see new things that she had only read about.

Most of the family came to visit us in Albuquerque. June's little brothers were with us for a short while, my mother and father took the train from Los Angeles to Albuquerque for a week stay, Ralph and Luciele and their kids came down for a trip and visit. We went out to White Sands National Monument and visited Alamogordo, the place where the first experimental atomic bomb had been fired. Our big trip was down to El Paso to visit relatives. June came from a polygamous family on her mother's side. June's grandfather Joseph Jackson had three wives. He was one of the Mormon's who fought the polygamy laws and fled to Mexico. One of his wives refused to go with him to Mexico. June said that when Grandpa Jackson went to Mexico he had two wives with him, one of which was Grandma Jones Jackson. She had three children, June's mother Nell, Joe and Fred, who were all born in Mexico in Chihuahua at Colonia Dublan near Casas Grande. We were in El Paso to visit Uncle George and Aunt Florence Payne and their daughter Roma. Aunt Florence was June's mother's half-sister.

June's mother had died about three years before we married. The great source of information about the Jackson's life in Mexico came from Uncle Joe, who was slightly younger than June's mother. After they moved to Mexico to escape the new law banning polygamy, Grandpa Jackson settled in Mexico. According to Uncle Joe, Grandpa Jackson set up one spouse in Casas Grande, the town wife, and Grandma Jackson at Colonia Dublan, the country wife. Colonia Dublan was but a hamlet. Grandpa Jackson established his mill there where he ground wheat into flour. Uncle Joe said the mill prospered, but trouble was on its way. It was a time of revolution in Mexico and Pancho Villa was raiding towns on both sides of the U.S.-Mexico border.

Villa's raiders burned down Grandpa Jackson's mill two times. After the second, Grandpa Jackson packed up his families for a return to the states-back to Ogden.

Uncle Joe told me the story of that move. He said that they took the train from Mexico to the United States. The train was made up of freight and livestock freight cars, and passenger cars at the rear of the train. Joe was riding up near the front of the train with his father looking after the stock in one of the cars. Mounted bandits raced along side the train, fired their rifles, and the train came to a grinding halt. Raiders were also firing at the train from the hills. Joe jumped down from the cattle car, his father shouted at him to come back, but Joe raced the length of the train, the bullets screaming overhead, to the passenger cars at the rear.

"All I wanted to do was get to my mother, sister and brother, and make sure they were okay," Joe said.

After a lengthy stop, the bandits let the train steam north to the border.

I was fascinated by the colorful stories Uncle George Payne told of life in Mexico in the Mormon colony when he was a child. Several members of the family continue to farm land around the place were the old flour mill stood.

The day trips we took into the Sandia Mountains, to Santa Fe, Taos and the pueblos were a welcome break from the stress of working in the tower. My favorite trip was 60 miles north to Santa Fe where we would browse in the shops, tour the historical sites, and look for new, good Mexican restaurants. On our first trip to Santa Fe we went to San Miguel Mission. When I walked into that old church it felt like I was coming home. June was holding Jeanine, and she had Rosanne by the hand at her side. We walked down the aisle before the altar. I knelt, made the sign of the cross, and said a quick Our Father and Hail Mary. A lump gathered large in the back of throat and it was an effort to keep the tears back. I stood. June clasped my right hand. I turned to her. She looked in my eyes, and I could feel the tears on my cheeks. In silence we turned and walked towards the door, I dipped my fingers in the holy water font near the door, turned, made the Sign of the Cross again, said goodbye.

We walked out into the bright New Mexico sun. June kept looking at me with concern. She was feeling some of the pain that I was at that moment, but I obstinately refused to accept that the spiritual values ingrained deep in me were of great importance. I thought I could live without faith, and be happy. After all, I had June and two beautiful daughters, a good job and life was good.

Our life in Albuquerque was filled with different activities, but I took on a new part-time job to earn extra money. I was always looking for something to do to earn extra money to put in savings, or to pay off bills. In Hanksville I helped a contractor put a new addition on the communications station, and got paid for it. In Salt Lake City I loaded freight on airplanes. Clark Couch, one of the watch supervisors at Kirtland Tower, told me about doing insurance inspections, a part-time job he did for many years. I began doing insurance risk investigations for the Retail Credit Co., and the extra money was something we looked forward to.

Chapter 14

Boise

At the end of 1955 I got another promotion. This time it would be closer to Ogden and June's family. We packed up to leave for Boise, Idaho, where I would be working in the combined control tower and communications station at Gowen Field. The move meant that I would be stepping up a grade to a GS-10. Reaching that grade meant that I could bid on journeyman controller positions at many places in the western United States. What I wanted was to eventually return to Salt Lake City.

It seemed as if we were always moving over Christmas and New Years, and June didn't like it a bit. One bright spot in the move was that we would be able to stop off and visit Uncle Joe and Aunt Catherine in Colorado Springs. Joe had accepted a job as chief baker with a big bread company there. Our stay with Uncle Joe and Aunt Catherine was marked by only one mishap. We were having a big New Years dinner. Aunt Catherine had baked a big ham as the meal entree. We sat down for dinner. Rosanne was standing next to me and I lifted her up to my lap. She had grabbed the tablecloth as I lifted her, and she pulled the serving dish with the ham over the edge of the table, and it crashed to the floor. Without pause, Uncle Joe reached down with this napkin, picked up the ham from the floor, put it back on the dish and put it on the table. Aunt Catherine wiped off the ham with napkins, sliced it, and we ate. Uncle Joe and Aunt Catherine made no fuss, and acted as if such a disaster was no big deal. Our next stop was Ogden for a short visit with the family before reporting to duty at Boise.

After stopping off to visit Ralph and Luciele in Ogden, we made the 300-mile trip north to Boise, our new home. We found a place that was very convenient for us, on Butler Street, about two miles from the airport. The only drawback was that it was next to the railroad tracks. That wasn't too bad because there were only about two trains that went by every day. When they did it caused a quick racket, but we got so we could sleep through all of the noise.

The year 1956 was a trying one for us. We were happy, getting along well, but everything bad seemed to be happening about the same time. June was pregnant again, and the baby was due in July.

"I guess that old wives' tale is a bunch of hogwash-that you can't get pregnant if you are nursing a baby," June said.

To compound the situation, I stepped into an air traffic control facility that had the reputation of being one of the worst in the western U.S. Harry Bergey was the chief and he was known as a hard man to please. He had sent a lot of controllers down the road, and he had a bad reputation. I got along great with all of the controllers, with the exception of George Hedstrom and Lloyd Jensen. Hedstrom and Jensen were Bergey's right hand men, and they did most of the training. The other staffers were Delphine Aldecoa, one of the few women controllers, and a fine one; Cecil Holmes, Henry Bray, John Maas and Phil Sonenstein. Boise was one of the few facilities that was a combined station-tower. We operated a full-phase communications station and control tower together. The only thing we didn't have to do was take weather observations, because we had a U.S. Weather Bureau station right next to us in the airport terminal building.

My check-out training progressed satisfactorily until we got to the approach control phase. Boise had a unique position in the air traffic control system. It was halfway between the Seattle and Salt Lake City Air Route Traffic Control Centers that separated and facilitated en route flights along the airways. A section of the airspace between Boise and Ontario, Oregon, was delegated permanently to Boise Tower to control aircraft below 7,000 feet. It was like we were a mini air route traffic control center, a tower and a communications station all in one. Bergey had delegated my training to Jensen and Hedstrom. I didn't have any problem in learning the area, the instrument arrival, departure and en route procedures. A big problem arose over use of standard air traffic control phraseologies. The CAA's air traffic control bible at the time was the ANC Manual. In it were described precise procedures and terminology to be used so that pilots and controllers nationwide would be using a standard system. It minimized confusion and traffic conflicts. Jensen and Hedstrom had devised their own local terminology for some standard procedures. I refused to use them, and continued using the standard phraseology taught to me at Salt Lake City, Albuquerque, and from the ANC manual. One day Jensen called me in for a talk before my check-out.

"Frank, I am worried about your progress. If you don't do things our way, the Boise way, you are not going to make it," he said.

The next day, when Harry Bergey was in his office, I confronted him. I told him that there was a problem with the way Hedstrom and Jensen were training me. I explained the standard phraseology question to him.

"I am going to continue using language as set out in ANC. If you are going to flunk me out, I am asking for an evaluation on my case by the Regional Office. One of the questions that is sure to be asked will by why I managed to get through the tough training programs at Salt Lake City and Albuquerque towers, places with much higher traffic counts, and not being able to make it in a podunk place like Boise," I said.

I must have been shouting, because Harry put his hands out and made a patting motion as to calm me down.

"I will look into it, Frank. I haven't heard anything about this," he said.

I completed taking the check-out tests, using standard phraseology; I passed, and nothing more was said. Hedstrom and Jensen continued to use their custom instructions and the rest of us used the standard ANC phraseology. My relations with Bergey, Hedstrom and Jensen improved over the next two years, because I wouldn't take any crap off of them and let them bully me.

Boise was a lot different in the types of aircraft I was used to working. During most of the year, except for the summer, things were pretty quiet. We had many bush aircraft flying back into the primitive areas of Idaho. Many ranches there depended upon the bush pilots to bring in supplies to them, and take people out in emergencies. We had United, Western and West Coast airlines operating out of Gowen Field, and there was an active Air National Guard Squadron that was flying the F-89s. In the summer, Air National Guard squadrons from the western United States, mostly from California, came to Boise for their annual two-week tour of duty. They were all fighter squadrons, mostly flying F-86s. Our traffic count jumped tenfold during these busy traffic periods. We would easily log over 1,000 operations a day. One operation was counted as a takeoff or landing. At peak periods we were running from 60 to 120 operations an hour. In 1957 we had a big bunch of National Guard fighters come in. We were short-handed, and one day I ended up working the day watch with only two people to help me. Bergey, the chief, had to work the flight data and ground control position, and a trainee who had been checked out in communications worked that position. It was up to me to work the local control position for eight hours straight. I would dash down-stairs for a restroom break, then back on the high stool at the local control position. I was so busy I didn't have time to eat lunch, just have coffee at the desk. It was an 8-hour day in which I logged more than 1,100 operations. That was repeated several times that summer, and I was not alone. Other controllers faced the same situation. We were not only working all the fighter planes, but bringing in airliners, small local civilian training flights, the bush pilots, and U.S. Forestry Service airplanes working forest fires.

We liked life in Boise, it was relatively close to June's family, and we had plenty of outdoor activity to enjoy in my time off. But 1956 was a hard year for us. My stomachaches persisted and I ended up by going down to Ogden and having Dr. Clark Rich operate on me to remove my gall bladder. Then my beloved Dad died. Dad suffered a heart attack April 26. He was at work, walking across the tarmac at the Douglas Aircraft Plant on the airport at Long Beach, California, when he was struck down. He was alive when they put him in the ambulance, but he died before reaching the hospital. June, our two little girls, and I left immediately for Salt Lake City where I took Western Airlines to Los Angeles. When I got there Mom was distraught, but most of the arrangements had been made for Dad's mass and funeral. The day of the funeral I had a letter from June. It was the most touching and loving letter that I had ever received.

"My dearest Frank,

"You sounded so lonely and defeated on the telephone. I felt so guilty about letting you go alone. There are many things in this life, my dear, that are so very private that in reality they must be borne alone. Pain is one, and deep grief is the other. I feel that I am essential to you in all things, great and small, but the adjustment to your tremendous loss must be made within yourself. Though my sympathy and love reach out to you-even over the miles-and I ache to put my arms around you and hold you tight, there is very little anyone can do to help you.

"As you said last night, you have found a new maturity these last years. It is this quality that gives me the confidence to trust you in everything and to depend and lean on you. I am sure that out of this maturity you will find the strength

for yourself as well. Please hurry home to us. We all miss you
and love you so very much. Until we see you, remember-we
are all in your hip pocket.

My love,
June"

I have memorized those words, and they have never failed to ease my
anguish in grief. June's letters helped, but I turned to my old friend, the
bottle, to help me through Dad's death. I stayed with Mother during the
time, and I was never drunk during the day when she had to do all of the
things so new to her. At night it was a different story. I drank myself into
oblivion, and paid for it with a huge hangover in the mornings. I helped
Mom straighten out some of their affairs, helped her with a budget, and
made sure she had enough money to live on. Dad's insurance took care of
all of their small debts, and she would have a small Social Security sur-
vivor's pension. She decided to stay on at the apartment in Long Beach
until she decided what she wanted to do.

I flew back to Salt Lake City, and June, Ralph and Lucielle picked me
up at the airport. Then we were on our way home to Boise. Then June
became really sick. She was hospitalized in St. Alphonsus Hospital with a
diagnosis of pancreatitis. She gradually recovered and came home, weak
and concerned that she might lose the baby. But all went well, and it was
time again to go back down to Ogden for the baby to be born. Melanie
was born July 10, 1956. The baby was all ready to be born, but June's
labor pains hadn't started yet. She asked Dr. Curtis if labor couldn't be
induced so that Melanie would be born on my father's birthday. It happened just the way she planned it. In 1956 it seemed that about every two
months something big was going to happen. Two months after Melanie
was born June became ill again. This time her trouble was diagnosed as a
gall bladder problem. In October she went into the hospital again, was
operated on, and quickly began to recover. She was almost fully recovered,
when we got the call from Ogden on Dec. 7, 1956, that John Van De
Graaff, June's father had died. June and I were convinced that alcoholism

had played a big part in his deteriorating health, but some of June's brothers and sisters had a hard time accepting that. Like many people, they believed that alcoholism was a physical or moral weakness, not an illness.

June and her brothers and sisters gathered immediately after funeral to decide what would happen to Fred, Ken, Merrill and David, the four youngest brothers who were at home when Pop died. The day Pop died, the four boys left the family home to Ethyl, and moved in with their married brothers and sisters. We all decided that we would pool any money that came in the way of an inheritance, and use it for the care and education of the four boys. That day we set up the fund that would be used to educate the boys. Fred and Kent would go to live with brother Bud and his wife Donna, and her two kids, in Hooper, Utah, about 10 miles southwest of Ogden. Merrill and David, the two youngest, would live with Ralph and Luciele in Riverdale, a suburb of Ogden. We wanted to keep the four boys as close together as possible. Younger brother John, who served in the Army, would finish school, get married, and go on to dental school at Northwestern University in Chicago. After he graduated he established a successful dental practice in Chicago. June and I promised the family that as soon as the opportunity came up, we would try to get back to Utah to help in caring for the boys. June was the eldest, and her opinions carried a lot of weight with her brothers and sisters. They appreciated her love, sense of family loyalty, intelligence and knowledge.

Surprisingly, John's children were criticized for their action of solidarity. They were accused by some of the older family members of being insensitive in making plans for the boys right after the funeral. We told them that was the only time all of us were going to be together, and we had to make a decision in a few hours after the funeral. Some of those same family members came to us later and told us how right we were in our cooperative action.

"I just wish some of us older folks would have acted the same way you guys did when John died. We sure didn't when Grandma Van De Graaff passed away," Uncle Joe said.

When we got back to Boise it was with a growing desire to return to Utah, close to Ogden, so we could be with June's family to help with the four younger brothers. For the two and one half years we were in Boise, we had the boys come stay with us during vacations and holidays.

Meanwhile we had been looking for another house in Boise. We wanted to get into a place of our own. We found an old, small house, that had been built in 1900. It was in excellent condition, and only required some cosmetic work to make it into a lovely, small home for our growing family. The single-level frame house had two bedrooms, a full basement, one bath, a big sleeping porch, and a detached two-car garage. It was located on North 16th Street, just off Harrison Blvd., an upscale neighborhood, and was right next door to the Gem Market, a neighborhood grocery store. Over the next two years we became good friends with the folks that owned the store. They had a small meat counter in the store, and they did wonderful work for the folks in the neighborhood. The butchers would vie over giving June special service. She would take her meal problems to them and ask for recommendations on the meat cuts she should use. One great result a crown roast of pork with dressing. It became her premier dish when we had company for dinner.

We worked hard on the house, had a new natural gas wall furnace installed to replace the fuel oil system, replaced doors and windows, and painted. The sleeping porch did not have a foundation under it, the sill was rotted and resting on the ground. I jacked up the porch, cut out the rotted wood, installed a new sill, and set the porch on concrete blocks. We had a fine-looking place when we were finished.

My mother, after a long trip back to Port Huron, Michigan, to visit all of the family back there, had packed up all of her stuff in California and was ready to move. Her first choice was to come up to be near us. Tony was still in the Air Force, and Pete was in the middle of changing jobs in Southern California. June and I thought we had found the ideal place for my mother. It was right next door, an apartment over the Gem Market. We made arrangements with the owners to clean the place up and paint it.

We did that and put down the rent so Mom could move in. When my mother arrived in Boise, she thought she would be staying with us, and when we showed her the apartment next door, she turned up her nose, and said that she didn't want to move into such a dump. It was a nice, clean modest three rooms, and I couldn't see anything wrong with it. I could feel the tension between June and my mother. June resented Mom's attitude after we had tried so hard to get her a place right next to us. My mother told us that she was going to try and get a job, so she could take care of herself. I was all in favor of that. She soon found work taking care of an elderly, infirm woman in east Boise. Mom moved in with her, and became her caretaker. That situation was temporarily resolved.

After the disastrous year of 1956, we were playing catch-up with our finances. I continued doing the part-time investigating work for Retail Credit Co. and took on a new client, the American Service Bureau. I managed to make enough money part-time, about $200 a month, to go towards our medical bills. We soon had all of those paid off.

One of our neighbors in Boise was Bert Simer, an old guy who must have been in his 60s. We thought everyone who was over 50 was old. That has changed a lot since I have become a septuagenarian. Bert noticed how interested I was in rock hunting and prospecting, a holdover from our Hanksville days. We had traveled to several places rock hunting, like for fire opal out in the southwestern part of Idaho. Bert was a retired miner and prospector. He came to me with a deal for buying a placer claim that he had over by Salmon, Idaho, his home for many years. Bert's placer claim was on Boyle Creek, also called Tower Creek, about 10 miles north and east of Salmon, just off the main stem of the Salmon River. The claim was located on the small creek, just below an old played-out mine that belonged to the Hecla Mining company. The old Hecla mine was in a quartzite formation that was heavily mineralized. It had a lot of galena ore, also copper and gold. Bert's claim was about 200 feet wide and about 500 feet long running down the creek bed. He wanted to sell it for $300. I asked Ralph and Luciele and June's Uncle Fred if they wanted to go in on the deal. They agreed, so we bought the claim that we named the Princess Placer Claim. We had to do at least $100 of work on the mine each year to keep the claim in force. It was on U.S. Forest Service land on the west slope of the Bitterroot Mountains. Bert claimed that we could get color every time we panned. I doubted that claim. So Ralph and Luciele, and their family, June and I, with our brood, made arrangements to go up to the mine with Bert to see how good it was.

Bert's claim was true. You couldn't get much gold, but if you took a magnifying glass you could see the golden trace in the black sand at the bottom of the pan. Bert called it "flour gold,' but occasionally you would find a small flake, or a nugget, in your pan. After we found out that there was really gold there, we told Bert we would buy the claim. The mine became a favorite vacation spot over the next ten or so years. We would travel to Salmon in the summer, and have a great time camping, hiking and panning gold.

While we were in Boise, Fred Jackson, June's uncle, moved to Spokane, Washington. June was thrilled. That mean that another set of relatives was going to be within easy traveling distance of Boise. June was close with her Uncle Fred. He wasn't much older that she, and when June was young her Uncle Joe and Uncle Fred had lived with her family. Fred and Jeanette Jackson, and their kids, Chick and Barbara, moved from Oakland, California, to Spokane shortly after we had arrived in Boise. We made several trips north to Spokane to visit them. The trips were always an adventure particularly in the wintertime. Heavy snows, blizzards and freezing rain were the norm. I particularly liked visiting Fred. He had a great well-stocked bar. I could count on having plenty to drink when visiting Fred.

I developed the habit of stopping off for a couple of drinks, usually beer, at the Boise Air Terminal restaurant after I got off a swing shift. I told June I just wanted to relax. She said I should come home to relax, there was beer in the refrigerator, and besides it was cheaper to drink at home. I agreed, but if I drank at home she would then know how much I was drinking. June said that she realized I had a little bit of a drinking problem when I didn't want to watch my favorite television show. I waited each week for the next installment of "Run Silent, Run Deep," the continuing series about the submarine service. One day I had been drinking on a bottle I had hidden in the garage. After dinner I went on the porch, sat on the steps, and looked out at the street. June came out and told me that it was time for my "submarine show."

"Ah hell! I don't want to see it. You see one, you have seen 'em all," I said.

"Right then I knew something was wrong," June said.

June asked if I had been drinking. I told her about the bottle in the garage. She went out and got it. There was only about two inches of booze left in the fifth. She put it in the cupboard.

"Leave your liquor in the cupboard. You can have it any time you want it. You don't have to hide your drinking from me," she said. "Lord knows I have done enough of it myself."

June didn't have the compulsion that I had. She could take it or leave it alone. I couldn't go very long, only a few days, a week at the most, without drinking. Once I started on a bottle I had to finish it. And I had to hide it because I was ashamed of that nagging need.

Faith, spirituality and religion were a jumbled tangle in my mind. Right after Rosanne was born, I told June that I thought the kids should be raised Mormon. I firmly believed that I was excommunicated from the Catholic Church, and June was a silently devout person who had been raised a Mormon. The kids were all baptized in June's church. Everywhere we went, the Mormon missionaries would find us. Two young men visited us in Boise and asked if they could come back to visit with me each week. I knew that they were trying to convert me, and I decided I would see what they had to say. They left material for me to read and study. The concepts were much different than the faith I had learned as a Catholic kid at the Our Lady of Guadalupe chapel at home. After six weeks, I sat down with June and told her I couldn't go through the things with the missionaries any more.

"It's tearing me apart," I said. "I think I want to believe, but I can't. I feel like a traitor when I have these thoughts."

I told June I wanted to please her, but the spiritual price tag was too high. I would have to deny everything I believed in, and become someone I didn't know. By the time I finished I was in tears. June rushed to me, hugged me hard, and said she didn't want me to change anything, that she wanted me just as I was. She called the missionaries and told them not to come back.

Chapter 15

Bountiful

In 1958 word came down the line that a job was opening up in Salt Lake Tower for a journeyman controller. I bid on it, and was accepted. June was ecstatic. That meant we would be going back to Utah and we could be closer to the four boys still in school. We put the house up on the market, and soon sold it for $6,500, a nice $2,000 profit for our hard work on improving the little home. We had to carry a note for about $1,000 that the buyers paid off at $20 a month for many years. June and I decided that we would move ourselves this time, instead of having a moving company do it for us. We could make about $500 by doing it ourselves, and that money could go towards a down payment on a new home in Utah.

Again Ralph and Luciele came to our rescue. I rented a U-haul truck, and Ralph came up to Boise with his pickup and a large trailer. It took us two days to load all of our household effects in the truck, pickup and trailer, and then we were off to Ogden. We would stay with Ralph and

Luciele until we found a house. My mother would follow us down after we got settled. The trip down was slow but uneventful until we hit the Utah Department of Transportation weighing station in Brigham City. Ralph and Luciele had gone on ahead of us and were already at their home in Ogden. We had a truck licensed in Idaho and it required a trip permit into Utah. I didn't have any cash on me, just our checkbook. The office at Brigham City would not accept an Idaho personal check, so I had to call Ralph to come up and rescue us. I was short of cash by 85 cents. Ralph and Luciele brought the cash, all of 85 cents, so we could complete paying for the permit. We drove on down to Ogden, unloaded the truck, pickup and trailer, and put all of our stuff in Ralph's garage.

Within a month we found a place in Bountiful, about eight miles north of the Salt Lake City Municipal Airport. June and I thought it was our dream house, and a brand new one. We had a little trouble getting the money together for a down payment on the three-bedroom, brick, one-and-a-half bath home, but we finally signed the papers and moved in. We had to do a lot of landscaping on the new house-put in a lawn, trees and shrubs.

June quickly became active in the Mormon Church. Her mother had been an active, devout member, and June said that she wanted to carry on that tradition. It wasn't long before June was a Primary and Sunday School teacher, instructing little children in the elements of her faith. Every time we went on a trip, June would buy postcards at places we visited, and write to each one of her tiny students. Later, their mothers would tell me how much those postcards meant to their children. Our days were filled with activity: working on the yard, exploring Utah and nearby states, my job, and June's involvement with her church.

She didn't expect, or ask me to change my habits. She accepted me for who I was. For years I had been smoking a pipe, and sometimes a cigar. On special occasions she would buy me a cigar. Grandma Van De Graaff liked me to smoke my cigar when we visited her. She said, "The house smells as if Grandpa were here." My favorite activity on weekends was lying on the couch, watching a ball game on television, with my pipe and a beer. I had a hard time keeping Jeanine away from my beer. She would grab the can and start drinking out of it. One Saturday I was in my favorite position on the sofa. Jeanine sneaked up grabbed my beer, and the doorbell rang. Jeanine toddled off to the front door, opened it, and there stood the Mormon home teachers. June was quick to the door, grabbed the beer can from Jeanine, tried to hide it behind her back, and asked them in. I scrambled off the couch and dived into the basement to my workbench to wait out the visit of the home teachers. They left in about 30 minutes, and a storming, pink-faced June ran into the basement.

"Damn you, Frank King! Keep your beer away from the babies," she shouted.

I really felt bad about it, and I promised I would keep an eagle eye out for my beer-snatching child.

We quickly made friends in the neighborhood. Rosanne, Jeanine and Melanie had plenty of playmates. One of Rosanne's little friends asked her about her parents, what her daddy was like?

"He's tall, has black, wavy hair, and my mother is a lot fatter than he is," Rosanne said.

June, who had been eavesdropping on their little talk, wasn't too happy with her eldest. Being June, she knew how to square things.

Jeanine had developed a strange affinity to the commode. We would be sitting in the living room watching television, or reading, and we would hear weird chuckling and splashing coming from the toilet. We would rush in and Jeanine would be splashing her hands in the toilet bowl, having a grand time. We had to keep cups and glasses out of her reach, or she would dip them into the bowl.

Rosanne was a bossy kid, and she ordered Jeanine to go get her a drink of water. Jeanine toddled off on her mission, and returned with a brimming cup, water sloshing out of the top. Rosanne drank the water.

"You know where she gets that water, don't you?" June asked.

Rosanne said, "Out of the sink," and June, with a satisfied smile, told her of Jeanine's favorite source.

Rosanne gagged, gagged and gagged. Not quite throwing up, but every time June would remind her not to accept cups borne by her younger sister, she would gag.

Getting back to the tower after three and a half years to where I had first trained as an air traffic controller was like coming home. The old ASR 2 radar was working well, but a lot of changes were in the planning stage. I quickly went through my area ratings, and checked out on all of the positions of operation in the tower cab and the radar room. There were some new faces at Salt Lake Tower, but many of the old crew were still there. Norm Andreason, Bob Erickson and Horace "Sully" Sullivan were watch supervisors and the ones who trained me when I came from Hanksville. Norm was a stickler for "by the book " terminology and procedures, Bob was a relaxed, but efficient controller who could really move traffic, and Sully had the most experience with different aircraft types, airline personnel and equipment. Norm taught me the right way to do things. From Bob, I learned how to work under fire. Sully passed on his experience and means of dealing with difficult airline pilots, dispatchers and en route air traffic controllers. I had a treat waiting for me when I reported for my new assignment. My good friend and best man Emil Henich had been assigned to Salt Lake Tower, and I would be working with him.

The layout in the tower was crazy. The local control, flight data and ground control positions were in a ring around the front of the tower facing the runways. Just in back of those positions was a black tent that enclosed the radar scopes. The departure control, arrival control positions-and the IFR flight data position-were in the tent. Shortly after I arrived in June 1958, work began on a new terminal building that would be across the field from us. The new terminal would have a control tower, with a radar room below, and plenty of space for tape recorders-that recorded all of our transmissions and phone calls from us to the pilots, the communications station and the Salt Lake Air Route Traffic Control Center. The new facility would also have a big training room, and offices for the chief, assistant chief and training officer. It would take more than a year before we would be in a modern facility.

Some of the equipment we were working with in 1958 and 59 had been in use for years. We had old military equipment, like radio receivers and direction finding equipment, that was used during World War II. Some of our desk microphones we used in the tower looked like something that Alexander Graham Bell would have designed. The old equipment had its faults. With the desk microphones in particular, if you would pull the plug out of the jack about one-quarter of an inch it would close the circuit and the mike would be hot. One day Sully was waiting to be relieved by Ken Stirk, one of the controllers. Ken climbed up the stairs about five minutes late. Sully quickly pulled out the phone plug as Ken moved over to the control position. Ken picked up the binoculars and zeroed in on a stewardess who was sitting in the seat next to the door of a United DC-3 parked on the ramp. Her legs were crossed.

"Boy, would I like to have some of that!" he said, the glasses pushed close to his eyes.

"So would I," blurted out of the speaker on the console.

The United DC-3 captain had his head out of the window looking up at the tower. He held out his microphone and pointed to it.

Sully raced for the stairs to escape Ken's wrath.

Ken Stirk was also our resident lothario. He was always chasing after women, even though he was married and had children. One of his romances was with a waitress in the coffee shop at the terminal. One night, Ken and his paramour were parked on one of the remote roads out near the airport. The Salt Lake City Municipal Airport was located out west of the city on the way to Saltair and the Great Salt Lake. The couple had been making out for awhile when one of the state policemen drove up in his patrol car. The patrolman was a friend of ours, and visited with us frequently when he stopped off at the tower on his patrols. He said that he parked his cruiser and walked over to the car. The windows were all steamed up and he couldn't see into the car's interior. He rapped on the roof with his nightstick, and quickly opened the driver's door.

"All I could see were elbows and assholes," he said.

For several years the commercial jet transports had been under development. The technology that fostered a couple of generations of military jet aircraft was being applied in the civilian aviation industry. The first Boeing 707 rolled off the production lines in the early 1960s and new jet transports were being delivered to the air carriers. Some of the first commercial airline jet transcontinental flights were from Los Angeles to New York City. The aviation safety folks quickly realized that the air traffic control system had not kept pace with the rapid jet aircraft development. We had no en route radar to safely control aircraft over the great expanses of the United States. As an interim measure, until they could design, manufacture and install civilian en route radar, a compromise measure was adopted. Civilian controllers would staff military high-site, air defense radar stations and provide flight following service for the new jet transports. We could not issue vectors, or headings for the transports to fly, but we could give them traffic information. We could tell them the location of traffic that could interfere with them, and it would be up to the pilots to spot the traffic visually with the information we provided.

One of the first efforts to provide the jet transport flight following service was at Angel Peak, Nevada, on a mountaintop about 40 miles northwest of Las Vegas. A team of two controllers, one from Los Angeles Tower and one from Salt Lake City Tower, would staff the military radar for one week. After seven days they would be relieved by another team from the same facilities. We could work the aircraft directly by VHF transceivers that had been installed for the project. When the Los Angeles En Route Traffic Control Center would hand the aircraft over to us at Angel Peak, we would identify them, follow them and issue traffic advisories, then hand them off to the next radar facility to the east. The flight following system continued until the big system of en route traffic control radar sites blanketed the country with positive radar coverage for the controllers.

The break in routine from regular tower duties to Angel Peak was a welcome novelty. It was exciting to be in on the first commercial jet transports flying cross country. I couldn't help but look back at how far aviation had progressed in the short time I had been involved with it. I was in my mid-30s and I had seen us move from the tiny 45-horsepower J3 Piper Cubs to the DC-3 Douglas transport, jet fighters and now commercial jet transports. I remembered being at Uncle Frank's after graduating from high school, the carpenter's job, and standing on the roof of that new house watching the first flight of the Douglas B-19, an experimental bomber, and a huge aircraft for its time. It could park, with room to spare, under one wing of a Boeing 707.

One thing I didn't like about the trip to Nevada was leaving the family behind. June didn't like it very much, either. June became pregnant again, and she was looking forward to the baby coming. About three months into her pregnancy she had a miscarriage, the first she had ever had. June was devastated, and quickly sunk into a depression. I had never seen her like this before, and I didn't know what to do.

"I thought the one thing that I was good at was having babies," she said. "I can't even do that anymore."

I was scheduled for a tour at Angel Peak, but I didn't want to leave June and the family then. We made plans to have her and the kids come with me, and have them stay in a motel. I would be able to come down off the mountain about every other day, to see how they were doing. After my seven days at Angel Peak we would leave for a visit to Southern California to visit my family and take the kids to Disneyland. I told June we would try and get a motel in Boulder City, about 40 miles southwest of Las Vegas, because I knew how much she hated cities that didn't turn their lights out at night. We found a great place in Boulder City, with a fine swimming and wading pool, so the kids were real happy.

We left Boulder City, did what we planned, and then drove down to Calexico to see Wayne, June's younger brother, and his family. We had a great time in Calexico. Wayne was an agent with the U.S. Border Patrol.

He spoke Spanish fluently and was well known in the community. He and some others had started a free clinic for Mexican children who needed medical care. They would have children brought up from Mexico's interior, children who had tumors, club feet, cleft palates and gross deformities. They took them to children's hospitals in the Los Angeles area for treatment, arranged care for them with families after leaving the hospital, and returned them to Calexico and their homes in Mexico.

Wayne and Josie had hired a Mexican lady, Ampara, to help care for their children. Ampara's family in Mexicali was caring for two small children, a girl about four and her brother, two years old. Wayne said that the children were going into an orphanage, because their mother, a prostitute, had abandoned them.

That night I woke up about 2 a.m. and June was sitting at the edge of our bed crying. I asked her what was wrong?

"I can't get those children's faces out of my mind," she cried. "They looked so lonely, so sad. They need a family."

Right away I knew which direction the conversation was going, so I decided to beat June to the question she was going to ask.

"Are you saying we should try and adopt those kids?"

She nodded, reached for me, and I held her until she finally drifted off to sleep.

The next morning we asked Wayne what we would have to do to adopt the little boy and girl. He said that the first step was getting a lawyer, which we did. After we returned to Bountiful, we sent Wayne a retainer for the lawyer and the drawn out process of adoption began.

We phoned Wayne and Josie about every week to find out about the kids' condition and how the adoption proceedings were going. After a couple of months, Wayne called and told us that the mother of the two children had returned to Calexico, and petitioned the courts for their return. It was granted. Wayne said that the woman had taken her children and disappeared. June wasn't as upset as I thought she would be. She was happy that the mother was reunited with her children, and she prayed that the kids would be well-cared for, happy and healthy. Several years later Wayne told me that both of the children were dead, that their mother had abandoned them again, a fatal consequence for the two little ones.

The summer of 1959 was a great one. The house was looking good, the grass was green, and the flowers blooming. June insisted that we plant roses along the side of our driveway. I bought her a Peace Rose, her favorite, and it bloomed a little that first year. We both continued with our reading, and the monthly book club offerings were eagerly awaited. About that time, some of the more controversial books were being imported into the United States. Among them was *Lady Chatterley's Lover* by D. H. Lawrence. I bought the book, and read it when I was working a graveyard shift at the tower. June picked up the book and read it during the day as quickly as I did. The day I got home from working a day shift was the day she was reading the book. She shooed the kids out into the back yard, grabbed me by the front of the shirt and pulled me downstairs into the basement. We had put a small bed down there for me to nap on before going on watch during the hot summer. June pushed me over to the bed, pulled my shirt off. She had on a loose house dress, and no underwear.

"Don't be bringing books like that home to me, unless you are ready to do something about it," she growled.

She shoved me on the bed and climbed on top of me.

The written word had a great affect on June. She could read a poem that would maker her cry, articles that would make her howl with laughter, and books that could deeply move her. I had read plenty of stuff by the author that got me in so much trouble in my youth, Irving Stone. I read his *Darrow for the Defense*, and *Adversary in the House*, biographies about famous defense attorney Clarence Darrow and Eugene V. Debs, the American socialist. June, like the rest of her family, was a pretty stalwart Republican. Pop, Bud and I would have some rousing political arguments that the younger boys would love to listen to. June's and my political philosophies were quite different, and she was curious as to why I believed so deeply in the labor union movement. I asked her to read the Darrow and Debs books. She told me later that she had never heard of such things before as the abuses imposed on working people by the robber barons of the late nineteenth and early twentieth centuries. When she read of the shirtwaist factory fire, the Pullman strike and the Haymarket riot in Chicago, she was moved by Stone's descriptions of the conflicts. June changed into an independent voter. She would never register as a Democrat; it would be denying her heritage.

If books moved June, some pictures could madden her, particularly if they were center spreads in *Playboy* magazine. I made the mistake of bringing home an early *Playboy*, "because they have great interviews in them." June took one look at the bare-breasted beauties, flung the magazine at me, and tore through the house screaming at me. If I ever wanted to sleep with her, I was not to bring such trash into her house again. I thought it was funny, and started laughing. Big mistake. June became almost hysterical; the crying and the sobbing came from deep inside her.

"You don't know what it is like to be big, fat and pregnant, and have you bring home a book with photos of women like that," she cried.

June had a way of making me feel small enough to crawl under a snake's belly, particularly when I knew I was wrong. Words didn't help. I got rid of the *Playboy*, and never brought one back in the house. My *Playboy* reading was done only at the tower, when my colleagues brought the book to work. Even then I felt guilty.

June was pregnant again, and she we began looking forward to the birth of our fourth child. Christmas of 1959 was a good one. Christmas Eve, I had a hard time reading Luke 2: 1-20. It was a tradition June insisted on, and I read it with three kids on my lap, and June sitting at my feet. The words burned into me as I read, and visions of midnight mass, the carols, candles and cloudy incense haunted me. I had a hard time reading, my voice was quivering so bad. June gazed at me soundlessly, her eyes filling up, as she silently acknowledged the pain I felt.

That pain got greater when my mother asked me to drive her to mass on Christmas Day. My mother had followed us down to Bountiful from

Boise, and got a job looking after an elderly patient in Salt Lake City. She later would return to the Los Angeles area and work as a cook for a community of priests. I took her over to St. Olaf's in Bountiful, and I even walked into the church with her with the intention of leaving, then driving back to pick her up. I thought that would be a waste of time, why not stay for mass? I did, and my mother was ecstatic. She finally got be back to church. The ritual of the mass hadn't changed, but I was all mixed up. I was strangely comforted, but I felt as if I didn't belong there. It didn't get any better as the day went on, but it all slipped into the background when I had the first drink of the day when we got home.

Winter crept out, and spring tripped in with its blossoms, lilacs and apple blossoms. I tried really hard to be a better husband and father. I always had a quick temper, and when I would blow up it always made June and the little girls feel bad. June was having troubles with her pregnancy, and about two months before the baby was to be born she started bleeding. She had to take it easy, and I helped out as much as I could. One day she was at the kitchen sink peeling vegetables, when something ticked me off. I think it was something that the kids got into. I flipped my top, and ranted for a while before I calmed down. June stood at the sink, her shoulders shaking and the tears running down her cheeks. I put my arm around her and asked her what was wrong?

"You have been so good during this pregnancy, and it just tears me apart when you lose your temper like that," she said.

I felt rotten. I promised to do better, and I really meant it. Things were pretty dicey at work. There was a lot of traffic and the pressure began to build as the flying increased. Some of the time, I would stop off at the Palm's for a drink after work with Norm. Norm pressured me to have drinks with him after a swing shift. I would call and tell June that I was going to stop for a couple of beers before I would be home. She would calmly state that she understood why I would rather spend time with Norm than with her and the girls. When she said that I would always go right home. But I was drinking secretly.

When working at Salt Lake City Tower we were obligated to wear a tie. June had a fresh shirt ironed for me every day. On evening and swing shifts I usually wore my old Marine Corps flight jacket, the leather one with the fur around the collar. She had just finished ironing my shirts, was hanging them up when she brushed against my flight jacket hanging in the closet. Something hard banged against the wall as she put a shirt on the hanging rod. She looked for the source of the noise, and noticed that I had a rather large, hard object in the breast pocket of the flight jacket. It was a half-pint bottle of vodka with about three inches of liquor left in it. June called to me and I went into the bedroom, and asked her what she wanted. She pulled out the bottle and held it up.

"I don't know what is going to happen to you if anything happens to me," she said.

She stood, the bottle in her hands, looking down at it, and cried. Again, I felt as if I was in the gutter looking up at her. I didn't know what to say, so I just held her. I promised her I would try to do something about controlling my drinking.

Two weeks after that scene, June began bleeding and I drove her up to Dr. Curtis in Ogden. He put her in the hospital, and her labor pains started immediately. She had been in labor for a couple of hours and went into the delivery room. Dr. Curtis rushed out, and said that June had to have a caesarian section. The placenta was coming out first, he had tried to hold it in place, but it wasn't working. If the situation continued they would lose the baby. June wanted to have the C section to save the baby. I held her and kissed her before they wheeled her into the operating room.

Dr. Curtis came out and told me the procedure had been a success, and June and I had a new little baby girl, our fourth. He assured me that June was doing fine, was responding well and would be in the recovery room for a short time, then they would take her up to a four-bed maternity room. Meanwhile. Lucielle, who had been there for the birth, went home to look after all the kids after Dr. Curtis told us that June was going to be all right.

Soon a crew wheeled June into her room. There were no other women in the three empty beds. June looked pale and drawn, and the nurses said that she was awake but very weak. I held her, crooned to her how much I loved her and that she would be well very soon. She began breathing very hard, and gasping, the breath rattling deep inside her. I shouted for the nurses. They took one look at her, called an emergency, and doctors, nurses and equipment dashed in the room. I tried to hold onto her, as they pulled me away. A nurse said June was in serious distress. I went crazy. I dashed out to a phone, called Dr. Rich who was having dinner at a restaurant up Ogden Canyon, and told him to do something. I ran back to the room, and the nurses let me hold June who had stopped breathing. The rest is a blur. I remember holding her, until I was again pulled away. I remembered her words when she found the bottle of vodka in my flight jacket.

"What am I going to tell my kids, and Luciele,?" I cried.

I later learned that June had an acute allergic reaction to the sodium pentathol anesthetic she had been given. Simply put, her lungs filled with fluid and she was unable to breathe. The irony of the situation was that both her obstetrician, Dr. Curtis, and her anesthesiologist, Dr. Dee Dixon, had gone home, because she was stabilized and doing well after the C section. June knew Dee Dixon. He had lived in her neighborhood and gone to school with her.

First I had to tell Luciele and Ralph, which was hard enough to do, but I put off telling the kids until the next day. I wanted time to calm down, if I could. The next morning, after the girls had had their breakfast, I tried to explain to them as gently as I could about what happened, that they had a new baby sister, but their mother was not coming home. That she would never be coming home. I tried all of the stories: that she was in Heaven with her Mommy and Daddy, that she would always be with us, and that we would never forget her. My own grief was so great that I thought I could not bear it, but when I had three children to console, sisters and brothers-in-law to comfort, I had precious little time to let go. I wept in private, and became more angry as the minutes ticked by.

I drove out to a remote field by an irrigation ditch, climbed out of the car, stood and looked at the star-filled heavens. I shook my clenched fists at the sky and cursed God. I mean I called him every mean, dirty word that I had heard Grandpa Smith use. I told him that he did not exist, and that if he did I was not having any part of him. If He was God, he had no right to take my wife and my children's mother.

I had a new baby, and three little daughters to think about. That night I called my mother and told her what had happened. She said that she would come up and help me with the four kids. Lucille insisted that she take the new baby and care for her until I was able to make arrangements. I named her Lisa June. June and I had already decided on her name. The lovely, new baby would be named after a pen pal of June's, a girl she had been writing to since they were in grade school. I arranged to take off two weeks from work, so that I could get everything settled. The funeral would be at the Bountiful Fifth Ward, June's home church. Church members, neighbors and friends brought so much food over to our house that I had to give a lot of it away, so that it wouldn't go to waste.

June and I had discussed death quite a bit, particularly after both of our fathers had died in 1956. I told June that when I died I didn't think that I wanted to have an open casket funeral, where people came and looked at me after I was dead. She felt the same way. I remembered those words when it came time for June's funeral. I decided that it would be closed casket. Aunt Till was very upset by this. She asked me if something was wrong with June, that her appearance was so bad that no one could see her? I told her no, and about the agreement that June and I had. Aunt Till asked if she could see June, just once, to say goodbye. I agreed. We went to the funeral parlor, and the attendant opened the casket for us. June looked beautiful, at peace. Aunt Till leaned over and kissed her, and I put one of her full-bloomed Peace roses on her breast. Then the casket was closed.

Also, I didn't want to put the kids through the ordeal of the funeral. I had my mother stay at home with them. Looking back, I don't know whether that was a wise choice. Even small children must have a chance to grieve. My girls never got over their mother's death, and I wonder to this day if going to the funeral, and being with all of June's family at that time would have helped the children. Lucille was so shaken and distraught by June's death that she couldn't go to the services.

The funeral was a real struggle. Merrill, June's younger brother, was in bad shape. The funeral ceremony followed Mormon tradition. When the bishops spoke on eternity, and how I had to be converted to Mormonism, to ensure my place at June's side in Heaven, Merrill became visibly upset. When we were walking out behind the casket, Merrill broke down.

"Those dumb bastards don't know what they are talking about, Frank," he cried. "Don't pay any attention to them!"

I held him and his brothers in my arms until Merrill calmed. June and Merrill had always been close, and their letters flowed back and forth up until she died. Merrill had developed a great reputation as writer, winning all kinds of prizes in high school. He was awarded a full-ride scholarship to Amherst College, where he was still in school. June reveled in his descriptions of New England, his poetry, and talks with Robert Frost. Merrill was complaining to June of homesickness, and told her how much he missed the Utah mountains, and the place he grew up. June answered him with a loving letter that contained a sprig of sage brush. The smell that reminded him so much of home. Merrill got that letter the day June died.

Then he wrote:

"Elegy For My Sister June: Died In June, 1960
The Peace Rose bloomed in your garden
The day you died,
Each day you had watched the sun's gentle touch
Coaxing the rose to disrobe.
You wrote about it,
And I was answering your letter when they called
And said your baby lived but you were dead.
I had never learned to wail, but I did then.

I borrowed money for a flight home,
And the girl beside me in the 707 jet
(flying to a vacation in Las Vegas)
Said she was sorry.
Perfectly alone, I sat swollen
In a pressurized compartment three miles
Above the sun flashed on steel roof.
The family waited for me at the airport.

I met them, but I scarcely knew their weariness
For my own senses were muffled
As the air closed inside your coffin.
At home, the Peace Rose adorned a table,
And your body, suffocated under greenhouse roses,
Adorned a chapel. The funeral came.
A town lady sang "That Wonderful Mother of Mine."
I insulted the speaker, said he didn't know about eternity.

June produced a Rose, June,
And I was sorry you couldn't see it.
But it doesn't matter so much:
No Peace Rose could know you had died anyway."

After three weeks, Lucille called me and said that I had to come up and get Lisa June.

"If I keep her for one more day, you are never going to get her back," Lucille said.

Lucille had become very attached to the new baby, but I knew that I had to bring her home with her sisters. I relieved my mother of the hard housework. Diapers had to be washed daily, and also clothes for three very active little girls. Mom would do the washing, and I would hang the clothes up for her when I got home. I didn't have a dryer. Not many people did in 1960. I also helped out with the cooking and the house-cleaning. Most of my mother's work was in watching the kids when I was at work. I tried to get on as many day watches as I could because of the children, but it was mandatory that I work a rotating shift.

Surprisingly, the day shifts were the hardest for me. I would work all day, then come home, be with the kids, maybe cook dinner, and do the dishes. They I would put the kids to bed. For a year after June died, I had three kids in bed with me all night. They begged to sleep with me, and I didn't have the heart to turn them down. When I would get them to sleep, I would creep out of bed into the living room. I would tell Mom that I was going out for a while, then head down to the closest tavern. There I would drink beer until closing time, and wobble off home to bed. I got so I knew all of the sad songs on the jukebox by heart. Work, take care of the kids, drink, and that was my routine. After two months, my mother needed a rest. I could tell that the children were wearing on her. I asked David, June's baby brother who was 13, if he would come down and help out. School vacation was still on so he had the spare time to do it. David was a big help, and I managed to get all of the housework done without any trouble. Every once in a while David would come down and spell Mom and me, and I have always been grateful for his eager help.

The Utah State Fair had become a big thing with June and me, and I was determined that was not going to change. So at fair time, I bundled up the kids, along with a stroller for Lisa, and I took them to the fair. I had entered a tablecloth June had embroidered for me, and an afghan that Grandma Smith had made, in the arts and crafts division. I was really pleased when June's beautiful pine cone Christmas tablecloth won a third prize in its category, and Grandma Smith's afghan took a first place in the senior citizen crafts section. After gloating over the winning ribbons, the kids and I proceeded to the part of the fair they liked the most, all of the animals. I was pushing Lisa, and Rosanne, Jeanine and Melanie were next to me holding hands. I wend over a bump in the blacktop and my camera case fell off the stroller I was pushing. The top of the case came open, and out tumbled my little, half-pint of vodka. It skidded and bounced across the blacktop, but didn't break. Rosanne raced after it, picked it up, and handed it to me.

"Here Daddy," she said, "Here's your medicine. It didn't break!"

The glares of the nearby good Mormon wives burned into me. I kept a little bottle of vodka under the front seat of the car all of the time. I would take a pull off of it, and tell the kids that it was medicine I had to take to keep me well.

Even though it was an election year, I had not been paying too much attention to politics. John F. Kennedy was running against the hated Tricky Dickey Nixon. Grandpa Smith, in his 80s, was in high form. He would bombastically rant about the collusion of Nixon, the railroads, insurance companies and the banks. Every time we talked politics, and that was every time we talked, Grandpa would gleefully, again, tell of chasing Nixon out of his shop with his shoe hammer. The way my life was going, I was convinced that the Democrats would lose the election. June had developed a real affection for JFK and his family. For the first time she broke with her family's Republicanism and actively supported a Democrat. When John Kennedy won the November election, I was surprised, happy and grateful. I knew June would have been happy. It did a lot to lift my spirits. I believed that maybe there was light at the end of the tunnel, and it wasn't an oncoming train.

At work we moved into the new control tower, and it was great working in a spanking new facility. It felt strange that I was able to care for the kids, work at my job and do normal things. Part of me was in this world, and the other part, the encapsulated fiery pain of June's death, was hovering nearby. Every once in a while, the pain would erupt and I would go off by myself in a nearby canyon and drink. My work and the changing locations kept me busy. The only problem was that we still had a lot of the same old equipment that they moved over from the old terminal building. We formed a chapter of the Air Traffic Control Association, and I was one of the charter members. Norm Andersen pushed me into a lot of work with the new chapter. As vice chairman I was responsible for publicity. We developed some workshops and meetings on local air traffic control problems, and we wanted to get all of the aviation community involved. I would write the news releases and send them to the *Salt Lake Tribune*, the *Dessert News*, the Mormon Church's official newspaper, the radio and television stations and the community newspapers in the area. I was really pleased when the press picked up on the releases. Many people from the airlines, general aviation fixed base operators, corporate and private plane owners and pilots attended those workshops.

The first holidays after June died were very hard. I was determined that the children would have a great Christmas. During the holidays, we made a quick trip down to California to see Grandpa and Grandma Smith and Lada. My Uncle Louie had died in 1954, and after his death my aunt made some big life changes. Lada had become a nun. She always wanted to be a nun when she was young, but Grandpa Smith had been dead set against it. That all changed after Grandpa became a Catholic. So back in 1956 and 57, she left a long career with Mandrel's, and took herself off to a Carmelite nunnery near Santa Barbara. She was there for some time, and then returned to San Gabriel Valley where she founded a new branch order of Carmelite nuns. She was very devout, but she always wanted to be the boss. Lada established a home for retired, infirm people in El Monte, Cassia Del Carmen. At one time her order had about 15 nuns caring for the people in the home. Grandpa and Grandma Smith had their own small cottage at the Casa. Meals were served in a central dining room. Food was carried on trays to the various residences to those too ill or lame to get the dining room. The Casa had a small chapel where a priest said mass on Saturdays and Sundays.

My drinking had become a lot worse. I couldn't sleep unless I was at least half-drunk. We had an ATCA convention in San Francisco, and I went over there with Norm. It was a disaster. I was drunk most of the time, and had to come back to Salt Lake to dry out so I could go to work. The big Christmas party that all the FAA people had that year was also a mess. I went with Emil and Glory Hence, who took care of me, and I don't remember any of It. I was in a blackout from shortly after we arrived at the party until I woke up at home, in my own bed, the next morning.

I still had to work rotating shifts at the tower, but I managed to keep the same days off-usually Sunday and Monday. The only time I had to change was if there was some sort of an emergency. We worked a shift we called the "scrambler," two swings from 4 p.m. to midnight, two days from 8 a.m. to 4 p.m., and then we would return in eight hours to work the graveyard from midnight to 8 a.m. That meant that I would go to work on a Tuesday afternoon at 4 p.m., work through the week, and get off graveyard on Saturday at 8 a.m. I had a weekend that lasted from Saturday morning until Tuesday afternoon. I liked the shift because it gave me plenty of time with the kids on weekends so we could do things together. I insisted that the girls go to their Mormon Sunday School and Primary. Every time they had a program I was there to watch them. It was the same way with school. Rosanne was the only one in school, but I was there for her registration, the PTA meetings, and all of the activities. I may have been half-loaded, but I was there.

June had been gone for almost a year when my mother and some of June's family said that I ought to get away on a vacation for a while. Wayne was working on the bracer program, the one where they were screening Mexican workers so that they could come to the U.S. to work on farms. Wayne had to go on assignments into Mexico's interior to work on the program. He invited me to come along with him. I took two weeks off and flew to Arizona where I met Wayne. We drove down to Guaymas where I would live for two weeks. Wayne and I had a room in an old commercial hotel in the downtown area. For two weeks I enjoyed the sun, fishing and great seafood. But I missed my children and I was anxious to get back to them. That two weeks with Wayne in Mexico meant a lot to me. There was a huge Catholic church within a block of the hotel. One Sunday I went over there and watched the people. The same feeling that I had at Our Lady of Guadalupe chapel in Beaumont swept over me. For an instant I felt a touch that could have been serenity, something I couldn't define. It quickly vanished when the anger, remorse and grief struck me again. I was still furious over June's death, and I blamed God.

I got home laden with Mexican toys that I had bought the girls. They and my mother were glad to see me. Rosanne clung to me and wouldn't let me go. She told me a little later that she thought I wasn't coming back, and she wouldn't have any parents and she and her sisters would have to go to an orphanage. I made a promise then that I wouldn't leave them again for such a long time.

Ron Barnes, who is about 10 years younger than I, became a very good friend. Ron had a little Morgan sports car that my daughters loved. When Ron visited they begged him to take them for a ride. They were queens of the neighborhood when Ron would parade with them down the local streets with the top down in the little red sports car. Ron also had a 16-foot-long boat with a 50-horsepower Johnson outboard engine. It was the perfect rig for water skiing. We made several trips with Ron up to Bear Lake, where some of the guys I worked with in the tower owned summer cabins. Ron Barnes was a bachelor and there were plenty of women, mostly airline stewardesses, dispatch clerks and reservation agents, who were after him. I wasn't very interested in going out again. The thoughts of dating, having to court some girl just left me cold. Ron tried to fix me up with some of the women he knew, but I just couldn't get interested. I tried dating a few women my around my age in their late 30s. The dates were disasters. The women were all divorcees and all they could talk about is how much they hated their former husbands, and that marriage was about the same as going to jail. None of my dates went beyond the first one.

Drinking played a big part in my social life, as well as my personal life. When we went water skiing with Ron, there was always a case of beer on hand. When I went on a date, I always brought along a bottle. Utah was a semi-dry state. You could only buy your hard liquor and wine at the state-owned liquor stores. You took your bottle along with you on the date, and the clubs would provide you with set-ups for your drinks. It's odd, but I found it easier to get drunk in Utah than in California, New Mexico, or Idaho. I realized that my drinking was increasing, but as yet it had not been a problem with taking care of my family or my job. When I went on hunting and fishing trips with my friends from the control tower, I was the unofficial designated driver. I could drink to a certain level, get that high feeling, and maintain it without ever losing control. I could name a dozen co-workers who drank much more than me.

Chuck DeFond, one of the men I was working with at the tower, had been after me for a long time to go on a blind date. He wanted me to meet a woman who was a good friend of the girl he was dating. Just to get him off my back I agreed. I picked up Carma Morrison Sellers at her house in Bountiful. She lived about a mile south of where my mother, my daughters and I lived. Carma and I went on our first date to a private club called the Stardust. We soon realized we had a lot in common. My wife had died, and so had her husband, Don. Carma, her husband, and their son, Michael, were living in Denver when Don had a fatal heart attack. Carma was born and raised in Richfield, Utah, and she returned to Utah to be closer to her family. Her son Mike was 14. At the time I was 39, and Carma was 45, but the age differences didn't seem to matter. After that first date we began seeing each other regularly. Neither of us was ready for any kind of long-term commitment, but we dated steadily because we enjoyed each other's company. After about six months we decided to get married.

Carma and I were married at Zane and Joyce Morrison's house in Bountiful. Zane was Carma's youngest brother. Merging two households proved to be a troublesome undertaking. Carma decided to sell her house that her oldest brother Val had built for her. Carma and Mike moved in with us on the place at 400S. 350 West in Bountiful. Just the logistics of such a merger was a puzzle. There were two of everything: electric frying pans, kitchen appliances, washers, dryers, pieces of furniture, etc. The big project of selling, trading and giving away stuff started. We soon realized that my small three-bedroom house was not going to be big enough for Carma and me, my mother, Mike and the four girls. We started looking for another place, and almost immediately found what we were looking for. A big three-bedroom, two-bath brick home with a full basement that could be converted into another bath, two bedrooms, recreation room and utility room. The price $21,000, seemed astronomical, but our payments would only be about $120 a month, and I was making well over $10,000 a year then-good money for the early 60s.

We moved into house on South Bonneview Drive, high on the east bench overlooking Bountiful and the Great Salt Lake. Our new house had a big deck that was roofed over and was an extension of our living room. Underneath the deck was a big, two-car carport that led into the full daylight basement. Carma and I got off to a rocky start. She wasn't very thrilled in becoming the mother of four small girls, the youngest of which was still in diapers. Carma had the same trouble with my mother as June. Mom could be temperamental, and her mood swings were hard to deal with. But she had done so much for me after June died, that I felt I would owe her for the rest of my life. She had come to my rescue when I needed her most. Carma decided to keep her job. We asked Mom to stay on as before, in her own room, and take care of the kids. We would do most of the housework and cooking, and Mom's primary duties would be taking care of the kids during the day.

Life was a rocky for us in adjusting to our new relationships. Right away Mom and Mike had trouble. My mother was used to governing the four girls with pretty much of an iron hand. She only tried to tell Mike what to do once, and there was an eruption. Mom was furious that Mike would not obey her order to do some chore. Mike sulked in his temporary room in the basement. Carma and I were caught in the middle, as we tried to smooth things over.

Amazingly, Rosanne, Jeanine and Melanie thought that Mike was wonderful. They had an instant older brother. They would follow him around, try to listen to his music when he shut them out of his room, and stared at him when we ate our meals. Mike, unnerved by their steady gazes, would holler at them to quit looking at him. There was a lot of work to do around the new house, and Mike helped me landscape. We planted a lawn, trees and shrubs, and installed an irrigation system.

In 1962 Rosanne was in the second grade and her teacher called the house and wanted to talk to me. I went in for an appointment, and she told me that Rosanne was having much difficulty seeing the blackboard in class, was becoming emotionally upset, and had to leave class frequently to go to the restroom. I called our pediatrician, and we went in for an appointment that same day. I was floored when the doctor said that Rosanne's tests had been positive for diabetes. Right away I went into the denial mode, and asked that if it couldn't be some other condition. The doctor said that he would ask for a second opinion, and he did so. It was the same with the consultant, diabetes. We put Rosanne into St. Mark's Hospital in Salt Lake City for regulation. Then started the process of learning about injections, diet and exercise, and how much of a tightrope a diabetic has to walk just to survive.

In a 1982 Father's Day letter to me, Rosanne wrote:

> "…My health also played a big part in my dependence on you. I was scared a lot, and I still am. How many mornings before dawn did you pack me up in my pajamas and drive me to St. Mark's for blood tests? We'd stop for breakfast at the little café by the Stinky Mountain (the North Salt Lake Hot Springs), pajamas and all. How many times did I hear you say, ' I wish I could do it for you' when there was another test, another shot? How many times have you wondered if I'd make it? How many days have you sat in hospital rooms and watched the same thing, over and over?

> "You were always strong for me, though. Where has it always come from, Daddy? The Higher Power you believe in so strongly in must be based on the power of love. I've never seen anything quite as powerful…"

My Higher Power at that time was booze. If I had any spirituality, I think that it was buried deep inside me. Booze helped take the edge off the grief;

Rosanne's precarious health; the deep flowing, but unspoken contention, at home, and the grinding stress of work at the control tower. It became habit to drink on day watches and weekends. After coming home in the afternoon I would start on a bottle, and weekends were open for drinking. I only had one bad physical experience due to my drinking. It was wintertime and we loved to have a fire blazing in our fireplace. I had a load of pinon pine delivered, but it still had to be split. I would split the larger pieces with a hatchet, so they would fit in our fireplace. I was chopping away down in the carport one evening, after a half dozen drags on my vodka bottle, and I got the thumb on my left hand in the way of the hatchet. I had chopped down and almost severed half of the thumb. I wrapped a towel around my hand, and had Carma drive me down to St. Marks Hospital in Salt Lake City. I told the doctors to cut off the section of thumb that was dangling, but they said no. The thumb is the most important digit on one's hand, and they must take heroic measures to save it. I was in the operating room for seven hours as an orthopedic surgeon did microsurgery on my dumb thumb. I spent four days in the hospital. When I told the guys at the tower what happened, I laughed it off as being a klutz with tools, but I knew that booze had impaired my judgment and actions that night.

I was developing a drinking pattern that would continue for several years. I drank secretly, mostly at home, and I would hide the bottles. The tension between my mother, my wife, and my children was something you could feel in the air. I tried to be the peacemaker, and usually was caught in the middle of some conflict. Drinking helped ease the tension. In the evenings after a day shift I would drink after I got off work until just before I went to bed. A lot of stuff was going on in those periods when I was anesthetized with vodka and beer. Things were happening between Carma and my kids that I should have been aware of, but booze was putting up a foggy barrier between me and reality. I always recovered enough to make it to work the next day.

Work in the tower was continually punctuated with hilarious moments, when humor did much to relieve the stress of the job. We had a great, easygoing relationship with the airline flying crews, the local commercial and instructor pilots, and the corporate pilots who flew the aircraft owned by businesses and industries. We had a "Gotcha!" game going continually. We would ask pilots to report when entering the traffic pattern, on downwind or base leg, or on final approach. We would many times ask for a report over a geographical fix. We would try to give them a geographical point that was so obscure that they would have to ask us its location.

For instance: "United 400 report downwind over the Pig Farm."

"Uh...Tower, where's the Pig Farm?"

Gotcha!

Pilots would play the same game.

"Salt Lake Tower, this is United 400 entering the valley and now over The Floor Mat."

"United 400 please say again your position."

"Passing The Floor Mat and coming up on Little Mountain."

Then you would have to holler at someone asking where in the hell Little Mountain was so you could give traffic instructions. Little Mountain is on the east shore of the Great Salt Lake close to Fremont Island. You would later find out that The Floor Mat was a tavern in Clearfield near Hill Air Force Base, 30 miles to the north. That would be a score for the airline pilot.

John Kimball, one of the newer controllers I helped train, teased me about my Catholic background. John was from a prominent Mormon family, and he had married an Italian Catholic girl. John was always complaining about the rosaries hanging from his car's rear view mirror and Jesus on the dashboard. I told him that Mormon missionaries were religious Fuller Brush salesmen. He and I got along great. With his sharp wit he was never at a loss for words. One day he was working a pilot flying his brand new Beechcraft Musketeer. The dialogue went something like this:

"This is Musketeer 12B on final approach."

"Roger, Mouseketeer 12B cleared to land"

"Tower! That's MUSKETEER 12B."

Silence on the air, but we were giggling in the tower.

The plane landed, and John cleared him off the runway.

"Mouseketeer 12B cleared to the ramp."

"I can't hear a word you are saying, Tower!"

"Roger. It must be that Mickey Mouse radio you have."

The enraged pilot called the tower and complained to our tower chief, Ted Martin. Ted counseled John in gentle terms, telling him to be more tactful with sensitive pilots.

John was a great trader, always on the lookout for collectible items. He wanted a rifle that stepson Michael had and was dickering for it. We traded rifles so Mike could have a good deer rifle and John brought it over to the house. Along with it he brought a puppy, a 10-week old Brittany spaniel bitch. John said he was throwing the dog in on the deal, because he got such a good bargain. That was a lie. He just wanted to get rid of all the puppies he was feeding. The kids wouldn't let me giver her back, so Dandy became part of the household. She also developed into a great drinking companion. I could talk to Dandy about my troubles, worries and failures, things that I would not reveal to another human being. Later on, Dandy and I did some serious drinking together. She didn't like hard liquor, but she loved beer and wine.

The control tower crew's favorite hangout was The Palms, a tavern next to the airport. It was there we would end up after a watch, talking over the day's air traffic. The bar's owner, Kip James, was a famed drinker. He loved to attend the University of Utah football games. The University of Utah and Utah State University were to meet for a big game in Salt Lake City, and Kip had tickets. He was in a quandary, because he wanted to take booze with him, but bottles were prohibited in Ute Stadium. He hit on a great solution. He would fill a hot water bottle with martinis, strap it to his body under his clothes. He would have a little rubber tube leading from the inside of the hot water bottle to the outside. He could hide the tube. All he had to do was put the tube in his mouth, squeeze the hot water bottle with his arms, suck on the tube and he got a good shot of martini. It worked, only too well.

The next day, looking really bad, Kip was tending bar.

"How was the game?" Ron asked.

"Don't know," Kip replied. "Last thing I remember was the kickoff."

My drinking had got bad enough that I thought I should try and do something to cut down. Out by the airport the Utah Council on Alcoholism had a huge billboard next to Highway 40. The billboard read something like: "Do you have a drinking problem? Maybe we can help." There was a phone number to call. I went to a phone booth outside of the terminal building and called the number. A man answered and asked if I had a drinking problem. I told him that I thought that I did, but I had to be very careful about who knew of my problem-because of my job. He in turn gave me another number to call. I did, and it was the Alcoholics Anonymous hotline. I quickly hung up without answering.

The only person really close to me who told me my drinking was start-ing to be a problem in my life was my Grandma Smith. She did it way back in 1945-46. Grandma flat out told me I was drinking too much, and that it could be a problem in my life. I think that there were some heavy drinkers on her side of the family, but none were considered alcoholics. When we drove down to El Monte for Grandma's funeral I remembered her words, and I prayed that I would stop drinking.

June's death really made me take a look at my life. I knew that I wanted to be a writer, but how would I do that? The ATCA's Journal of Air Traffic Control was asking for articles, and I thought that maybe I could do something like that. But I didn't know where to start. I was O.K. when it came to simple news stories and press releases, but I had never tried a full-length magazine article. The journalism department at the University of Utah offered a night course in magazine article writing. I signed up for the class that was taught by Milt Hollstein, the chairman of the department. That course changed my life. We learned all about non-fiction magazine article writing, and our term project was a query letter to an editor and a

2,000-word article. I queried the journal, and got an approval for an article, "A New Approach to Fog Dispersal." At the Salt Lake Airport we were testing a new fog dispersing system, seeding winter fog with dry ice. After seeding, the super-cooled water droplets would turn to ice crystals and drop out of the fog as snow, and the visibility would increase.

The article appeared, with my byline, picture and bio. I was hooked. I knew that was what I really wanted to do. So I signed up for more classes at the U-public affairs reporting, advanced news writing, radio news writing, photography, editing and typography. In about three years, I took just about all of the journalism courses the university offered.

Then Norm Bowen, the city editor with the *Deseret News*, lectured to one of my classes. He said that the paper was looking for good part-time help. I asked him about the job, and he said that my tower schedule would conflict with what they had in mind. He also said that if I wanted to submit freelance articles he would take a look at them. I thought about it, and decided to start out small. I asked the editor of the Davis County Clipper if I could do an article for him on peach harvesting and canning. He gave me the green light, and my article appeared along with a nice photo. One problem. The byline on the article read "by Frank White." I hoped that was not an omen of how my new career would progress. Then I started doing articles for the *Deseret News*, and Norm Bowen bought every one of them. I only got paid $10 an article, but I was building up a portfolio. When I would write a successful article it was as if I were undergoing a little spiritual experience. When my pieces appeared in print I felt very close to June and my Dad.

The Civil Aeronautics Administration had changed into the Federal Aviation Administration, a different name but the same organization. We had several publications:a newsletter, "Intercom", published in Los Angeles at the regional office; *FAA Horizons*, a national employee magazine; and *FAA Aviation News*, an aviation monthly directed toward an outside public. In addition to writing freelance stuff for local papers, I did some work for United Press International. Then a new FAA Area Office was built in Salt Lake City. The area manager asked that I do the publicity on the dedication, and design a brochure for the new office. All of this stuff went into the portfolio I hoped to use some day to make a change in my occupation. The stress of working in the tower was becoming more pressing as traffic increased and the days went by.

Nov. 22, 1963, another tragedy struck that deeply affected me. I was at the departure control position in the radar room when the first news came through that President John F. Kennedy had been shot. I felt sick, as if I was losing a family member. I was working traffic, several aircraft were on departure at the time, when someone burst into the radar room and said that the president was dead. I forget who it was, but someone made some wise crack about it was good that there was one less politician to bother us. I lost it. I slammed my headset down, turned around and screamed at the offender to "shut your goddam mouth or I will do it for you!" The crew, struck silent, gaped at me. I put the headset back on, and calmly began working traffic again, tears running down my cheeks. JFK's death hit me hard. His ascension to the presidency was a battle I reveled in. His inaugural words inspired me. I was proud to be a federal employee, working in a demanding job, in a government that was at long last beginning to put people first, instead of economics and the military. When I watched the funeral and saw Jackie Kennedy, with Caroline and John Jr. at her side, the pain of losing June became more acute. In those days I lost the fire that I needed to be a hard-charging air traffic controller.

One other incident also helped put out that fire. I was working departure control again on swing shift when the Air Guard scheduled some night flying. An F86D took off to the north, and had clearance to make a left turn and climb southbound to 20,000 feet. I spotted the target on my scope. He was moving quickly down the runway, when the tower called and gave me his departure time. The pilot called me, and I told him I had him in radar contact. He already had his clearance, and made a left turn and flew south. Over Antelope Island his target disappeared from my scope. I tried calling him and got no answer. I continued calling. No answer. I called the tower and asked if they could see anything out over Antelope Island, that I had lost the F-86D from my scope. They could see nothing. The Air Route Traffic Control Center was notified, and Air National Guard operations. At daylight the search started. A pilot saw the crashed F-86D. Nothing much was left of it. Apparently the pilot had rolled off into a left turn, became disoriented, and went into an inverted position. He thought he was climbing, but he was descending, and crashed into the island. I was the last person to talk to him before he died.

Several job openings came open for duty officer in the Western Regional Office in Los Angeles. I bid on the jobs, and finally I was considered for one of the positions. I was even called in for an interview, but I didn't get the job.

Then a job announcement came down the line notifying us that a new position had been opened up in the Western Regional Office Public Affairs Office. The new job, a GS-11 public information officer slot was being added to the staff there. There were three people in the office, Gene Kropf, the chief, Cliff Cernick, his assistant, and Barbara Abels, the editorial assistant. I was one of about 40 applicants for the job, and that was narrowed down to 10 finalists. I was notified that I was one of the 10, and told to come down to the Regional Office for an interview. The night before the interview I booked into a motel near the airport, and got drunk. I was so nervous I didn't think I could sleep, and the booze helped. The next morning I had a horrible hangover, and I knew my breath stunk from the booze. I used plenty of mouthwash, and chewed breath mints by the handful. I took my portfolio with me. I knew Cliff, because I had submitted some of my articles to him and he got them in the FAA publications.

I was interviewed by Joseph H. Tippetts, affectionately known at Joe T., the regional director for the FAA's Western Region. The Western Region encompassed the 11 western states, and had a staff of almost 4,000 people in air route traffic control centers, towers, communications stations, electronic maintenance facilities, aviation safety and airplane manufacturing type certification offices. Joe was also the chairman of the Los Angeles Federal Executive Board (FEB). The job I was applying for would be a support position as Joe T's executive assistant on the FEB, which would take up about 50 percent of the time required for the job. The other 50 percent would be working in the public affairs office. Gene Kropf and Cliff Cernick also interviewed me and looked at my portfolio. I flew home on Western Airlines, with the butterflies flying in my stomach. I went to work as usual in the tower, and I really believed that I wouldn't get the job.

Two days later Gene Kropf called me and told me the job was mine if I wanted it. Wanted it? I would have killed to get it, but I couldn't have stopped drinking to get it. Joe T. also called and congratulated me. He said that I had been picked over journalists who had a lot more experience than me because I "knew one end of any airplane from the other, and was part of the FAA family." There was a push to move older controllers into other occupations, and my selection was in line with that new FAA policy.

Just before I had been called down to Los Angeles for the job interview, I got a call from the Salt Lake City UPI bureau chief Don Reid. He asked me to come down and talk to him. I thought I had goofed on a story I had done, but Don said everything was okay but he wanted to talk to me in person. After he greeted me he asked if I would like to go to work for UPI. I was floored. He liked the work I had been doing for him, and he had noticed the features that I had been doing for the *Deseret News*. At the time, Don and his assistant, Steve Smilanich, would be busy covering the University of Utah and Brigham Young University basketball teams who had good teams that year. They needed the extra help and he offered me the job. I thought hard on it, and decided to stay with the FAA. I had more than 20 years in federal service, including my military time, and I didn't want to lose the retirement, health and life insurance benefits I had accumulated. Also my federal pay was about two times what I would get with UPI. I turned down the UPI offer with great regret. It was something I had been dreaming about for years.

Carma and I put our house up for sale, packed out stuff, and got ready for the move to Los Angeles.

Chapter 16

Back to L.A.

All of us, except Mike, would be making the move to Los Angeles. Mike, who was 18, didn't want to leave his friends, and he believed that he would have to go into the Army very soon. He would stay on in the house until it was sold, then he would move in with his Uncle Zane and Aunt Joyce. Carma, Rosanne, Lisa, Dandy and I would drive down in our little station wagon. My mother, Jeanine and Melanie would take the train down to Los Angeles. Tony would pick them up at the depot. The plan called for Mother, Jeanine and Melanie to stay with Tony and Edna, and their kids, until we found a permanent place to live in the Los Angeles area. Carma, Rosanne, Lisa and I would stay with Zonna and Art Johnson in Huntington Park. Zonna was Carma's older sister.

Within a month we found a house in Granada Hills, in north San Fernando Valley. It was a flat roofed, four-bedroom, two-bath house with an attached garage and a big swimming pool in the back yard. The back yard was fully enclosed by a concrete block wall, so Dandy would have plenty of room.

Carma soon found a job out next to the Los Angeles International Airport, a short distance away from where I worked at the FAA Western Regional Office. She got a job as a secretary to a group of engineers at Vickers Corp., a company that manufactured all kinds of pumps. It was 30 miles from our home in Granada Hills to the airport. Taking the freeway to work only took us 30 minutes to drive to the airport in the early morning. Coming home it was a much different story. On a day with normal traffic it would take us one hour and 30 minutes for the same drive. On Fridays that same drive took about two to three hours. The traffic was horrendous. I would get off work, pick up a half-pint bottle of vodka, drive over to Vickers and wait for Carma to get off. I would finish the bottle before she got to the car. I had to have at least eight ounces of vodka in me just to face the freeway battle. That continued for most of the time while we were in Los Angeles, except for one nine-month period of sobriety.

Learning to work for Joe T. was a delight, and a great education. He was one of the most spiritual persons I had met. There are three people whose spirituality I envied: Joe T, my father and June. All three had that deep trust and belief in a Supreme Being that I could not understand. They were also people who lived in what they believed. Joe T., like June, was a Mormon. He was born in southern Idaho, to a very poor family. After high school he went into the Navy, got into communications work, and ended up with the old Civil Aeronautics Administration. With only a high school education he ended up with one of the top jobs in the FAA after a distinguished career in the field. He was the most people-oriented boss that I had ever had. He was a legend in aviation circles. Joe would be on a business trip to some place like Seattle, and he would show up at the tower, the air route traffic control center, or the communications station, bang on the door, and shake hands with all of the workers. He would stay for hours, talking about the job, his plans for the region, and writing down the comments of those who complained. I traveled with him many times. We would be walking up the ramp ready to get on a flight and Joe would spot a mother trying to carry a baby, a purse and diaper bag, and pull another youngster along by the hand. Joe would rush over, ask if he could carry the baby or the diaper bag, and help her on the plane and get seated. This was normal behavior for him. He treated his subordinates, colleagues and superiors with identical courtesy and concern. Joe T. was a lot like my Dad, and I loved them both very much. Joe T. was a Mormon, had been a bishop and active his church everywhere he served. He made no action to try to convert me, and for that I was grateful.

The Los Angeles FEB was highly involved in recovery work after the Watts riots. Joe explained to me that the FEBs were first established by President Kennedy and continued under President Johnson. The boards were set up in the headquarter cities of the old Civil Service Commission,places like New York, Chicago, San Francisco, etc. Under President Johnson, several other important cities were added like Los Angeles. I think there were about 15 major cities at that time that had Federal Executive Boards. The boards were established to provide a direct line of communication between the Office of the President and the field headquarters of federal agencies. The director or manager of each local federal agency was a board member on the Federal Executive Board. Our members included the commanding officers from military, naval and Coast Guard bases; directors of the Internal Revenue Service; Secret Service; FBI; the departments of Agriculture; Interior; Labor: Commerce; Health, Education and Welfare; the Small Business Administration; National Aeronautics and Space Administration and many more, all together about 30 members. The theory was that policies, instructions and advice could be sent directly from the president to field offices for rapid implementation, bypassing the sluggish bureaucracy.

My job supporting Joe T. with the FEB was exciting, and I learned a lot. One of my jobs was to arrange all of the meetings, conferences and seminars. I also had to prepare an annual report that we published in booklet form. We had a weekend seminar once every six months. I had to book the facility, get commitments from members, and make reservations; in short, all of the logistic work. Joe had delegated one of his secretaries to help me, Dimple Lewis. Dimple was a wonderful black lady who had several children. Joe T., Dimple and I got along great and I thrived in that environment.

The board members had all donated towards a "recreation fund" that I had to maintain. The little account was to pay for the bar I had to set up at the seminars. I had to buy the liquor and keep the bar stocked on the weekend conferences. That was like putting the fox in charge on the hen house. I didn't abuse my responsibility as the keeper of the keys of the booze stash, but I didn't go thirsty either. At one of the board meetings a member voiced concern that the booze pantry was being depleted at an alarming rate. I told them that they had a quite a few members who drank copious amounts, and it wasn't up to me to limit their drinking. That was the truth. There was an Army colonel who would take bottle of Scotch every night of the conference and finish it off by himself, in his room. My dear Joe T. said that it couldn't be me because "Frank is a teetotaler." Again the guilt was almost overwhelming. I was hiding my drinking very well. I hid it from June, and now I was hiding it from Joe T.

I guess I was doing my job well, because I was getting complimentary notes from Joe T., Gene Kropf and Cliff Cernick on my work. About 70 percent of my time was devoted to FEB work, and the rest to public affairs duties. I continued to write articles, set up displays, and provide public information duties. After I was in the job less than a year, I got a promotion to a GS-12, and a performance award.

Living in Los Angeles was a lot more stressful than the bucolic environment of Bountiful, Utah. There was liquor everywhere. No state liquor stores. I was back in heaven. Disposing of the empties became a big problem. I had all of the available dumpsters behind the grocery stores scoped out. I would have to make a stealthy bottle run about every two weeks. I limited my intake to half-pints of vodka. I figured if I only drank half-pints I couldn't be an alcoholic. I drank two or three half pints a day during the week, plus beer and wine for appearances sake. On weekends my consumption increased. I tried tossing some of the little bottles under the hedge next to the garage, but that didn't work. One day Carma complained about the horrible neighbors next door, the Gillespies. They had been throwing their empty liquor bottles over on our property under our hedge. I didn't do anything to dissuade Carma from that belief. There was finite space under the hedge for empty bottles, so I had to find a new dumping spot.

Rosanne's health was always a concern, and her diabetes would suddenly shoot out of control. That meant trips back to the hospital for regulation. Jeanine also came down with pneumonia. She had two bad cases of it, and at one time she and Rosanne were in Holy Cross Hospital, near our home, in the same room. They gave the nurses fits. Jeanine couldn't go back to school, and had to stay in bed at home. The school arranged for her to take classes over the telephone, and a teacher would visit every week. She did well under that system, and eventually got her health back. She became bored staying at home all of the time, so Carma and I made arrangements for her to take guitar lessons. Jeanine had talent, and music became a big part of her life.

Mike had been drafted into the Army, went through training, and in 1967-68 he was in Vietnam. He went through the big Tet offensive, and we were really worried about him. His letters were eagerly awaited. He would write to us, telling of the fighting and what he was doing. He told us how much he missed us, how much he loved us, and how much he missed his sisters. It sure didn't sound like the same rebellious Mike who would do anything to avoid the annoying little girls who tagged along behind him in Bountiful. When Mike got back to the states, he made directly for our house in Granada Hills. He took all of the money he saved in Vietnam and bought a Chevy Corvette convertible. He drove the girls, top down, all through the neighborhood so their friends could see them in the Corvette.

The girls were all doing well in school, and Lisa started first grade while we were in Granada Hills. Rosanne, in junior high school, told me that she wanted to be a writer like her daddy. She began taking journalism classes, and entered a news and feature writing contest held by the Los Angeles County Schools. One Saturday I was lying on the couch, watching a game on television, and Rosanne came running in the front door clasping a trophy to her chest. The trophy was almost at tall as she. She had been at the awards ceremony and was ecstatic with the results.

"I did it Daddy! I did it! " she cried.

Rosanne had won first place in both the news and feature writing competitions and the trophy was for the school to display in their awards case. Rosanne got some nice certificates for the honor. She was following in her mother's and my footsteps in writing. I later found out how much she was like me. Rosanne, even at 13 and 14, was sneaking drinks, and some of her diabetes control problem was due to drinking and experimenting with drugs.

About this time I got some news that devastated me. I was going to lose my boss, Joe T. He was being recalled to Washington, D.C., where he was to be the FAA's Associate Administrator for Personnel and Training, one of the agency's top jobs. Joe T. wasn't very thrilled over the assignment. He said that he really wanted to stay on as director of the Western Region and retire out of that job. But Joe T. was a good soldier and he took his orders very seriously. He accepted the assignment and moved to D.C.

I continued as the FEB's executive assistant under the new chairman, Bob Kamm, the NASA boss in Los Angeles. He was a fine administrator, and I enjoyed working with him. When I came on board with the FEB I knew that I had to provide support for a television series. "Your Federal Executive Board," was run on KCOP/TV, channel 13, in Los Angeles on Sunday mornings at 10 a.m. It was a 15-minute public service interview show moderated by Florence and Suzy Thalheimer. It was my job to schedule participants to be interviewed, schedule the taping session, develop the viewing schedule, and take the videotape from the studio to the television station. The job developed into the producer's position, and in the two and a half years I was with the FEB I produced more that 50 shows.

When Joe T. left there was a big hole in my professional life, and I knew that I had to do something about my drinking. It was an obsession that was getting out of control. One noon I took a government car and drove over to Manhattan Beach, a town a few miles from the Regional Office. There was a club there for recovering alcoholics, and I thought I would sit in on a meeting and see if I could learn anything. I parked the car about two blocks away from the club and went in. The meeting was just starting and I was startled and amazed at some of the stories. Some were very close to my own. Others were much worse, and most of the men and women at the meeting were a lot older than I was. I remember one pretty little lady who looked as if she was in her 70s. She had carefully coifed blue-white hair, and a quiet, gentle voice. She told of being drunk on lower Main Street in LA, Skid Row, waking up naked in a hotel room with a man beside her who she did not know. It was hard for me to believe-she looked just like my Grandma Smith. A man related how once he also was on Skid Row, and would go to bed naked in his flop house hotel. He had heavy hair growing all over his body. He would get sick and throw up all over himself. When he woke up the vomit had dried into a case on his body. When he managed to sit up, he said, "I would crackle."

I wasn't that bad yet. I didn't go back to meetings at that club, but the feeling I got stayed with me. I felt that I was at home in that place. The serenity, and courage, that those folks had was something I wanted, but I didn't think that I was an alcoholic of their caliber. I went without a drink for a whole month after attending that meeting, the longest period I could remember of going without a drink.

I really missed Joe T., as a boss and a person. I liked working in the public affairs office at the FAA. After all, it allowed me to make a great change in occupation, something I had been working towards for a long time. I found out about a position open with the U. S. Army Corps of Engineers Los Angeles District as a public affairs officer. I inquired about, and discovered that it was a chief's job, at the same grade I had, with a staff of three people. Col. Norm Pehrson, the district engineer, interviewed me. A few days later I was told I had the job. I accepted and made arrangements to leave the FAA, after almost 18 years as an aircraft communicator, air traffic controller, and public affairs specialist.

I really wanted to do a good job, so I decided the best way to get on that track was to try and cut down on my drinking. I found a place where alcoholics held meetings, the same as the location in Manhattan Beach did. I would go to the meetings on Sunday mornings, and I managed to keep from drinking during the week. I was amazed at how good I felt when I didn't drink, and my energy level soared. I was able to get more done in a full day's work than I ever had before. Early in the morning I would drive into the Corps' offices in the Federal Building in downtown Los Angeles, and work straight through until 5:30 to 6 p.m., about two hours after normal quitting time.

My staff was made up of Pat Hannon, a former WWII P-47 Thunderbolt pilot, public information specialist; Eleanor McCarthy, the editorial assistant, and Geraldine Fitzgerald, a clerk-typist. Pat, of medium height, red hair, and a florid face, was a full-blown alcoholic, with all the symptoms; shaky hands, flushed face, and an alcohol-laden breath that would knock you over the first thing in the morning. In his bottom desk drawer he hid a bottle of vodka that he would sneak nips from throughout the day. His lunch hour ran from 11:30 a.m. to 2 p.m. Geraldine Fitzgerald, a pretty, petite black woman, with six kids, was a bright, talented, funny worker. She also had a drinking problem. She wouldn't show up for work for days at a time, then she would appear as if nothing had happened, take up her duties and work like a crazy woman. One night about 2 a.m. I was rousted out of bed by a phone call from Geraldine. She wanted me to come down to the L.A. women's jail and bail her out. She was drunk, assaulted a policeman who tried to arrest her, and thrown in the drunk tank. Her bail would cost $100. She only had one phone call, and it was to me. I talked to the jail officials, and they said I couldn't bail her out until 8 a.m. the next morning. I was at the jail the next morning with the bail bondsman, and she was released into my custody. Poor Geraldine, usually so neat, stylish and trim, was a frowzy, dirty, smelly mess.

"I never wanted you to see me like this!" she cried. "I didn't know who else to call."

I drove her home, and I didn't mention anything about her drinking. I didn't say anything to Pat about his drinking, either, and that is something I regret. I was staying sober, but I could tell that my sobriety was shaky, tenuous thing. I was afraid to involve myself in other folks' drinking problems. I really felt bad about Pat. I knew that he was a talented flyer. He flew hundreds of sorties against the Germans in his Thunderbolt fighter plane. After the war, he was a contestant in the very dangerous Cleveland Air Races for a couple of years. I think that I didn't mention his drinking problem to him because I was intimidated by his flying record. He was a hero. I didn't want to be the one to diminish his stature. It wasn't very courageous on my part, and not facing him on his drinking problem is something I regret.

Eleanor McCarthy, a native Californian, an Irish virago, wanted to mop the floor with Pat and Geraldine. She would wait until everyone had left the office at quitting time, stride into my office and demand that something be done about those "boozers." As diplomatically as I could, I tried to tell her that Pat was a war hero, and Geraldine's race were a big factor, that both had very hard lives, and we had to work with them and try and help them. Also, under the current regulations, it would be almost impossible to fire either of them. I asked her to be patient, and see how things developed. She would stomp out of my office, not before criticizing my wimpy response through a cloud of smoke in ladylike language. Eleanor was a hard worker, and a harder smoker. She had a lit cigarette dangling from her lips, or her fingers, every hour she was awake.

Shortly after I began working with the Corps' Los Angeles District, I became convinced that the organization needed a good employee newsletter. We held an employee newsletter naming contest, and managed to get the finance people to approve a money prize. The winner would get a $25 U.S. Savings Bond. The winning name for the newsletter was "Newscastle." The official symbol of the Corps of Engineers is a turreted castle. Eleanor became the editor, and she did a good job. She graduated from the Defense Information Agency's public information officer's course at Fort Benjamin Harrison, Indiana. She had the tools to do the job, and she soon showed how good she was. "Newscastle" became a success, and it has been continually published until today. The District had to complete a history. To accomplish this, I hired Dr. Anthony "Tony" Turhollow, chairman of the History Department at Loyola University. Tony became an important member in the public affairs office. He tried to work on the history, but was continually pulled off it to work on research for the district engineer and other executives. "A History of the Los Angeles District, U.S. Army Corps of Engineers, 1898-1965," was published in 1975, long after I had left.

When I was at the FAA public affairs office I managed to get into several college courses. There was a middle management course at the USC public administration school; a public relations course at UCLA and a short story writing class at Valley College in Van Nuys. I didn't manage to get in much freelance article writing, but I did a lot of features for the FAA magazines. At the Corps of Engineers I wrote two full-length articles for the *Military Engineer* magazine.

My job was to gain public understanding and support of the Corps' mission, its programs and projects. We were in the process of establishing a small craft harbor at Port San Luis on the central California Coast. We needed a short, about 15 minutes, slide show or motion picture to describe the project. The show would be used at public hearings, service organization meetings and other public presentations. Merle Gould was a talented photographer who was skilled in all of the visual arts. He had done a lot of movie work. He urged me to develop a movie treatment, then a shooting script. I had never done one before, but Merle and I came up with a 15-minute color moving, with dubbed sound, that did a good job of describing the project. That project started a friendship that would last until Merle died of a heart attack three years later. Merle learned about movie making by doing feature films on his own. He had enjoyed some modest success in producing some off-the-wall movies about para-normal healing, witch doctors, and spiritualists. He said there was a good market for that kind of stuff. and he tried to get me to go after some big bankroll to back his brainstorm. I declined. Merle couldn't understand why I wouldn't risk a few bucks on such an undertaking. He had been in business several times for himself; a printing shop, photography studio, producing movies. He said I hadn't lived until I took the risk of owning my own business. I told him I had better things to do with my life, like keeping a job, earning good money, and getting a safe retirement income. Despite our differences, we were fast, good friends.

I was well into my job at the Corps when we got disturbing news from Utah. Carma's father, Bill Morrison, was dead. We later found out that he had committed suicide by shooting himself in the chest. He went up into a remote canyon above Richfield where he took a rifle and ended his life. I got along great with Carma's father. He and his brothers had been horsemen all their lives. They had sold, traded, trained and raced horses in Utah and California for many years. Bill, and his brother, Leith, trained polo ponies for luminaries such as Zane Grey, Will Rogers, Clark Gable and other movie stars. Some of the cousins told me that Bill Morrison was known as "Windy Bill" and "Blanket Bill" among the horsemen of central and south Utah. Windy Bill, because he could talk a mile a minute in dealing for a horse, and Blanket Bill, because he would even trade his saddle blanket to get a good horse. Bill had visited us in Granada Hills shortly before he left to go back to Utah. We tried to get him to stay, but he thought we had too much responsibility already with four kids at home, along with my mother.

We went up to Richfield for the funeral, and all of Carma's brothers and sisters and we stayed at the same motel. The night we arrived I went to the liquor store and bought a half-gallon of vodka and brought it back to the rooms. Others then brought in bottles and we had a fine wake for Bill Morrison. Carma's brothers and the brothers-in-law became roaring drunk. That night when I went to bed, Carma was on her side facing away from me. She was shaking with quiet sobs. I reached over turned her to me an asked what was wrong?

"I can't stand it. When I needed you so much, you weren't there for me. You were drunk, and you got my family drunk," she said.

Her words were enough to keep me sober for another five months after I went back to the Sunday meetings.

When I left the FAA, Carma quit her job with Vickers, because I was working in downtown Los Angeles. She got a few part-time jobs, and managed to bring in some extra money. We were depending on her income to help pay for our house in Granada Hills. We were faced with a big payment coming due, and we didn't have the money in the bank to pay for it. We decided to look for another place to live that would be cheaper and closer to work. Maybe I could even take the bus into work if I had to when Carma needed the car. We really hated to leave the place, primarily because of the swimming pool. The kids had all learned to swim, and we couldn't keep Dandy out of the pool. Someone would go out to go swimming, dive in the pool, and Dandy would follow with a big jump and splash. Even my mother loved the pool. She would come out in an old-fashioned black swim suit, with skirts on it, and climb carefully into the pool. She would hold on to the edge, and carefully make her way all around the pool. After two or three circuits, she would get out and dry off, smiling all the way.

We found a three-bedroom apartment in North Hollywood that would fit our budget perfectly. It was in a five-unit apartment house, and we would get a reduction in rent if we managed the place. Carma took over that duty, and we made the move. We found a nice, economical one-bedroom apartment for my mother one block away from where we moved. The girls would stop off and see her every day on their way home from school, and I would go down to see her almost daily.

The kids quickly made friends in school, and Rosanne, Jeanine and Melanie became midget political activists. Rosanne, in high school, campaigned ferociously for Tom Bradley, the black candidate for Los Angeles mayor. Later she was an active demonstrator in the Latino worker boycott campaigns on lettuce and grapes. With their long hair, longer dresses, guitars and folk songs my three oldest daughters took on the aura of clean little hippies. If they wanted the dirty, scruffy look so cherished by the hip community, their grandmother and stepmother would not stand for it. That's one thing the two matriarchs agreed on. Dirt was evil. Whenever the girls left the house they were scrubbed clean and shiny. I feared for their safety sometimes, but they insisted on demonstrating their beliefs. They learned their lessons too well.

Rosanne wrote: "Political activism, and more importantly, political conscience were served with dinner. Do you remember the impassioned discussions at the dinner table that upset poor Mom so much? I was not only encouraged to develop my own opinions, I was forced to develop them. How I learned to love it. Politics, sociology, foreign affairs …all of it remains one of my greatest loves and I thank you for the special, irreplaceable gift of free thought."

The kids' continued attendance with the Mormon Church and its activities kept them busy. My mother insisted that we all go to mass with her on Christmas and Easter. We were walking examples of Pope John XXIII's ideal of ecumenical concert. Vatican II turned the whole Catholic community on its ear, and changed, forever, the mass that I knew. We went to a folk mass at Loyola University that Christmas. No organ, but three guitars and long-haired students singing in the congregation. The mass was in English, not Latin. The priest stood behind the altar, not in front of it with his back turned to the congregation. It was strange, but at the same time, familiar. I liked it, Mother hated it, the kids loved it, and Carma couldn't understand what the fuss was all about. The kids asked me why I was crying. I couldn't tell them. I didn't know. Every time I would attend mass, at my mother's insistence, the tears would flow.

After nine months of being sober, with a one-day lapse at Bill's funeral, I began drinking again. I don't think there was any reason for it. I know I had an argument with my mother about that time, but I was always fighting with her over some damn thing. I had gotten into the habit of drinking to blot out the contention out at home. It wasn't anything overt, but the tension between the kids and Carma was something that I could feel. Many years after I finally sobered up, and the kids were grown, they told me of some of the things they did to Carma.

Carma had always complained about having an allergic reaction to daisies and zinnias. I know she didn't like the smell of them.

"When Mom was gone, we would steal daisies and zinnias from neighbors yards," Melanie said. "We would sneak those bouquets into the parents' bedroom, vigorously shake the flowers under the bed, and all over the room. Once, we even left some under the bed. Mom never exhibited any reaction. We were mystified. We wondered if she was practicing some kind of black magic."

One night, as usual, I had a lot to drink before going to bed. I woke up about 1 a.m. and had to go to the bathroom. I staggered into the bathroom, tripped over the throw rug, and plunged head-first into the wash basin. The impact knocked me to the floor. I could feel blood dripping down my nose.

"Oh my God! Look at your head!" Carma cried.

I had a two-inch gash in the middle of my forehead just above my eyebrows. At about daybreak I went to the hospital emergency room and had the slash sewn up. Both eyes had blackened and I looked like a chubby raccoon. I wore dark glasses for two weeks. First I cut off part of my thumb, then I banged up my head in alcoholic hazes, but I still didn't think I had much of a problem.

As the skin around my eyes started to lose its purplish tint, and change into a greenish yellow, I backed away from a fight one night. I told myself I didn't want my eyes blackened again, that it would result in a terrible image for the Corps' public affairs office. We were awakened by a thunderous banging. Carma was out of the bed first, ran to the front door, squinted out into the hall through the little peep hole. She drew back in horror, and frantically motioned for me to look. I staggered over, looked out, and there was a wild-haired mad man trying to break in. He was raving, froth foaming around his mouth, and eyes rolling. I braced myself against the door, and told Carma to call the cops. We had an off-duty policeman living in the house next door, and he heard the racket. He ran over, struggled with the guy, pulled him out of the hall, threw him down in the driveway, and cuffed him. I went outside then. I was ashamed that I had not helped the cop, who was a friend, subdue the guy. We later learned that he was high on drugs. Carma wasn't too impressed with my valor that night.

"I wonder what we would have done if he had got in our house?" she said.

I received a shock at work soon after that incident. I was told that Perry Davis, the guy who I had replaced in the public affairs office, was exercising his return rights. He had been in Saudi Arabia on assignment for 18 months, and now wanted to come back to his old job. I was dumbfounded. I hadn't realized that my job was subject to that right that Perry had. After stewing about it, and complaining, I was given several choices. There were GS-12 PAO openings in Huntsville, Alabama; Rock Island, Illinois; Omaha, Nebraska and Walla Walla, Washington. Of them all, Walla Walla appealed to me the most. The Walla Walla District Engineer Col. Bob Geisen arranged for me to fly up there for an interview. When I got to Walla Walla, the personnel officer picked me up at the airport and took me to the motel. The interview was scheduled for the next day. Then I found out I was returning to hell-another place with state-owned liquor stores. After checking into the motel, I called a cab and the driver whisked me a few blocks to the liquor store. Fortified, I could face the interview the next day.

I was picked up by the public affairs officer who was retiring, Tex Witherspoon. He was a florid, tall ex-Texan, a WWII fighter pilot who looked like Teddy Roosevelt. Tex had flown with the Royal Canadian Air Force before we entered the war, then switched over to the U.S. Navy after Pearl Harbor. His communications background was in broadcasting, and he was a pioneer in that field. He was as loud as Teddy Roosevelt. I expected him to explode with "Bully!" what I thought was Roosevelt's favorite expression, but Tex's expletives were much more profane. We hit it off immediately. I really liked him. He drank more than I did. The interview with Col. Geisen went very well, and he told me I had the job if I could get the approval of the Division Public Affairs Officer John Ulrich, who was in Portland. Col. Geisen placed a call to John, I talked to him over the phone, and handed the headset back to Col. Geisen. The colonel then told me I had the job.

I flew back to Los Angeles, drove back out to North Hollywood, and broke the news to the family. We would be moving to Walla Walla.

Chapter 17

Walla Walla

No one wanted to move. I thought they all hated California and would be glad to move to a place like Washington. So it was with a lot of anger, tears and bitterness that we packed our things for shipment to Washington. Mom decided that she didn't want to move, and would stay on in her little apartment for awhile. She would soon move out to Tony's place in Simi Valley, and stay with him, Edna and the kids for some time.

After a nice farewell party arranged by Eleanor at a Mexican restaurant on Olvera Street, we started out on our trip north. We drove up the coast much of the way, and all were impressed with the scenery, except Rosanne. She was weeping in the backseat, crying because she was leaving her boyfriend Glenn Harvey. She had met Glenn at the Mormon Church youth group in San Fernando. After two days on the road we stopped in Wilsonville, about 18 miles south of Portland to spend the night. The next day I stopped by the Corps's North Pacific Division Office to meet

213

John Ulrich; then we started up the Columbia Gorge to eastern Oregon and Washington.

The scenery through the gorge was spectacular. Rosanne even stopped crying long enough to look. When we got to The Dalles, all of the faces in the car except mine became longer and longer. It was a hot August day, and as the cliffs next to the river became more dry and forbidding so did the temper of my family.

"Where are you taking us?" Rosanne cried. "This is horrible!"

I told her to shut up, and kept driving. We left the Columbia River and the dry river canyons at Walulla Junction, and headed up the almost dry Walla Walla River to our new home, only 30 miles to go. When Carma and the girls saw the desert-like brown hills we were going through, a heavy silence settled over the five of them. The tension eased when we hit the Walla Walla Valley, and green fields stretched before us. We settled into the Capri Motel for a week before we found a house that was suitable. We moved into a home at 814 South Howard Street where we would stay for almost eight years.

Another family was moving out as we moved in, Jack and Barbara Metzger and their children. They were newcomers also, but had found a house more suitable for them. Jack was a psychology professor at Whitman College. Our children, being strangers in town, hit it off immediately. My kids and Carma hated Walla Walla at first.The children had been involved in many school activities in North Hollywood, and they missed their friends and the challenging activities they were involved in when we were in California. Jeanine said that Walla Walla was like dying and going to hell.

We got to Walla Walla at the end of August, just before school started. Rosanne went to Walla Walla High School, or Wa Hi as it was called, Jeanine and Melanie into junior high school, and Lisa to grade school just up the street. Rosanne had even quit crying long enough to sign up for the school paper. She became its editor, the first junior who was editor of the paper. The girls quickly became involved in Mormon Church activities.

Tex Witherspoon was making plans for retirement. He planned to stay until the first of the year. He would have four months to work with me on breaking into the new job. The Walla Walla District was established just after World War II to design and construct big dams on the Columbia and Snake rivers. Their first big project was McNary Dam on the Columbia, about 55 miles by road west of Walla Walla. That was followed by John Day Dam, completed in 1968, between McNary and The Dalles dams. The Walla Walla District then did the four lower Snake River dams: Ice Harbor, Lower Monumental, Little Goose and Lower Granite. Those were all multi-purpose run-of-the-river dams that generated electricity, had navigation locks for shipping, and parks for recreation. Only a couple of the dams had minor flood control storage capacity. The district was also building a huge storage dam on the North Fork of the Clearwater River near Orofino in north Idaho. Dworshak Dam was the largest concrete straight axis, gravity dam in North America. A concrete gravity dam is just a huge block of concrete that dams the flow of water, as opposed to the thin arch type dam that gets its strength from its shape as much as the concrete mass.

Tex retired, and died of a heart attack within six months. He and his wife had moved to Brookings, Oregon, where Tex entered local politics. I don't know whether it was the hard living, booze or politics that killed him, but I resolved then that I would never retire. Retirement killed people.

Tex had introduced me to Jim Schick, the editor of the daily *Walla Walla Union Bulletin*. Jim and Tex had made it a habit of having coffee every Saturday morning at the Red Apple Café. After Tex left, Jim and I became very close friends. He had been a reporter, and editor, at the Union Bulletin for almost 30 years. All of the news releases that I wrote about our dams, studies and projects got good coverage in the news media in eastern Oregon, Washington and north Idaho, particularly in the Walla Walla paper. The Corps of Engineers had about 600 people working at the district office and another 600 in the field that covered eastern Washington and Idaho, most of Idaho except for the exteme northern part, and tiny slices of north Nevada and western Wyoming. Our district encompassed the entire Snake River basin, and a short stretch of the Columbia River from John Day Dam upstream to the confluence of the Columbia and Snake rivers.

Col. Geisen was only with us for a short time, until he retired and moved to Whidby Island in Puget Sound. He was replaced by Col. Richard M. Connell, a West Pointer, whose management style was much different. Connell was a hard-charging engineer. He was ambitious, and didn't want anything interfering with the progress of Corps projects. He ran headlong into environmental groups, agricultural interests and property owners who had land next to rivers and streams. The Vietnam conflict was in the news constantly. The colonel, and his deputy, a lieutenant colonel, were in uniform all the time. They were the only two military persons in our district. The uniforms drew a lot of animosity, particularly among younger people opposed to our involvement in Vietnam.

Walla Walla High School had a big ROTC program, and it was strongly supported by the school district's families. Every year they had a big review, and usually it was the colonel from the Corps who inspected the troops. Rosanne warned me that there might be a demonstration that year, and I so informed the colonel. We arrived at the athletic field where the reviewing stand had been set up. The colonel and I walked over to the stand and there was a large group of students with placards parading around the field. The ROTC troops were in place. The picket line of demonstrators walked in file around the field. Rosanne was in the lead with a big "Get Out of Vietnam Now!" sign. She walked up to the stand, I climbed down, took her by the hand, pulled her up and introduced her to my boss. The colonel smiled warmly, they shook hands, Rosanne climbed down, and resumed her marching. On the way back to the office Col. Connell told me he had a son in college who was also opposed to the Vietnam war.

Rosanne said that I had done a courageous thing, and she would never forget it. I thought it was a dumb reaction. I just didn't know what else to do. I wasn't about to chase her off. The whole damn outfit including the ROTC students probably would have lynched me. I worried a lot about the kids, and I feared for their future. A lot of it was unreasonable fears fueled by my drinking. I can remember lying in bed at night, silently crying into my pillow, wondering what would become of my four girls if anything happened to me. It didn't occur to me then that if I would sober up, maybe my life would get better. That would come a little later.

About a year after we got to Walla Walla, Carma noticed an advertisement in the paper announcing cast try-outs at the Walla Walla Little Theater. Carma and the girls talked me into taking them up to the theater that same night. I didn't want to go, because it would interfere with my drinking, and I would have to stay sober enough to drive. Bea Mortenson, the drama instructor at Walla Walla Community College, was the director of "Three Men On a Horse." We watched the try-outs and Jeanine and Melanie were fascinated. Carma and the girls urged me to read for a role, and I reluctantly complied. I read for one of the minor racetrack tout roles. I was shocked, and scared, when Bea announced that she gave me the lead role of Erwin Trowbridge, the harassed greeting card poet. Erwin's hobby was handicapping horse races, an avocation that brought him fame, fortune and trouble.

One of the funniest parts of the play was a drunk scene. Three tough gangsters found out about Erwin's horse doping talent, and they wanted to use him. The best way to get information was to get him drunk. And they did. Bea Mortensen coached me on acting the part of a drunk. I knew that I had plenty of experience, but I thought, "Let her have her say." Bea said that when most people act drunk the over-exaggerate with slurred speech, staggering walk and hand actions. She said that the secret in doing a credible drunk scene was to try and act like "you are *not* drunk." Try to keep people from finding out that you have drunk too much. That wasn't any problem with me. I was already doing that. Bea was very pleased with my interpretation of Irwin deep in his cups.

I hadn't been on stage since high school, and I was terrified. How was I going to learn the lines? Perform? Stay sober? The kids helped me with the lines, and I managed to memorize my part. Bea was an excellent drama coach. She had her master's degree from Occidental University, and was a product of the Pasadena Playhouse. I developed a routine to stay relatively sober throughout the production. I would buy a half-pint of vodka and stash it in the car. I wouldn't drink at all during the day, so my head was clear for the daily rehearsals-except for Sundays when we did not rehearse-that ran about six weeks. After the last line of rehearsal, I would dash out to the car, past the smokers, and take a quick belt. The harsh burn of raw vodka flowing into my gullet was quickly replaced by that warm glow in my belly spread out to my nose, toes and fingertips. I was then ready to face Bea and the nightly critique. She was in a fury when she found a half-full beer bottle backstage during one rehearsal.

"Booze has no place in the theater. If you are going to drink, do it after rehearsals and performances-not before, and certainly not during the play. Booze gives you a sense of well-being, that you are doing a great job of acting, running lights or props," she shouted, "But you are not. You have to be fully in control to do your job on stage. No booze!"

I had beat her to it. I knew that everything she said was true, but I still didn't think I had a drinking problem. I only drank after performances. We opened to a sold- out house, and that first performance was a blur. We got a good review in the *Union Bulletin*. Every performance went well, except for the second when Gene Alexander, who played the part of Patsy, the lead gambler, played a thoughtless prank. For the drunk scene we used liquor bottles filled with tea, for that rich whiskey look. Before the scene started Gene filled my glass with straight bourbon. The curtain opened as we were seated at the table, the three gamblers and I. I spoke my lines, grabbed my glass, lifted it to my lips, and gulped. I strangled slightly, my eyes bugged out, I gagged, and coughed. The audience howled. Every line I had learned fled from my brain. Gene and the others looked at me expectantly, mentally urging me to come out with my line. Finally it came back, and we finished the scene and the act. Backstage I learned that Gene was the prankster, and I grabbed him by his shirtfront.

"Don't you ever pull a stunt like that again, you stupid jerk," I shouted. "I forgot everything when I tasted that booze!"

Jeanine and Melanie got their first taste of theater during that play. Jeanine worked on lights, and Melanie did props. They loved it. Both would go on to great things in local theater. Carma attended every rehearsal, and helped with costumes. Rosanne was busy with her school newspaper job, and Lisa was too young then to get involved. Later, she, too, would do many things with Little Theater and the Walla Walla Community College Players.

After that first play we jumped into involvement with the community theater. That led to more work with Bea Mortensen and the Walla Walla Community College Players. I was named to the board of directors of the Little Theater, and Melanie and Jeanine worked intensively in the youth summer theater programs taught by Bea Mortensen and Joanne Rassmussen. Carma and I were named producers of "Brigadoon" in the 1970-71 season. We struggled through the two months of preparation, and I continued in the same drinking pattern. I was much more lax for "Brigadoon" because I didn't have to appear on stage. The musical was a moderate success and made money for the Little Theater.

Surprisingly, there was a lot to do in Walla Walla. We became active in the town of 30,000 people, and after a year it didn't seem nearly as provincial as it did when we arrived. Rosanne was really involved as editor of the school paper, and the rest of us increasingly active in community theater. At work I continued Tex's Snake River Editors Conference. That was an annual meeting, briefing and tour of selected projects for the local and regional news editors. It proved to be a very successful effort, and provided us with a lot of news coverage on Corps programs and projects. The Walla Walla District did not have an employee newsletter or newspaper. One of the first things I did was to start "Intercom", a newsletter that came out every two weeks, on payday. It was a success from the start. I also began a weekly phone-in information service. Every Monday, immediately after the staff meeting, I would record information, in a news format, on our projects, installations, personnel changes, retirements, and anything of interest to our workers in the field. The field people could call in and get the latest information directly from the District office. The service was called "Telecom," and continued for several years after I left the district.

The Corps of Engineers saw some big changes in the late 1960s and early 1970s. Almost every federal agency would be affected by new laws that were coming from congress and the president. It was the time of the great environmental, social and cultural revolution, and the rule book was being thrown out. One of the strangest things would be to see the Corps thrust into the role of protector of the environment. Some of the old hands had a lot of trouble with that new image. We also became very involved in public participation in our planning process. That meant we had to be trained. In 1970 I attended, along with other folks from the District, a course on public participation at Georgia Tech in Atlanta. I had to fly to Chicago, then to Atlanta. There was some glitch in the reservations, and I was given a seat in first class on a jumbo jet. I was in hog heaven. Free food and booze all the way to Atlanta. I was determined that I was not going to drink, because for the past two weeks I had been sober. I had been going to meetings of recovering alcoholics, and I thought I wanted to stay sober. I could tell that it was beginning to affect me some. I went to the meetings in Kennewick, Washington, about 45 miles from home. I didn't want anyone seeing me go to a meeting with a bunch of drunks trying to sober up. I stayed sober until we were over Wyoming. We went to an Atlanta hotel. The first thing I did was buy a fifth of booze, put it on the dresser my room, and watch the level of liquid miraculously go down. I can't remember drinking it.

Daughter Rosanne had continued her relationship with Glenn Harvey by correspondence, and begged to visit him and his family. Carma and I relented and she went for a month's visit. In early 1971, after a great record in school, she announced that she and Glenn were going to be married, and she was quitting school and moving to California. We had the wedding in Walla Walla at the Mormon Church. I don't remember much of it, but I was going through something that felt like that terrible grief of losing June all over again. Rosanne and I had always been so very close, in the way that we thought, our interests, and talents. I didn't know it then, but she was already walking the same alcoholism trail that I did when I was her age. I felt that I had lost her when she and Glenn left for California.

I wanted to quit drinking, but everything I tried didn't work. When my drinking began to affect my writing, I made a promise to give up booze, some day. I had to do a !,500-word article on salmon runs. I wrote the article on one Saturday afternoon and evening. I fortified myself with a six-pack of Becker's beer and a pint of vodka. I fantasized that all great writers drank: Hemingway, Steinbeck, F. Scott Fitzgerald …and Edgar Allen Poe was even a dope addict. We needed that extra something to fuel our creative engines. I talked myself into believing that it was O.K. to drink if it would make me a better writer, be better at my job, be paid for it, put food on the table for the family. I breezed through that article, put it in my desk drawer, and staggered off to do something else. I don't remember going to bed. I do remember Carma shouting, shaking me as I stood in the corner of our bedroom. I thought I was in the bathroom, but I had been peeing on the wall.

Hung over, ashamed, full of remorse, with a queasy Sunday morning stomach, I went to my desk. I took out the piece I had written the night before. Good lead, nice transition into the body of the story, then it began to deteriorate. I could see where I had started on the beer, drank more vodka, and finished off all the bottles. When I got to the last page I couldn't read my own writing…and I had been using my trusty Smith Corona electric typewriter.

I was determined to stop drinking. I quit every day, up until about 2 p.m. when I miraculously got better. My daily routine called for me to drive home for lunch. It was only 10 minutes from the Corps's offices at the airport to home. After lunch I would stop at the liquor store for my pint bottle of vodka. About 2:30 in the afternoon I had my tea break. I would go out to the car, drive a short distance out into the wheat or pea fields, and have my first snort of the day. I would lie down on the seat of the car so I couldn't be seen drinking. In the hot spring, summer and autumns of Walla Walla, the temperature in the parked car could climb into the 100s. Drinking hot vodka, lying on my back in the front seat of the car, is not a dignified position. One chokes a lot. The hot vodka courses down the throat, can't run uphill, gags one, and vodka explodes out of the nose and mouth. Despite the choking I would get enough of the white lightning down so I could finish my workday.

At home I would climb into my recliner in the front room, doze for an hour, then adjourn to the basement where I finished off my pint of vodka, then have dinner. Most of the time I couldn't remember what happened from the time I got out of my recliner to drink until I woke up the next morning. It was a blackout almost every night. I was drinking a pint or more of vodka every day, and a fifth a day on weekends. One Tuesday night I followed my same pattern, and suddenly woke up about 9 p.m. Clad only in my shorts I dashed out into the living room and shouted at Carma.

"Why didn't you wake me up! I had a Little Theater board meeting at 7 p.m.!"

"I called them, said you were sick. I tried to wake you, but you wouldn't get up," she said.

I felt so small.

"I have to do something about my drinking. I will call someone tomorrow," I promised.

"Yes, I think you should."

The next day I called in at work and took a day of annual leave. I called the Alcoholism Information and Referral Service in the Denny Building. My call was answered by two ladies, Blanche Stafford and Rosemary Smith. They asked me to come down and talk to them. I did. We talked about an hour, and I told them my story. Blanche and Rosemary agreed that I should contact a Jim Dennis, who was a chaplain at the Veterans Administration Hospital. He would probably be able to help me more than anyone else in the community. Blanche and Rosemary made an appointment for me to see Jim. I don't know what I expected. He had an Irish name so I thought he might have been a Catholic priest. Jim was a Baptist minister. It wasn't long before I told him he ought to change his name or his religion. We got along famously-until he said that I should go away for alcoholism treatment. Jim insisted that I go to a doctor who had been treating alcoholics, who proscribed thorazine. He told me to be very careful, because I could go into seizures, the delirium tremens, or DTs. The thorazine made me a little spacey, so I quit taking them.

I told Jim that I couldn't go away to treatment for six weeks because I had the dedication of the Spring Creek Fish Hatchery to run. I promised him that I would go up to Sundown M Ranch on the Yakima Indian Reservation at White Swan, Washington, the day after the dedication. I had my last drink on May 10, 1971, three days before my first meeting with Jim Dennis.

On June 20, 1971, I drove from Walla Walla to White Swan. The hop fields were green, the sky blue, and fresh breezes blew down from Mount Baker to the Yakima Valley. I felt great, but I was very anxious because of the unknown, of what I would be facing in the next 21 days. The Sundown M Ranch treatment facility was located in buildings owned by the United Christian Missionary Society on the Yakima Indian Nation. It had been in operation for two years and had a good record. Its treatment philosophy was based on that of Hazelden, a recovery house in Minnesota that had a great international reputation of treating problem alcoholics. I drove up to the ranch, they told me where to park my car, and I checked in. They took away my car keys and my prescriptions.

"You won't be needing any thorazine here!"

Immediately, I met Merrill Scott, the director. He had been named to the post about six months before. He was a recovering alcoholic, and a former executive with a big department store chain. I learned that the treatment I would be getting would be intensive individual and group counseling, and meetings of alcoholics like me who were trying to sober up and stay sober. We would embark on a spiritual quest, tally up our faults, admit them, get rid of personal failings, and help other alcoholics. In other words, I was to change my behavior completely. Although I felt good, I had some doubts about being able to stay sober for any length of time. About six weeks of not drinking had made me into a new person. My energy level zoomed, and there were plenty of things I wanted to do. Before I left Walla Walla, we had auditions for "Taming of the Shrew." I had the part of Gremio, and I was determined I would learn all of my lines while I was at Sundown M. I wanted to do a good job, because my daughter Jeanine was playing the lead of Kate. Melanie also had a part in the play that was being produced by Bea and Joanne's Walla Walla Community College Players. I settled in and waited for my first counseling session.

On June 22, 1971, I was called in to see my counselor, Sister Pat Hauser. She was a nun with the Sisters of Providence, working in civilian clothes. I was a little uneasy because this was the first Catholic sister I had ever seen without a habit. She quickly set me at ease. Behind her on the wall was the Prayer of St. Francis of Asisi:

> Lord, make me an instrument of
> > Your peace
> Where there is hatred, let me sow
> > love.
> Where there is injury, pardon.
> Where there is doubt, faith.
> Where there is despair, hope.
> Where there is darkness, light,
> > and where there is sadness, joy.
> Divine Master, grant that I may
> > not so much seek to be consoled,
> > as to console.

To be understood, as to understand;
To be loved, as to love;
For it is in giving that we
    receive,
It is in pardoning that we are
    pardoned
And it is in dying that we are
    born to eternal life.

"I grew up with that prayer," I said, as I nodded towards the poster on the wall.

"It's a beautiful prayer," Sister Pat said, "and my favorite. Now tell me something about yourself, Frank."

Reading the prayer made a lump stick in my throat. I coughed, and began telling her about my job, writing, my family and June's death.

"Today, June 22, is her birthday, she would have been 48." I choked on the words.

I began to cry, then sob. That went on, I thought, for hours. Finally the tears were gone and I was spent. Pat walked over to me put her hand on my shoulder, and said that I had a lot of grief that I still had to deal with. Maybe I could work on that while I was at Sundown M. After the session with Pat I went out on the front lawn and sat in a chair looking out over the entrance to the ranch. I was completely drained, and felt as if I had a big hole in my gut. I closed my eyes, let the sun soak into me. A faint warm glow spread at the bottom of my stomach. It was almost as if I had a shot of vodka, and the slow warming filled the rest of my body. I don't know what it was, but at that moment a sudden flash of clarity struck me. That God that I had been fighting and cursing for 11 long years did exist. The fact that I was angry with him acknowledged his existence.

"O.K., You are there," I said under my breath.

For the first time in my life I really believed there was something there-a higher power, or God. To this day I can't define what I believe in. I can't put a face on my God, only feel the presence of a force greater than myself.

Years later, when I reconciled with my faith and began attending mass, a portion of the liturgy was very meaningful to me. During the eucharistic prayer the priest will call:

"Let us proclaim the mystery of faith."

That's what it is to me, a divine mystery, something that I cannot understand, but something that I can accept-my belief in a divine power.

My three weeks at Sundown M Ranch was unlike any experience I had been through before. In group they would tear you down, make you admit your faults and shortcomings, then they would put you back together again. After one session, one on one, with John McClure, a counselor, I told him of all the wrongs that I could remember, that I inflicted on my loved ones, including my kids, family, friends, neighbors, employers, and acquaintances. John McClure was a Protestant minister who had a lot of experience in hearing those client disclosures. To me it was a lot like going to confession when I was a kid. A great weight seemed to have been lifted from my shoulders. I intuitively knew then that I would try very hard to right the wrongs I had inflicted on those close to me. Those misdeeds were nothing overt, but if I remember my catechism properly, they were sins of omission, not commission. I had withdrawn into alcoholism to block out any pain and conflict in my family. I just hadn't been there for my kids and Carma when they really needed me. After my session with John, I felt as if I were walking four feet above the ground. I had never felt so good. Again, I went out to the lawn chair on the lawn, again, looked out over the ranch entrance, and that warm, swelling feeling inside of me grew. I was scared, because I knew it wasn't indigestion. That floating feeling has stayed with me over the years, only now I bounce along one or two feet above the ground.

Some eight years after I sobered up, we visited grandchildren in Northern California. We took Mike's daughter, Ambi, just a tiny tot, and Tory, his stepson, about 10, to see Star Wars. It had just been released. In the film, when Obe Wan Kenobe said:

"May the Force be with you."

I jumped up out of my seat and yelled, "Yeah! Yeah!"

"Sit down, Grandpa!" Tory hissed, pulling on my hand.

That one line summed up my belief. It is best described as a force that makes me want to live in accordance with my values. Now came the hard part, letting him, that Force, run my life from now on. After all, he had screwed up pretty bad until I sobered up for good.

Working with others was a big part of the therapy at Sundown M Ranch, and each of us had a job to do. The day after I got to the ranch Merrill insisted that I befriend, and work with, a man who was a little older than I. His name was Jimmy. He was a naturalized Scot, with a thick accent, a chemical engineer who had been a successful manufacturer's representative, and a flaming alcoholic. Jimmy had been sober for almost eight years, was active in an alcoholic treatment movement, and a well-known speaker on the subject. He got drunk, and lost everything. He was frantic, and I spent most of the day, and night, trying to talk him down from the self-destructive mode he was in. He said that all he wanted to do was go back to Seattle and walk off the back of the Bremerton ferry. Jimmy calmed, and so did I. I didn't realize it then, but in working with Jimmy I was not concentrating on my own pain and problems. I learned that alcoholics like me have big egos, and we have to get them down to a manageable size if we want to stay sober. A good way to do that is becoming involved with other alcoholics, and doing what you can to help them. I was told that you can't do it for them, that all alcoholics have to find their own way, but you can share your experience, strength and hope. Wise alcoholics who have managed to stay sober for a long time told me not to give people advice, or tell them what do, but tell them my story and how I got sober, and stay sober.

My assignment at the ranch was a cushy one. Merrill found out that I was a writer, and he had me do the copy for a new brochure for the ranch, and other writing chores. I also did a few office duties, while my fellow inmates mopped floors, washed the dishes, and raked the ranch yard. I lucked out again.

Jim Dennis wrote to me while I was in treatment, and said that I had been chosen as a board member for a new halfway house for alcoholics that he was trying to set up in Walla Walla. He also strongly recommended that I sign up, and become active with the Walla Walla Council on Alcoholism. I thought he was kidding. What in hell did I know about any of that stuff? It was sure to be like the blind leading the blind.

The three weeks passed quickly and I went in for a final meeting with Sister Pat, and to make my farewells with Merrill and the staff.

"Frank, I want you to promise that you will go to at least one meeting a week when you get home," Pat said.

I promised, and headed back down the ranch lane to the highway and back to Walla Walla. Everything at home was the same, yet different. I was fully awake every hour of the day, and I knew what was going on. My first week home was drawing to a close and I hadn't been to a meeting yet. I remembered my promise to Sister Pat. You don't lie to nuns. The fellowship that I was soon to become a member of had only one meeting a week in Walla Walla. It was in the downtown state welfare office. I was damned if I was going to go to a meeting in a welfare office. I would have to parade before all of the inquisitive eyes downtown, and everybody in Walla Walla would know I was an alcoholic. I couldn't hide my alcoholism very well when I was drinking, but now that I was sober it seemed to mean a lot. O.K., no meeting at the welfare office, but where could I go? I discovered that there was a meeting in the minimum security section of the Walla Walla State Penitentiary on Saturday afternoons.

I decided to go to the pen for my first meeting away from Sundown M because I didn't want anyone knowing I was going to a meeting of recovering boozers. I walked into the reception area. A guard took me to the minimum security foyer and had me sign in. He then directed me to a door leading to the room where the meeting would be held. I walked in and was greeted by shouts. Two guys I worked with at the Corps of Engineers greeted me with hugs, Russ S. and Ed D.

"Boy, are we glad to see you. We didn't think you would ever get here," Ed said.

The meeting was a lot like those that I had gone to at Sundown M, but the inmates at that first meeting were really inmates. When they told their stories it soon became apparent that booze and getting drunk were their primary problems. All of them were in there for crimes committed while they were drunk; murder, rape, assault, theft. Many said that they had been sober for years, in prison. It was harder staying sober in the joint than it was on the outside. Booze, illicit home brew, or Pruno, along with every known street drug was readily available in prison, if you had the money. I felt that if those guys could stay sober, I could, too. After my first meeting in the prison, it wasn't difficult to show up for the Tuesday night meeting at the state welfare office. The folks there made me feel welcome. I really felt as if I was with my family.

I went back to work at the Corps as if nothing had happened, but Goldie was impressed with my energy level. I was able to get more work done than ever before. No one had noticed that I had gone away for alcoholism treatment. I had taken regular vacation time for my stay at Sundown M instead of sick leave. I told Goldie and a few confidants, but my alcoholism treatment was not general knowledge. Then the missionary zeal struck me. I wanted to sober up drunks. I even went down to the Pastime Café, sat at the bar, and tried to get drunks out of there to meetings, and to our new halfway house, Newhouse. That didn't work too well, I calmed down, and was able to take a more rational approach in ridding the world of alcoholism.

Carma said that the first 12 months that I was sober was the worst year of her life. I was off trying to help drunks at all hours of the night, I brought very strange people into our living room for meetings, and I began watching the checkbook. For years, I had turned over the family finances to Carma, as I had with June. Carma calmly accepted the responsibility of paying the monthly bills, and balancing the checkbook. Now that I was sober I began noticing more things, and I criticized how she spent some of our money. That went over big. We ironed that out and noticed that our finances were improving dramatically. We had more money that ever before. Booze was expensive, and that was one expense I didn't have to face anymore.

"The Taming of the Shrew" was a success, and I was very proud of Jeanine. She did a masterful job of interpreting the stormy Kate. Carma and I had also been busy with other things in the theater. We were the producers for "Camelot." It was much different with "Camelot" than "Brigadoon." I was sober, much more productive, and it was a much smoother production. I even filled in one performance for one of knights who had been sick. Without rehearsal, I went on, said the lines, and got through it successfully-something I never would have been able to do while drinking. I was so proud of the work that Melanie and Jeanine were doing in the theater. Jeanine had a great role in "Arms in the Man" and Melanie would go on to do great lead performances in "Guys and Dolls" and "Gypsy."

In the seven years we were in community theater, we did everything. Produce, act, stage manage, build sets, and in our last effort Carma and I directed a play. I really enjoyed acting, and in addition to "Taming of the Shrew", I was the Prince of Morocco in the "Merchant of Venice," bit parts in six plays, was the Rev. Dr. Chausuble in "The Importance of Being Ernest," and Sam Nash in Plaza Suite's "The Visitor from Mamaroneck." The most intense role I played was Rev. Alfred Davidson, in "Rain," the story of Sadie Thompson.

"Rain" was the most demanding, and satisfying, play that I was in. The title role of Sadie was played by number two daughter Jeanine, and Melanie, my number three daughter, played my wife. I had to play the part of a Bible-thumping, narrow-minded missionary fallen to fleshly delights that he had been criticizing in others. He was a bigot. Jeanine was brilliant in her interpretation of Somerset Maughm's Sadie Thompson, and we got great reviews.

Some of those meetings in our living room were with the strange men-whom Carma feared-who were residents of our new halfway house for men alcoholics. Jim Dennis, true to his promise, really got me involved in fighting alcoholism. Jim had commitments from me, Kelly Wylie, a businessman and Dean Culbertson, a wheat farmer from Prescott, Washington. Others who helped were Bill Tugman and Art Hawman, lawyers and former county prosecutors who saw alcoholism as a major societal illness. Jim's scheme was to buy a big older house-of which there were plenty in Walla Walla-and convert it into an alcoholism treatment facility. We began organizing and our operation started shortly after I came home from Sundown M Ranch. Jim, Kelly, Dean and I took out a $4,000 loan that we all co-signed to make a down payment on a house that cost $16,000. We got a fine old house on Main Street next to Whitman College. It had about six bedrooms, with two baths, and that meant that we could house at least a dozen clients and a house manager. Our first clients were those who had gone through a brief detoxification and treatment program at the Walla Walla Veterans Administration Hospital. We stayed solvent through grants, and initially by making the clients pay for board and room out of their pension checks. The checks would come in the mail around the first of the month, and either the house manager or I would be there to meet the mailman. We would hand out the checks, march the guys down to the bank to cash them, haul them back to the house and demand their rent. We were very forceful. I like to think of it as helping them learn responsibility. Their cries and moans as we took their money were great. That was money that could have paid for a good drunk. Amazingly, most of the guys we had in the house stayed sober. A few ran off, and some ended up in the hospital with serious health problems that came with years of drinking. Then we began to get referrals from sources other than the VA.

After six months of operation we designed a treatment system that each client was obligated to follow:

- Each was assigned a counselor with whom he met once a week.

- He had to attend at least one Alcoholic Anonymous meeting a week.
- AA members held a Tuesday night meeting at Newhouse. Clients were urged to attend, but they could go to any meeting in town that they wished.
- If a client was prescribed Antabuse, the counselor had to monitor his taking the daily dose, to make sure he was taking it.
- All prescriptions and medicines were held by the house manager to dispense.
- Residents had to attend the monthly house meeting.
- Residents signed a treatment contract when they entered Newhouse. This outlined and described treatment, routine and house rules.
- Work and recreation was scheduled as an integral part of the recovery program. Free time was built into the program.
- Lecturers from local colleges and community services provided presentations on alcohol and chemical substance abuse.
- Clients were referred to other human service agencies for programs to augment the Newhouse program, programs such as occupational training, public assistance, or social security benefits.

After our first six months we found we could do the same things that larger treatment facilities could do in places like Spokane, Seattle and Portland. We did not have the money for a large, full-time staff. We relied on volunteers; medical people and counselors from the Veterans Administration, community alcoholism services personnel, AA members, and volunteer nurses and doctors. It took a lot of adjusting and tweaking of schedules to accommodate the willing volunteers, but it was worth it.

I started out as one of the founders of Newhouse, then I became vice president, then president. It was one of the most satisfying things I had done in my life, and I learned a lot. But it wasn't all hearts and flowers. Our house managers kept getting drunk and running off. Barney was a tall, lanky, easygoing fellow who was popular with the guys in the house. Barney was married, and his wife was still drinking. They had an apartment close to Newhouse, and Barney would stay overnight at their place. One day Barney didn't show up. He had run off, left his wife, and no one knew where he was. He was followed by Bud Miller. Bud was a good manager for about a year, then he disappeared. By that time I was president, so a lot of my time was spent at the house doing the things the manager was required to do. Eventually we got through those trying times, and management became more stable.

I learned how to work my way through the maze of paper-the applications, justifications, the bureaucracy, to obtain money to operate. We managed to get the house licensed as a residential care facility, and that meant we could apply for additional funds through the state. My association with Newhouse led into active work with the council on alcoholism, and then the Walla Walla County Alcoholism Administrative Board, then the county's Human Services Administrative Board. The early 70s was a time of great decentralization of federal services, and substance abuse and mental health programs were being delegated to the states. The Walla Walla County Commission decided to place all of the mental health, drug abuse and alcoholism treatment programs under one board, and the Human Services Administrative Board was formed. We did the budgeting, evaluation and planning and made recommendations to the county commission. The first year, Ken Knopf, the Whitman College chancellor and former president of the mental health board, served as chairman, and I was the vice chairman. The second year, I became the chairman.

Juggling work and all of the community activities, theater and freelance writing wasn't too hard, and I had never felt better. The Corps had finished the huge Dworshak Dam project on the North Fork of the Clearwater River in northern Idaho, and was busy finishing up Lower Granite Lock and Dam on the lower Snake River. Lower Granite was the fourth and last of four Snake River dams from the Tri Cities area in Washington to Lewiston, Idaho. John Ulrich, who was the public affairs officer in the North Pacific Division at Portland, became a good friend. He was a former newsman and taught journalism at Washington State

University. John told me that if there was ever a question as to putting out bad information on your organization, do it as soon as possible, in your words. At his insistence I became a member of the Public Relations Society of America. In 1973 I passed that organization's demanding, two-day examination for accreditation.

John was a great exponent of truth in dealing with the news media and the public. He maintained that you could only cover up bad news so long, and eventually it would get out. You had to tell the story first, in truthful, unvarnished terms. I can remember two incidents in northern Idaho where I applied John's wisdom.

We had a serious fish kill at the steelhead hatchery at Dworshak Dam. Thousands of small fish had died. I learned of it at the Monday morning staff meeting, and I told Col. Connell that we should get a news release out immediately on the fish kill. The engineers went crazy. They argued that we would be cutting our throats by putting out the information that perhaps the public wouldn't even find out about. I fought back with the argument that it was impossible to keep the incident quiet, that we should act first, and tell the story in our own words. That way we would be acting on the information, and not reacting to pressures for information. The colonel agreed with me, and my first call was to Sylvia Harrell, a great reporter with the *Lewiston Morning Tribune*. I told her what had happened and arranged for her to interview Col. Connell. Then I did a general release, and phoned it to the media, including the wire services. There were big stories on the fish kill for one day, a few follow-up stories within a week, and that was all there was to it.

I applied the same procedure in a mishap on the Lewiston levee project. We were building a levee around Lewiston. It was a great project that would provide the city with a landscaped park on top of the levee, with picnic spots, jogging and bicycle paths. The contractor was excavating and dug into the skeleton of a fossilized mastodon. Ed Groff, our resident engineer, ordered the contractor to stop work in the area. The word wasn't passed to the bulldozer operator who continued working, dug up and broke a huge tusk. The contractor caught hell, and there was the potential of bad publicity. Again, I went to the colonel and told him we should lay it all out, just as it happened, and that would minimize our exposure. I called Sylvia, she interviewed Ed and the contractor, and the story came out. There was more in the following stories about discovering and preserving a mastodon than about the contractor's goof.

The four Lower Snake River projects were dedicated in a huge ceremony and we were knee deep in dignitaries. It was my job to set up a press conference for Idaho's Senator Frank Church in the Lewis and Clark Hotel in Lewiston. The conference was in a long, narrow, windowless room, the only one available. Church made an announcement that Sam Giancanna, the mobster who was a government informant, had been shot and killed. The press began firing questions at him, the TV lights were all turned up bright, and the cameras were whirring. Then the lights went out. Dead silence. Then the reporters began asking questions-and I guess taking notes in the dark-as if nothing had happened.

"This is the first press conference I have held in the dark," Church said.

The overloaded hotel circuits, probably due to the TV lights, had blown fuses, and the hotel staff scurried about trying to restore power.

A short time after I sobered up, I was sent on an interesting assignment. Hurricane Agnes had struck a devastating blow to the East Coast, and I was assigned to do public affairs work on the recovery effort in Maryland. I was in Annapolis and Washington, D.C., for two weeks. That was the first such assignment of many where I would work on natural disasters including floods in the Northwest and later the Teton Dam disaster.

The Teton Dam, a U.S. Bureau of Reclamation project in eastern Idaho, broke and flooded a small town downstream. Twelve people were killed, and hundreds were left homeless. The day after the dam break, I left for Idaho Falls where I would be working for three weeks. I worked very closely with the news media on stories on rebuilding essential services and cleanup in the area. We had a small dam near Idaho Falls, Ririe, and rumors began to spread that it also was about to fail. I called my boss, Col.

Nelson Connover, the district engineer, and said that we should inspect that dam, and issue a report on its condition. We had already been monitoring it closely, because of its proximity to Teton Dam. The engineers were in favor of a more comprehensive inspection, and a team of experts from Walla Walla, Portland, and Washington, D.C., flew in to do the job. When I tried to get a report on the dam's condition, our district engineering chief said that it looked as if the dam was in great shape, but it would take them two to three weeks to come up with a definitive report. I told him that we had to get the word out immediately on the dam's condition. He said that he wouldn't do that, because he wanted a complete report released to the public and it would take some time. I called the colonel and told him how important it was to alleviate fears that another dam was about to break, and we needed a preliminary report in minutes, not weeks. He agreed. I worked up a draft news release saying that an inspection showed that the dam was in good shape, did not have any apparent structural flaws, but that a detailed report on the inspection of the dam would not be available for about 14 days. I got the release on the wire immediately, and the response was great. We had requests for interviews and follow-up stories, and the rumors disappeared. Our quick response assured reporters and editors that we were honestly trying to get timely information out.

A few months after I sobered up, and returned from my stay at Sundown M Ranch I got a disturbing call at dinnertime from one of Mike's cousins. Mike was in jail in Farmington, Utah, on a drug charge and contributing to the delinquency of a minor. It had been a pot party, and the girl Mike was with was 17 years old, and he was 24 at the time. I returned to the dinner table, and Carma asked me about the call. I told her I would tell her after we had eaten. After dinner, when things were calm, I took her into the bedroom, closed the door and told her what had happened. She fell on the bed sobbing. When she calmed down a bit, I told her she should go with me to my meeting that night. It was a Tuesday. Blanche Stafford ran a meeting right next door to the one for recovering alcoholics. It was an organization for the spouses, lovers, children, relatives and friends of alcoholics, for those deeply involved in the lives of their boozing loved ones.

We each went to our meetings that night, and Carma told me what happened.

"It was as if I belonged right away. They knew what I was going through. The most important thing I learned was that I was not responsible for your drinking and Mike's drug use," she said. "I felt like the weight of the world had been taken off my shoulders."

After that meeting, Carma calmly made the flight down to Utah, saw Mike, and sat through his sessions with the courts. Mike worked his way out of that morass, Carma came home. She became a regular at her Tuesday night meeting, and I continued to go to mine.

Blanche became our trusted friend. She was a small, slender, white-haired, motherly person. She was bright, articulate and open. She said that she hadn't always been that way, that working with the loved ones of alcoholics and becoming involved in her own recovery program changed her.

"We get as sick, or sicker, than the alcoholic," she said. "Our whole life was centered around alcohol, and we reacted in sicker ways that the person who was doing all the drinking.

She told the story of one night when her husband Opie came home drunk after a day of drinking. He staggered into the front yard and passed out in the middle of the lawn.

"It was autumn, and I had raked the leaves into big piles on the front lawn," Blanche said. "Opie was lying there, on his face. I wasn't able to pick him up and carry him into the house. So I grabbed a rake, and raked a big pile of leaves over him so the neighbors couldn't see the drunkard in my front yard. I left him there all night."

When she woke in the morning, Opie was sitting at the kitchen table drinking coffee. He didn't remember what happened, but Blanche wasn't the least hesitant in telling him, loudly and in rich detail.

With both of us involved in a continuing recovery program, we were able to face big domestic crises, and deal with them. Rosanne left Glenn, returned to Walla Walla, and took an apartment close to us. She had gone back to school in San Fernando Valley, graduated from Monroe High School as a Gold Seal Scholar, and completed two years at California State University, Northridge. Rosanne admitted that Glenn couldn't deal with her independence and her drinking. She had continuing problems with her diabetes, and drinking caused her a lot of problems. She had become pregnant, and the doctor ordered an abortion. He said that with the severity of her diabetes, neither she nor her child would survive. After that, Rosanne's emotional health deteriorated, and she wanted to come home and be close to her family. Rosanne felt that Glenn should be able to marry again and have a family, because she couldn't have children. This devastated Rosanne. She was the little earth mother. After her mother died, she became the mother, and took care of me and her little sisters. She always tried to run interference for her sisters when they got in trouble with Carma or Grandma.

A phone call came from Pete and Nona in Southern California. My brother Tony and his family had moved to Florida, and my mother had gone to stay with Pete and Nona in Southern California. Nona said she couldn't deal with my mother any longer, and I had to come and get her. My mother, tearful and begging, asked to come and live with me, Carma and the girls. Carma and I agreed immediately, and within two days Mother arrived at the Walla Walla Airport. This time it was a lot different. For some reason I could live with my mother and not become as angry as I did before. Carma was the same. She said she felt as if she had a second chance to do a better job of getting along with my mother, and that was no easy chore. I had learned a lot in the few years I had been sober, mostly honesty, being able to admit my faults and saying "I am sorry," tolerance and acceptance. My mother couldn't help acting as she did. It was up to me to accept her, and love her as she was. The same loving, caring person that I loved as a child, was in her body that acted so differently as she aged. She adored, and doted on Lisa, the youngest.

Lisa developed a lot of problems. In her early teens he ran away to follow a boy up to Pullman, Washington. I dragged her home, only to find her missing. A short time later she ran away to California. She ended up at Rosanne's, creating havoc in that household. Rosanne forced her onto a plane back to Walla Walla. One night I got a call from the cops saying that my youngest daughter was in the Walla Walla County Jail. I said I would be down to pick her up. They said no. They were keeping her until the next morning and I had to see the judge. Lisa said that if I came down to get her, that I would beat her. I had never done anything thing like that before. We went down to the jail, saw the juvenile people, and Lisa was released on probation to our custody. I wouldn't let her walk close to me because she smelled so bad, and I made her sit in the back seat with the windows open. Lisa was in tears. She thought they were going to put her in a nice, comfortable juvenile home, but they threw her in the women's section of the jail, where she tried to sleep on a bare mattress.

Our next action was to have Lisa go to a private child psychologist for an examination and evaluation. We didn't know what else to do. The psychologist told us that Lisa was a bright, fully developed youngster who had definite personality problems. She could be a sociopath, a person who knew right from wrong, but just didn't give a damn. The psychologist said he saw three options in dealing with Lisa: to continue as we had been, to let her go on her own, or to institutionalize her. We opted for the first alternative. I told Lisa what we were going to do, and she was very unhappy. She wanted her "emancipation," wanted to leave and live with anyone who would have her, other than home. I told her she would continue to live in our home, go to school and try to get her life in order. I told her that Carma, her Grandma, and I would do everything we could to help her live a good life, but if she didn't conform I would go to the juvenile authorities and they could handle it. Maybe they would even put her back in jail. She was horrified, shocked and speechless. But things gradually did get better, particularly in her relations at home.

Jeanine and Melanie graduated from Walla Walla High School, enrolled in community college and were extremely active in theater. They both were part of the juvenile theater that Bea Mortensen and Joanne Rasmussen formed. They took their shows on the road and played at elementary schools all over eastern Washington and Oregon. Melanie had met Maarten TrompVanHolst in high school and their relationship became serious. Maarten had worked as a potter's apprentice at a respected studio in Pendleton, Oregon, and wanted to test his independence. He moved to Portland and set up shop there. Melanie followed him. They weren't married. Carma and I got a quick education in how to deal with the lifestyles that were dramatically changing. Melanie, my baby girl, was running off to the big city to live with artist. I dealt with that crisis a hell of a lot better sober than I did drunk when Rosanne left high school, married, and moved to Los Angeles. Melanie would later go on to a career in dinner theater and children's theater in Portland. She later returned to Walla Walla for a temporary stay, to play Anne Sullivan in "The Miracle Worker." She won Walla Walla's Actress of the Year Award for that stunning interpretation.

The crises in my life did not bring on the monumental fears that I had when I was drinking. I must have been doing something right, because I had lost the compulsion to drink right after I sobered up. Quick, fleeting flashes of memory would bring back scenes of cold, sweating beer glasses; the clink of ice cubes in a tumbler filled with vodka; or the deep, ruby red of sunlight glinting through a bottle of Burgundy. My sobriety was sorely tested one night when I got a call from Lada at Casa del Carmen in El Monte. My dear Grandpa Smith had died. He was 98 years old. Every year I had made the pilgrimage to San Gabriel Valley to see him and Lada. Grandpa was a drinker, but I had never seen him drunk. He had a bottle of Old Crow bourbon in the kitchen cabinet for as long as I could remember. He would have one drink out of it every day. Just a one-ounce jigger in the morning with breakfast. His usual breakfast was whiskey, a raw egg that he would down in a single gulp, a piece of lightly buttered toast, and three cups of black coffee. Right after we moved to Walla Walla Grandpa Smith had become seriously ill, and ended up in the hospital. He had bad abdominal pains, and the doctor operated on him for appendicitis. The doctor found mangled scar tissue where he appendix was supposed to be, and an infection had set in there. Apparently Grandpa had a ruptured appendix when he was young, and he lived through it. He recalled that when he was about 26 years old he had a real bad stomachache that put him in bed for a week. He was weak and shaky for two weeks after he went back to work, but recovered fully. My Grandpa Smith was the toughest old guy that I had ever met. He was a great teacher. I learned that loyalty, courage, honesty and hard work were manly attributes to which I should aspire. He and my Dad taught me the obligation to care for family above all else. "Charity begins at home," was their creed. I saw many deals my Grandpa made with other men with a handshake. His promises were cast in concrete. I think that my brothers and I were greatly blessed with the role models we had in my father and Grandpa Smith. Dad was the thinker, Grandpa the doer. Dad provided the intellectual stimulus, Grandpa the physical. They were so different, but so much alike. They had similar values, but different ways of doing things, and they had the same code of morals. You didn't cheat, steal, lie, gamble, or mess around with women other than your wife. When it came to drinking and smoking, you were on you own. It was that simple.

I fought off the depression that hit me when Grandpa Smith died, and dived into the activities that were keeping me busy.

Bea had talked me into taking publicity pictures for her theater. I had become interested in photography right after June and I were married. She bought me a Kodak Pony 35mm camera and I was hooked. I had taken thousands of pictures over the years. I took two photography classes at the University of Utah, and even set up a small, temporary darkroom while we were in Bountiful. In Walla Walla I had a big basement that I could use as a darkroom.

The basement, my drinking haven to where I went with Dandy in my drinking days, became another haven for me during domestic turmoil. I had to keep my wits about me when processing pictures, and I totally forgot, for a short time, all of the family troubles and tensions at work. My basement photo sessions, and my meetings with other recovering alcoholics, gave me mental and spiritual respite. I was even selling some of my photos. I took up photography because I needed pictures to with my articles. When I started freelance writing I missed making some sales because I didn't have photos to go with the articles. I could have bought photos to go with the articles, but sometimes the pictures would cost me more that I was getting for the article. So learning how to take and process my own photographs was necessary.

My writing success increased proportionally with my sobriety. When I was sober in Los Angeles, I managed to ghost two articles for the *Military Engineer* magazine on coastal engineering research and the floods of 1968-69 in Southern California. After I sobered up I was selling at least one big Sunday magazine piece a month, and lots of smaller articles every week. In the early 1970s I started selling articles to the Sunday Magazine of the *Spokesman Review* daily newspaper in Spokane. I developed a long, rewarding relationship with the editor, Jack F. Johnson. The first article for Jack, with photos, was "Cinderella on the Sagebrush Circuit," a story about the travelling children's theater my daughters were in. Then I did a score of pieces for Jack on a wide range of subjects such as prison reform, Indian burials, dams, salmon blood research and many others. I had pieces in all of the Pacific Northwest major newspaper Sunday magazines. The one of which I was most proud was a photo essay for the *Seattle Times* Sunday Magazine. "Off and running at bush tracks," was a big spread about a traveling starter gate operator who plied his trade at small horse racing tracks in Washington.

I was also doing some engineering articles and sold several stories to McGraw-Hill's *Engineering News Record*. That would eventually lead to writing for McGraw-Hill World News when we left Walla Walla.

Those of us in the Federal Civil Service were used to periodic cutbacks in the workforce, but things really started to change in 1976-77. A big effort was being made to reduce the federal payroll, and the Corps of Engineers was not exempt. We saw a lot of contracts being granted to private companies and individuals to do the work normally done by government workers. President Jimmy Carter, in his campaign speeches, had promised that he would protect the integrity of the federal workforce. I was caught in the downsizing grinder. There was a quota to be met, and I had to get rid of a model and display builder position in my office. That meant that Andy Anderson, who had that job, would be looking for a job after a long, dedicated federal career. I was furious. The folks in our North Pacific Division said that the work that Andy was doing could be done under private contract. I believed that was against federal regulations, at that time, to eliminate a job and then contract on the outside to have the same service. I appealed to our local, division and national budget folks, but was turned down. So I wrote a letter voicing my complaint to President Jimmy Carter. The bureaucracy managed to get around the system, and Andy was transferred into the Engineering Division as a model builder in the design branch. He did the same work on the same projects as before. But on paper, the Corps had got rid of a position, and met its quota. But I was still waiting for an answer to my letter to the president.

My old friend John Ulrich had left the Corps and was with the Bonneville Power Administration as their public affairs officer. He had been replaced by Ed Sanchez. Ed decided to retire in 1977, and his job would be open. I didn't even bid on it, because I thought I didn't have a chance, even though I had been getting outstanding performance ratings and awards since I quit drinking. I also thought that my name would be on the bottom of the list after writing to the president. I wondered if the letter had even gotten to the president. Someone in Washington, D.C.

had probably thrown the letter in the waste paper basket. The bureaucracy works in strange and mysterious ways. In February of 1977 I was notified that I was one of three persons being considered for the job of public affairs officer for the Corps' North Pacific Division. The division took in all of the Pacific Northwest and Alaska. Next, I went down to Portland, was interviewed by Major General Wesley E. Peel, his deputy, and his executive assistant. The day after I got home to Walla Walla, General Peel called and told me I had the job if I wanted it. I accepted. After all, it meant that I would be a GS-13 and get a big raise in pay.

They held a big going-away party for me at the Walla Walla Elks Club. I had joined the Elks right after we moved into town. The only reason I joined was that it had the best bar in town. After I sobered up I hadn't been in the lodge building, except for farewell and retirement parties for Corps employees. I was really touched by the comments some of the folks made. I really had no idea that they thought so much of me, particularly Mary Thomas, my second in command, our editorial assistant Goldie, artist Ruie Glaspell, and Phil Lane, a civil engineer. Phil is a Sioux Indian, and I got to know him well after I interviewed him on several stories. He was the one who started and sponsored the Confederated Tribes at the Walla Walla Penitentiary, and was active in Native American affairs. Phil gave me a beaded neckpiece made by his 90-year old aunt. I still have it, and it hangs in a place of honor.

When our personnel director at the Corps of Engineers learned I was so involved in alcoholism programs such as Newhouse, he asked me to take over the new alcoholism and drug abuse program coordinator position. It was a co-lateral duty and something I was familiar with. We had several people with drinking and drug problems, some in very responsible positions. My job was to get them into a treatment program, into a continuing recovery program, and assist them in the process. Some didn't make it, and opted for early retirement. Others did start on the road to recovery. The alcoholism and drug abuse program coordinator job was one that I would be taking with me in the new position at Portland.

I was sad that I would be leaving Walla Walla, but relieved. The job would be a piece of cake, and no more would I be the head of the Walla Walla Human Services Administrative Board, on the boards of the Little Theater, a group home for handicapped youngsters, the Walla Walla Symphony and Newhouse. What would I do with all that spare time? The hard part was leaving my recovering alcoholic friends that had become as dear as my family. I couldn't hold back the tears when I said goodbye to them at the Tuesday night meeting. That was the same meeting in the welfare office that I wouldn't go to at first. My ego almost kept me from one of the greatest experiences of my life-that deep sense of belonging, fellowship, understanding and love us ex-boozers have, those who are trying to stay sober and live a good life.

Chapter 18

Portland

I began my new job by working three days a week in Portland; Tuesday, Wednesday and Thursday; and two days in Walla Walla, Monday and Friday. That way I could be home for the weekend. The three days in Portland were spent with Ed Sanchez learning the office routine and becoming familiar with the Division Office. The Corps' North Pacific Division was the headquarters for the engineering districts in the Pacific Northwest: Alaska, Portland, Seattle and Walla Walla.

In May of 1977 Carma, Lisa, my mother and I left the house on Howard Street in Walla Walla and moved into the Heathman Hotel in Portland. Within a week Carma found a place in North Portland. We signed the papers to buy it, and moved in. The house was a Portland bungalow, two stories, full basement, four bedrooms, three baths, including one in the basement. Carma and my mother loved the old house that was built the year I was born. All Lisa wanted to do was go back to Walla Walla, the place she hated so when we moved there from Los Angeles.

There was a Fred Meyer shopping center, a big Oregon grocery-drug-department store chain, only about one mile from our new home.

"Do you want to up to Fred Meyer's to do some shopping, Mom?" I asked her.

"No! I will never set food in a Fred Meyer store. He got you drunk when you were 17, and that was the start of all your problems."

I tried to explain to her that it wasn't the same Freddie Meyers, but when Mother made up her mind about some things there was no changing her. She never did go to Fred's.

When I reported for duty in Portland I had a letter waiting for me from Maj. Gen. R. C. Marshall, the deputy chief of engineers in Washington, D.C. He answered the letter that I had written to President Carter. My office staff had been reduced because they thought I had too many people in the public affairs office.

Gen. Marshall wrote: "…Although there have been initiatives which encourage contracting for services, this was not the primary basis upon which the reduction was proposed…this reduction is not predicated upon any plan by the President to reorganize the government, and therefore, it does not fall within the purview of the President's remarks that loss of jobs due to his reorganization will be avoided…I appreciate your concern for conserving resources and for your conscientious efforts to serve the public. Also, I hope to see this reflected in your performance as the new Public Affairs Officer of the North Pacific Division."

A nice little dig.

Portland was a great city. I love the Willamette River cutting through the center of town with all the bridges and the great McCall Waterfront Park. The North Pacific Division Office in the old Custom House was within walking distance of most of the city's important features. The restaurants were great. I was soon involved in advising Gen. Peel on some knotty problems. He told me he had made one decision that was not going to be popular. The Chief of Engineers, the number one man in charge of all Corps' operations, had made an inspection trip of the western states. Out division had been included in his itinerary. One of the projects he visited was Lucky Peak at Boise, a flood control and hydroelectric power generation dam on the Boise River. On the face of the dam we had painted the slogan, "Keep Idaho Green," a caution on protecting forests and range lands from wildfires. The "Chief" was on a personal mission to improve the Corps' image. He wanted the castle, the Corps's official emblem, painted on all of our projects with signs that read, "The Corps Cares." Gen. Peel said that he had an order from his chief to erase the "Keep Idaho Green" sign and replace it with a big red castle, and the "The Corps Cares." I listened, and didn't have much to say then; I was in a state of shock.

I went back to my own office and really looked into the matter. Our design people, particularly the landscape architects, were all against dead set against changing the Lucky Peak sign. I also knew that if we changed the sign it would infuriate the Idaho congressional delegation, including Sen. Frank Church, and the people with the most political influence in the state. I explained this to Gen. Peel, and told him that if we erased the "Keep Idaho Green" sign on Lucky Peak, we could kiss goodbye to any projects we had planned in Idaho. Our field people would be tarred and feathered and run out of the state. If the press ever learned about how the three hundred gallons of paint that were needed, plus the thousands of work hours, we would be the laughing stock of the age. Gen. Peel listened to my pitch and his face got longer and longer. Finally he said that he had no choice, that he had told the chief he was going to put up the big red castle. Two days after I gave him my recommendations on Lucky Peak, Gen. Peel called me into his office.

"I have decided to put the Lucky Peak castle deal on hold," he said. "The Chief has only one more year, and maybe we can kill it then. God help me if he ever finds out."

Lee Turner, the executive officer with the Walla Walla District, wrote a nice note to me when I retired from federal service soon after.

"Thanks for helping us get the big castle off Lucky Peak Dam," he wrote.

I consider it my crowning achievement in public relations, keeping a dumb sign off a dam. I liked public relations, particularly working with the press. And it provided me with a nice salary that supported my writing habit.

Every year there were congressional budget hearings in Washington, D.C. We would prepare a presentation for the public works subcommittees of the House of Representative and the Senate. Initially, I was asked to help with the copy in the presentation. I made a lot of suggestions, mainly trying to keep the words down to one and two syllables and editing out a lot of the bureaucratic jargon. The folks in program development, who were responsible for creating the presentation, would come to the public affairs office looking for 35mm color slides to go with the general's speech. I reviewed the programs that they had presented in years past, and I saw a lot of room for improvement. I began collecting outstanding color slides of our work and project. I recommended that we change our whole approach. Instead of the dry, one projector slide show, why not put together a real good audio-visual presentation. I suggested we use the developing lap dissolve system in showing the slides. That would involve using two 35mm slide projectors and a unit that would change the slides. For example: a slide would be shown on the screen, and it would gradually phase out as the new slide brightened on the screen. It was a seamless method of presentation without the black screen between slides. If I could have figured a way to feed in music unobtrusively I would have done it, but the general said no to that. Our plan was for the general to read his presentation, and I would have an annotated script to go along with it. I just changed slides. A nice thing about the lap dissolve unit was that it didn't make the loud clicking noise when the slide changed. It was a clean, unobtrusive method of putting a good audio-visual show together. I had seen it used in slick audio-visual shows in displays at expositions and fairs.

The general asked me to come and run the audio-visual part of the presentation for him as he read his speech before the committee. I remember some of the legendary politicians who sat on that Senate Committee: Magnuson of Washington, Packwood of Oregon, and Eastland of Mississippi. Our presentation went off without a hitch, and Magnuson was profuse in his compliments. The general beamed.

Two weeks after we had returned to Portland, General Peel got a call from Magnuson. Maggie wanted to show our "movie" to some other congressmen. It was my job to send the slides back to D.C., and I arranged with our public affairs office for them to get the equipment together to show it again to Magnuson.

The trip to DC was not the first time that I had met Magnuson or Frank Church. I was introduced to them in Lewiston, Idaho, at the dedication of the Lower Snake River dams. In Washington, when I saw Magnuson early in the day at the congressional hearings, my heart went out to him. It was obvious that he had a drinking problem. His breath had the overpowering smell of mints and booze, he eyes were bloodshot, and he had that puffy look of the heavy drinker. I admired him for his great mind, his talents and ability, but I commiserated with him, too. I had been on the boozy road he was traveling, and I wanted to say something to him about it, but I was intimidated by his reputation. I don't know if he ever gained any sobriety before he died, but I sure hope so. For Maggie, and Pat Hannon, I regret not putting my ego on the line and not telling them my story, and how great life can be when you are sober. I thought a lot of them, and I don't know whether telling them my story would have made any difference in their lives. But I wish I had.

For some time I had been collecting information on taking some more college courses, with the hope that I would some day get a degree. There were a lot of opportunities to do that in Portland. I met Kay Stepp, who was a trainer and personnel manager with Portland General Electric, at a session she was conducting. She told me about a program for adult students at Marylhurst University. It was a program that could give you college credit through university courses you had taken, work experience and special training. I entered the program, and found that I had completed 122.5 credit hours over the years, and needed 57.5 hours, including 3.5 hours of math or science, to get my degree. I started working on my degree after General Peel departed, and it was something that would keep me busy for more than a year.

In 1978 General Peel got a new assignment. I sure hated to lose him as a boss. When he left, I started working harder on my freelance writing, along with my college work, hoping that I could make enough money on the side so that I could eventually retire from federal service. I was selling some good articles to McGraw-Hill's *Engineering News Record* on construction projects in the Pacific Northwest. In a discussion with one of the editors, he told me to get in contact with McGraw-Hill World News, that they had a lot of markets that I could sell to. I did, and that began a relationship that would last for several years.

I tried, unsuccessfully, to sell a short piece that I had done, "Whisper Words." I even tried to sell it to Andy Rooney at CBS's "60 Minutes." Here's the article:

> I grew up with whisper words.
>
> When you had to go to the bathroom you said it in a whisper.
>
> This was a problem when I started first grade. I never held my hand up all the way. I only raised one or two fingers head high.
>
> When my Mom and Dad, Grandma or Grandad were talking about someone being seriously ill, it was either *cancer, tuberculosis* or a *stroke.*
>
> Words like *abortion, homosexuality, incest* and *birth control* were never uttered. They would have frozen the vocal cords completely closed.
>
> When my folks were talking about you in whispers, it meant you were either sick or immoral.
>
> There are plenty of whisper words on television today. Whisper words are also in books, magazines or newspapers, but

when whisper words are in print, they are private. They don't go any farther than you. It is only when they are spoken out loud that they become whisper words.

It wasn't too long ago when *prostitute, illegitimate births* and *venereal disease* were banned from the lexicon of radio and television newscasters and announcers.

It is certainly different today.

I am not saying that it is either good or bad.

I think that some of our changes and attitudes are healthy and for the better, but I have trouble listening when some things hit me broadside from the TV tube.

My pet peeve is hemorrhoid preparation commercials. They should be whispered and the screen blacked out. It wasn't until I reached my teens that I discovered *piles* were hemorrhoids. *Piles* was in important whisper word. Grandma avowed that one was stricken with *piles* after sitting on wet grass and sidewalks.

A close second are *toilet paper* commercials. *Toilet* paper was always whispered, but you could say "T. P." out loud. I am uncomfortable with "squeezability" and seeing grown men sensuously fondling rolls of T.P. It makes me squirm.

Deodorant and *feminine protection* ads bring sweat to my brow. Particularly when a girl on TV drops her purse and *feminine protection* pops out. Two girls then clinically discuss advantages of that particular product. They should be talking in whispers. We didn't even have words for such devices when I was growing up. *Feminine protection* wouldn't have even been a whisper word. It, too, would have paralyzed the voice box.

Dad, Grandma, Grandpa and Mom are dead now. I am alive and well but getting deaf. I blame whisper words spoken out loud. My hearing started to go when new morality started to grow and show up on television.

I wear hearing aids now. I catch myself turning down the volume when I expect a whisper word to boom out from the television set.

I know that whisper words have taken their toll on me.

Rooney sent my article back, and I got the nicest rejection slip I had ever received.

"Thanks for your note and the piece you enclosed. All I am is a writer and I don't use anything written by anyone else.

"Did you ever hear the song Flanders and Swan used to sing? They were a British comedy team that was briefly popular about ten years ago. One of them died last year, but I'll see if I can find the words to the song and enclose them."

He found it, copied it and sent it with the returned article. Not many people are that considerate of freelance writers. I think that Andy Rooney is the finest of fine gentlemen.

At times in my life, certain things have happened that deflated my ego and brought me back to earth. I remember one Saturday afternoon when I got a mysterious telephone call at home. The caller asked me if I was the Frank King who was the public affairs officer with the Corps of Engineers in Portland. I said I was. The caller then asked me to hang up the telephone, and stand by for a call from Washington. I was really puzzled. Then my imagination really took over. Was it the FAA asking me to come back and take over a public affairs job in Washington, D.C.? Or perhaps one of the congressional committees asking me to go to work for them, after the great job I did with the audio-visual presentations? Or maybe it was a higher job with the Corps in D.C.? I anxiously paced while waiting for the phone to ring. It did about 5 p.m.

"Is this the Frank King who is waiting for a call from Washington?"

"Yes. What can I do for you."

"If you are waiting for a call from Washington, you will have to wait a lot longer. He has been dead for 200 years!"

I stared at the dead telephone in my hands, as I beamed back to earth.

"What's the matter? Who's dead?," Carma cried.

Through my laughter, I told her what happened. Not too many years ago it wouldn't have been very funny.

In late 1978 I found out that the University of Portland was looking for a new director of public information. I was eligible to retire from the federal service because I was over 55 and I had more that 30 years of service, 34.5 years to be exact. I went out to the university, which was in North Portland about three miles from our house, for an interview with Barbara Miller. Barbara was leaving the job, and taking over a fund- raising position with the university. I was asked to prepare a public relations plan for the university to demonstrate my knowledge. About a week after I handed in the plan, I was asked to an interview conducted by the school's executive vice president and Brother Rafael Wilson, CSC, the president. The University of Portland is a Catholic school that was founded by the Holy Cross priests and brothers. It had a good reputation, and was known as "the Notre Dame of the West." The Holy Cross order was also the organization that founded Notre Dame.

Shortly after I went through the interview, Barbara called me and told me that I had the job if I wanted it. Want it? I jumped at it. Here was the chance to leave the government for what I thought was a real job. After all, except for the break when I left the old CAA back in 1947-48, I had been nursing at the federal bosom from 1942 to 1978. Imagine! After 36 years a real job.

I had some qualms about working in a Catholic university. After all, I was an excommunicated Catholic who had gotten a civil divorce, and married twice more outside of the church. Vatican II had resulted in a lot of changes in the Church, but I didn't think it had changed so much that I would be allowed back into the fold. Working with the priests in the administration and faculty was great, and I soon came to like and respect them very much. Our public information office that I headed was responsible for designing and producing all of the brochures and printed materials used by the university, a news bureau and a photo lab. There were three of us in the office, Marilee Quesnell, who ran the news bureau; Bob Boehmer, our publications specialist, and Debbie Miller-Carter, the secretary. Bob was a former newspaper reporter, and a public relations man with the forestry industry. It was great working with him, and he did a wonderful job.

I liked working with Marilee, but I know that she didn't like me. I think that she felt her turf was being invaded. I liked to write, so did she. I liked to do my own photography, and so did she. We would bump heads over assignments, and I made a real effort to back off and accommodate her. There were some great stories to be done at the university and I soon found some to work on. I was most proud of the one that I did on Father Robert Francis Beh, a Holy Cross priest who was the chaplain at the Washington State Penitentiary in Walla Walla. Father Bob wanted to be a missionary after graduating from Notre Dame. He was assigned as a speech professor at the University of Portland, then became the Roman Catholic chaplain at the pen. He was an embattled figure, at odds with prison officials, the Washington legislature and Governor Dixie Lee Ray over treatment of prisoners at Walla Walla. The big controversy was between Beh and state officials over treatment and handling of prisoners during a riot and lockdown. Beh made public his battle with prison officials, and his efforts paid off in better treatment of prisoners. "A Chaplain In the Middle" came out in the Northwest Magazine of the Sunday Oregonian Sept. 30, 1979. That article resulted in the only prize I have ever won for writing-for feature writing excellence by the Oregon Communicators Association.

About six months after I began working at the University of Portland, I got my Bachelor of Arts degree from Marylhurst. After 38 years of taking my first college class at Santa Monica City College in 1941 I got a degree. I don't know if it really helped my career, but I sure had a lot of fun earning the sheepskin. It validated the knowledge I had gained through experience. General Peel was fond of quoting a statement attributed to Einstein-something like this: "Education is what you have after you have forgotten everything you learned in school." He and my dad were a lot alike in their attitude towards education. Now that I was a college gradu-ate I didn't want to become one of those "educated damn fools" my father detested. I could prevent that, I thought, if I continued to stay sober, work with other alcoholics and pass on what I had been given.

About this time I met John Armstrong, who was an adjunct professor of communications, teaching journalism at the U of P. He introduced me to Bob Costa, who headed up Portland Community College's business and management division. Bob asked me to teach a class in public rela-tions that was held in the evenings at Techtronics, in Beaverton. I accepted, and that assignment continued for three quarters.

Everything was going great. The job at the university was proving to be a challenge, and I enjoyed it. With my federal retirement and the salary from the university, I was earning a good income, and we were saving money. My mother had a couple of pretty bad illnesses, and had to go to the hospital for a short stay. She became seriously ill, went back into the hospital, and was there for 10 days. The doctors told us that she had been stabilized, she was suffering from congestive heart failure, and it was time for her to go into a skilled nursing facility-a euphemism for a nursing home. I had a lot of qualms about it, but the medical people suggested a place very close to a club in Northwest Portland that I had joined. The club was for recovering alcoholics and I went to meetings and social affairs there two or three times a week. If Mom was in that nursing home, I would be able to visit her every day. It was a traumatic experience for everyone. We would visit and Mother would be surrounded in a sitting room with a dozen old people in wheel chairs watching television. My mother would grab me when I came in.

"Who are these people? What am I doing here?" she would cry.

It tore me apart. Mom was one who liked her privacy, to be in her own room alone. She was comfortable with her family around her, but grew uneasy in the presence of strangers. All of the people in the nursing home were strangers. Carma was as upset as I, and said that we should get her out of that place and back home. I had a lot of reservations about that. How would we care for her? Change and bathe her? We had our health and accident insurance, through my federal retirement system, with Kaiser Permanente. We went to them for help. They said that Mom would be eligible for home care, once she got the approval of the doctors. About this time Mom took a turn for the worse and ended up in the hospital. We told her that she wouldn't have to go back to the nursing home. The news seemed to give her life, and in seven days she was back in good health. The Kaiser home health nurses came in and instructed us on how to care for Mom. Nurses and aides would come in twice a week and bathe her, and check on her condition. When we had any problems, we had a phone number to call for assistance. Mom was home for six months, happy and content in her own room. Her heart began failing again, and she went into Bess Kaiser Hospital. We told her that as soon as she was well, she would come back to her own room again. At the end of the seventh day I was visiting her. She was comatose, gasping for breath. I sat with her for hours, until she was given a shot that calmed her. On that beautiful starlit October night, I looked up at the heavens as I walked to the car.

"Please, God," I said. "She has had enough. Don't let her suffer any more."

I drove home, and Carma and I went to bed shortly before midnight. At 4 a.m. the phone rang, and the nurse told me that my mother had died quietly in her sleep. I didn't have to get drunk at my mother's funeral, as I did at my dad's. I was able to call Tony, Pete and the family, make all of the arrangements-a rosary to be said for her in Portland, a funeral mass and burial next to my dad in California. I learned something from my mother's death-be very careful about what you pray for.

The older I get, the more I sense that a renewal cycle is continuing in our lives. Before we left Walla Walla, Mike's wife Brooke gave birth to little girl, Ambi. She was our first grandchild. Brooke had a son by another, married, Tory, and he also became a big part of our family. Shortly after Ambi was born, my Grandpa Smith died. Then my mother died in

October of 1979. Just three weeks before I was ecstatic when granddaughter, Sanie June King, was born. Jeanine's little one became my sidekick and a frequent companion. After Sanie's birth, Lisa had Timothy Michael a year later, and he was followed by Jennifer Michelle. Melanie and Maarten would also contribute in adding to the family. Melanie lost her first baby, Ariel. Melanie carried the baby to term, it was born, and died 24 hours later. Ariel had a rare blood disorder. Then Melanie and Maarten had Ian William TrompVanHolst, followed by Katherine Marcella TrompVanHolst. With the exception of Tory, all of my grandchildren had been born while I was sober. I was there for my kids, not insulated from the pain and joy of childbirth by the invisible shield of booze.

I got along great with the Holy Cross priests at the University of Portland. Father George Bernard was the academic vice president, and he became a good friend. I had common interests with Fathers Harry Cronin and Jim Thornton. I asked Father Harry to conduct my mother's rosary before we left for the California funeral. Just before we started the rosary, Father John Hooyboer, one of the oldest priests at the university, showed up and asked if he could help Father Harry officiate. I was very touched. Father John had read about my mother's death in our newsletter, and he showed up on his own to offer his help.

As a staff member of the university I received a few perks, one of which was a reduction in tuition for me and direct members of my family. I decided to take advantage of it, and I enrolled in some graduate communications programs. I had it in the back of my mind to get a masters degree.

In the summer of 1980, I was called into see Art Schulte, the executive vice president. He quickly got to the point and said that if it were time for the university to renew my yearly contract he would recommend that they not do so. I had just signed a new contract in May. He said that it was wrong for me to be teaching for another institution, that I should have asked for permission first. He said that a member of my staff complained about that and other things that I had been doing. I asked if he wanted me to resign, and Schulte said that would probably be the best thing for me to do. He was very friendly and open in our discussion and he emphasized that there was no deadline on my leaving, to take as long as I wished. I told him that I would be leaving by October.

I was crushed. I had been fired for the first time in my life. I was growing a great resentment, and that was directed mostly toward the person who had blown the whistle on me to Art Schulte. In my heart I knew that I was wrong, that I could have done things properly, but I felt betrayed. I had been betrayed by a person with whom I worked. I complained about this quite a lot, until a friend, who is another recovering alcoholic, offered a solution.

"Pray for her," he said. "It probably won't do her a damn bit of good, but you will sure benefit. Resentments will get you drunk quicker than anything else."

My friend had been sober for more that 30 years, so I figured he knew what he might be talking about. His statement spurred one of the hardest chores I had ever undertaken. I started praying for the person who turned me in, at first with a lot of profanity, then in a gentler, calmer mode. Within two weeks the seething anger melted down, and Carma and I rationally assessed our situation. We were in solid financial shape, had a little money in the bank, and with a little cutting back we could weather the setback. In August, I gave Art a month's notice and said that I would be leaving.

I had made arrangements with my old friend John Ulrich to do some editing for him. John had moved from the Bonneville Power Administration back to the North Pacific Division Public Affairs Office when I left to go to the University of Portland. I started editing the water resource booklets for the Corps. That gave me a little extra money to make up for the job I lost at the university. I decided to keep on with my master's program at the University of Portland, and I soon had a graduate teaching appointment. That job defrayed the cost of tuition, and gave me a small monthly salary. So with the graduate teaching pay, the money for editing the Corps' pamphlets and my freelance work for McGraw-Hill World News, I was able to almost match my former monthly salary.

In every step I was taking to further my education I was aware of my father's attitude, and I did not want to become an "educated damn fool." I knew what I was, a recovering drunk who had been able to stay off the bottle for a few years, a want-to-be writer who was continually learning his craft, and a family man. I really liked the teaching duties. My teaching assistant duties consisted of grading papers, helping with some of the lecturing, and helping the professors who I was assigned to, John Armstrong, and Ken Edwards. Both were former newspaper men. John worked at Oregon weekly newspapers until he ended up at *The Oregonian* where he was an editor. Just before he came to the university he was news director for KOIN/TV. Ken had owned several chains of weekly newspapers, and had been a journalism professor at the University of Alabama before coming to Oregon. I learned as much working with them as I did from the graduate level classes I was taking. What really pleased me were the grades I was making-straight A's. Not bad for someone who couldn't get a C for charity in algebra and geometry.

My work with still practicing alcoholics really grounded me and kept me in the real world. The club where Carma and I had been going to meetings became a big part of our lives. Every Saturday night we would go there for dinner and the meeting. A good friend had urged me to serve on the club's board of directors, and I agreed to take on the assignment for a year. Then I was elected president of that board. The club needed a continual supply of new blood, and when someone new showed up they immediately got him active by appointing him, or her, president. Things went without incident for a few months, then things developed into a tangled mess. Our club manager couldn't be found. He had taken off for parts unknown, and it was up to the club officers to sort things out. We had an astronomical food and milk bill, and the withholding taxes hadn't been paid to the state and federal agencies for the past six quarters. We were in heavy debt, but we did have some savings we could draw on. I designed a recovery plan, got a club member to design a new computer-ized accounting system, closed down the kitchen, but continued to host the many daily meetings that went on in the club. Through the generosity of club members, intensive fund raising efforts, and careful budgeting we were able to recover by year's end, and show a positive bank balance.

I had a big resentment against Jim, the club manager who had run off, and it didn't seem to go away-despite my praying for him on orders of my closest recovering friends. That all changed about one year later. My grandson Timmy, who was about three years old, wanted to go to "Santa Claus's house again." None of the family could figure out what he was talking about. I had my grandkids in the car and was driving up to the club for something, and Timmy became very excited.

"There's Santa Claus's house!" he screamed.

It was the club. Jim, the departed club manager, had been a great Santa Claus for the kids every Christmas. It was something that Timmy remem-bers to this day. My resentment against Jim miraculously evaporated when I heard Timmy's cry. That resentment hasn't come back. I accepted the fact that Jim had done wrong, but he was a friend, and did a great job until he was overwhelmed. I could see then that the club officers and board also had to accept responsibility in the matter. We hadn't monitored the situation, and we let the problem develop. There was enough blame to go around, and it was time to put the incident in the past and move on.

On May 9, 1982, I marched in the commencement processional and received my Master of Arts Degree in Communications from the University of Portland. Acting University President Art Schulte handed me my diploma. I felt good. Just a few nights before we had a big awards dinner in downtown Portland for the communications department. Bob Fulford, the department chairman, presented me with an award for being one of two outstanding graduate communications students for the 1981-82 school year. Now I really was an "educated damn fool." I never felt closer to my dad than I did when I got my master's and that award. I could even see him smiling.

One thing really struck me when I looked back at what I had done in the 11 years I had been sober: I had got all sorts of awards and recognition from the Corps of Engineers, changed jobs, got fired, got two degrees, and was teaching community college classes. Unconsciously, I think I was trying to right some wrongs. When I was drinking I used to lie a lot. Back when I got out of the Marine Corps I had lied about how much education I had on employment forms, and had drunkenly boasted in bars and parties about the articles I had written. I can recall one incident where I became an airline pilot, but I never stooped so low as to claim I was a brain surgeon or an astronaut. My lies were plausible, but a heavy load. I was working hard at making those lies, really dreams, come true. One thing I have learned about my fellow alcoholics-men, women, and persons of all faiths and races-is that we are paradoxes. We aren't very happy with ourselves, we don't like what is inside and what we have become, but we have tremendous egos. We are the centers of our universes. "I ain't much, but I am all I have." Something amazing had happened in 11 years of being sober. I was more concerned about my loved ones, my friends and co-workers than I was with myself.

The summer following my graduation I worked hard at consolidating free-lance writing activities. My work for McGraw-Hill World News was growing in the office I had at the Board of Trade Building in downtown Portland. Then Bob Fulford asked me to teach a beginning journalism class for one semester at the university. Next came an offer to teach several journalism classes for Portland Community College at the Rock Creek Campus. I accepted both, and with my freelance income it all made a nice supplement to my federal annuity. Portland Community College then asked me to move to the Cascade Campus in Portland, and all together I taught for two years at PCC.

In 1983, after Carma and I had gone on a great trip to England, I began working part-time doing public relations, photography and advertising for The Grotto, The National Sanctuary of Our Sorrowful Mother in Portland. Even though I was 62 years old It was hard for me to be without a job, somewhere to go to work every day. At the Grotto I set up a nice little darkroom, using some of my own equipment, and began having fun. The Grotto is run by the Servites, the Order of Servants of Mary, an order that was founded in Italy. Fathers Jerry Horan and Steve Ryan hired me. My job soon became half-time, then full-time. I took over the direct mail program, and became involved in fund-raising. The Grotto was in the middle of a big capital fund raising campaign to raise money to repair buildings and enlarge the facility located in a beautiful section of east Portland. The name Grotto comes from the big cave-like altar that features a reproduction of Michelangelo's Pieta, Mary holding the body of her son after he was taken down from the cross. An amphitheater that held hundreds of people for outdoor services was at the foot of the cliff, the cave, and altar. The Grotto also included the Chapel of Mary, a big church, a beautiful garden with Stations of the Cross on the upper level, a monastery, gift store and offices. It took in about 80 acres.

In addition to Father Jerry and Father Steve, the co-directors, the original staff included Sister Donna Marie McGargill and Sister Ruth Arnott. They were great people, and I soon became good friends with Sister Donna Marie. We shared a lot of common: painful memories, mostly to do with alcoholism in our families. I told her of my disastrous first marriage, and my isolation from the church. She strongly suggested that I talk to a priest, who oddly enough was stationed in the parish near our home in North Portland. It took me about eight months to get up enough courage to make an appointment with him.

I told the priest my story-about my family, my alcoholism and my marriage to Donna, why we broke up, and my getting a civil divorce, and then marrying twice again. After a hearing me out he was silent for a time. Then he quietly explained that my marriage to Donna was not a true marriage in the eyes of the church, that it never existed. He said that my first wife had taken instructions in the faith, and realized what the obligations of matrimony were, and that having children was one of those obligations. The fact that she refused to have children made the marriage null and void.

I was dumfounded. All those wasted years of thinking that I was excommunicated, and I wasn't. Then I asked what I had to do to return to the church.

"What do you think you should do?" he asked.

"Go to confession?"

"We call it the Sacrament of Reconciliation now."

I asked him if I could make my confession in about two weeks, after I had time to do a complete, truthful accounting of my moral shortcomings, bad deeds and how I had hurt my friends, family and loved ones. He said that he would be glad to hear my confession, that he had done so many times before with other recovering alcoholics.

I really prepared for the session, and it was like going through the same process that I did at Sundown M Ranch. I made my confession. I was amazed that the priest didn't give me one million Our Fathers and Hail Marys.

"For your penance I want you to do something good for the Church."

He explained that my penance was to be an action. That was a toughie, but it was something that stayed on my mind, and it wasn't until a year later that I was able to put it into action.

It wasn't like it was up at Sundown M. I didn't come floating out of that confession like I did when I bared my conscience when I went through treatment. Instead, I felt calm, at peace, as if some indefinable obligation had been completed in my life. I found my faith on the front lawn of Sundown M Ranch, and it wasn't the conforming belief of my parents and grandparents. I had found a personal relationship with a God I could understand in my own way. God showed himself to me in the eyes of my children, grandchildren, in the love I had for recovering alcoholics in my group, and in my garden. Mine was a common, barefoot, carpenter God with whom I could converse, tell my troubles and triumphs to and thank him for my life.

So, again I found out that I dramatized things in my life. Instead of trying, years before, to find out where I stood with my faith, I assumed the worse. I took on the mantle of a martyr, cried over my loss, and sent myself into spiritual exile. I could have spared myself a lot of pain by doing what my mother and father urged me to do when I got the civil divorce from Donna. I should have followed through with the annulment thing with Uncle Steve. But I decided to play the martyr, and make a big problem out of it. I have found that the phenomenon of creating the Rocky Mountains out of a tiny sand pile is peculiar to alcoholics, and those close to them. A beloved group of people I know, made up of loved ones of alcoholics, have joined together to help themselves. They say that blowing things out of proportion is:

"Pole-vaulting over mouse turds."

As I racked up more years in productive sobriety my long vaulting pole shrank into a stout walking stick. I use it daily.

I had the opportunity to go to mass frequently at The Grotto. Like at the University of Portland, there were several priests who were recovering alcoholics. I became friends with them, and many times we attended noon meetings together in a refurbished chicken coop on the upper level of The Grotto.

My freelance writing was continuing, but I decided to turn over part of what I was doing in that area to Rosanne. She had developed into a great writer, and was helping me with some of the McGraw-Hill World News account. I turned it all, including the office and files, over to her. It could provide her with an income so that she could become independent. Rosanne also began writing for the *Portland Business Journal*, a respected business and industry weekly. She did some blockbuster stories for them that involved a lot of investigative work. She also wrote for the alternative press, mostly for *Just Out*, a gay publication. Rosanne made the solemn announcement one day to Carma and I that she was coming out, that she was gay. I told her that was O.K. because I was a very happy person myself. She didn't think it was funny.

After all we had gone through-her diabetes, early marriage, divorce, continuing health problems-this didn't seem like a big deal to me. I think

Rosanne was sort of disappointed that I didn't kick up a fuss. Carma's reaction was a little different.

"All you need, Dear, is a good husband to love you and take care of you," Carma told her.

"No, Mom! I've tried that and it doesn't work. I have found what I want," Rosanne said.

I had read in a book very dear to me about acceptance. This is what I had to do:- accept Rosanne for what she was and her choices. I found that I could have no serenity unless I accepted what her choices were. She was God's child before she was mine. I remembered that when I really sobered up I had to accept my alcoholism, and if I wanted to maintain my loving relationship with my daughter I had to accept her for who and what she was. I couldn't change her. God knows I have had enough trouble changing myself, and that doesn't work all of the time. What really troubled me about my daughter Rosanne wasn't her being gay, it was her progression into alcoholism. Her drinking caused her many problems, the worst of which was terrible insulin reactions when her diabetes would be uncontrolled. She would have extended periods of sobriety, then she would go back to drinking and end up in the hospital. In spite of her drinking, she was able to make deadlines and write good stories.

My second daughter Jeanine was also having her troubles with booze. She had married Kim Smith, one of the kids she had met in summer theater in Walla Walla. They had moved up to Husum, Washington, on the White Salmon River about 70 miles east of Portland. She called me and said that her drinking had become a problem and she wanted to know what she could do to sober up. All I could do is tell her my story, and what I had done. She sobered up for a while, but it wasn't to last.

I lost my dear companion, my beloved drinking buddy Dandy. She was 13 years old when I had to have her put to sleep. Dandy had become quite feeble, and I had to carry her down the front steps so we could take our little walk every night. One night she couldn't even stand. So the next morning I took her to the veterinarian and he said she had something wrong with her lungs, and was doomed to die within days. I told him to put her out of her misery, and I stayed there while she was put to sleep. Lisa was inconsolable. She cried for three days. Now, every time I see a lively, jumping Brittany spaniel I get a catch in my throat. I haven't been able to get another dog. I don't think I ever will. I was sad, but I felt good about Dandy. She had seven great years of sobriety before she died.

We had been in Portland for more than seven years in the place on North Montana Avenue. At one time, we had every one of our kids except Mike and Melanie live with us during that period. Carma and I developed a diabolical plot-to get a smaller place just big enough for the two of us, so we wouldn't have kids and grandkids with us all of the time. My friend John Armstrong, whom I worked with at the University of Portland, provided us with that opportunity. John and his wife Kina had a place in Lincoln City on the Oregon Coast. Kina's folks had owned property there for many years, and John was editor of the *Lincoln City News Guard* in 1946. John had a one-bedroom apartment that he was renting to a radio announcer. When his renter left, John said the apartment was available, so we rented it-for $150 a month-as a weekend place. We rented the place in August 1985 and spent several weekends there. We had our Portland house up for almost a year, then it sold suddenly. We had until November 1 to move out. We decided to live in our vacation rental apartment, put our furnishings in storage, and see how we liked living on the Oregon Coast.

Chapter 20

The Oregon Coast

Moving this time was to be like no other move we had ever made. When I left The Grotto, I left with their old pickup truck. I paid $200 for a 1979 Datsun half-ton pickup that was dented up and in pretty bad shape. I had to put in a new rear end and get it tuned up before I could use it. We used the pickup to move most of our stuff down to Lincoln City and put it in storage. I figured I made 10 trips with the pickup filled, and one trip with a rental truck to complete the move. We made it by mid-October so the new tenants, Elizabeth and Victor Aldaz and their children, could move into the house.

Our place on Schooner Creek gave me lots of opportunity to fish. During the fall you could see the salmon in the creek resting for their trip up the stream to spawn. I never did catch one of them, but I sure tried. In addition to fishing I did a lot of work around John's place. He had an old log cabin on the property that he was having rebuilt. John said that if

Carma and I planned on staying there for a few years, he would build an addition onto the cabin and we could move into it. That would give us a kitchen, bath, a large living-dining room, and small office in the cabin. In the built-on addition we would have a large sitting room downstairs, with a loft bedroom and bath upstairs. A contractor would do all of the rough work, and I would do the finishing in the addition. I started work on the project, and did a few more things as well. I enclosed an open storage area in back of the cabin, made it into a shop-storeroom, and put in a concrete floor. I also formed in a sidewalk all around the back of the cabin. When it was poured, Carma helped me finish it off. We had a nice, but odd-looking, house when we were finished. In addition to the building, I spent my free time fishing. I fished from Newport to Pacific City, in every stream, and lake, on the beaches and the jetties. I caught a lot of fish, and life was good, but something was missing.

I started going to church, and became a communicant at St. Augustine's In Lincoln City. I could now go to mass and not cry. I remembered the penance that had been imposed on me. Father Michael Lau, a little Chinese priest, asked for people to clean up the church, do the janitorial work on Friday before the Saturday evening and Sunday morning masses. I volunteered. After I went the first time, Carma asked if she could help me, so we did it together. We ran the vacuum cleaner over all the carpeting, dusted the pews, cleaned the toilets, and swept the walks. I figured that doing janitorial work for the church was a good thing, and I would be doing the penance that the priest in Portland gave me.

When we first started coming down to Lincoln City, I contacted some of the recovering alcoholics in the area who were involved in the same sort of recovery movement as I. I started going to a regular Sunday meeting, and it was as if I had never left Walla Walla, or Portland. The faces were different, but the stories and messages were the same. The center of my life, my recovery, had moved with me to Lincoln City. I was feeling good-physically, mentally and spiritually-until something odd began to happen to my body. I couldn't pee like I could when I was younger.

My urologist in Portland, Dr. Tom Carey, said that my prostate was enlarged and I should have a TURP-a trans-urethral prostate resection-a roto-rooter job. They would go in and ream out the center of the prostate. After a particularly painful urinary blockage, when I had to go into the Lincoln City Hospital and have a catheter plunged into me, I quickly agreed to the operation. About three weeks before I had heard of an opening for a coast correspondent for the Salem *Statesman Journal,* the daily newspaper in the state's capital city. Salem is about 50 miles east of Lincoln City. The folks at the paper wanted to interview me, but I was due for the hospital visit, so I arranged for the interview to be five days after my operation.

I was discharged from the Portland Bess Kaiser hospital on June 14, and drove the 80 miles back to Lincoln City, with Carma anxiously watching my every move. We got home, and I got a good night's sleep in my own bed. The next morning we drove to Portland for the interview. Larry Roby, the community editor, interviewed me. We had a great talk, he had looked at my portfolio and copies of my stories from over the years, and said he was impressed. I also met Dan Davies, the city editor, and Bill Florence, the executive editor. At the end of the interview, Larry said he had only one concern, my age. I was 64, soon to be 65, and he didn't know if I would be able to physically handle the job. He told me he would let me know very soon if I got the job.

Feeling good about the interview, I rushed to the men's room to urinate. I was still feeling the effects of the operation, and there remained a faint pinkish tinge of blood in my urine. I had just finished, was zipping up my pants and Larry came in.

"Have you ever been hired in a men's room before?" he said. "The job is yours if you want it."

I accepted immediately, was about to shake his hand, and decided to wash up first. First impressions are important.

That was the beginning of a job that lasted seven years, the most challenging, satisfying and rewarding job I ever had. I felt as if I had finally validated my dream of becoming a newspaper reporter. Granted, I wasn't a full-time, salaried, general assignment newspaper reporter, but I was close. I covered everything: fires, school board meetings, murderers, trials, church bazaars, the sinking of fishing boats and county commission meetings. And I got paid for how much I had published. I was still a true freelancer, and I felt as if I had truly found my niche. I am a believer in the Peter Principle of every person rising to his own level of incompetence. I sure did that when I couldn't make the 30 word-per-minute Morse code speed when I was with the CAA in Hanksville, Utah; I got fired as the public relations man for the University of Portland, and my fundraising work for The Grotto tarnished my silver ego. I finally came to the realization that public relations had been paying for my writing habit for many years. Now I had the public relations monkey off my back, and I could be a real journalist.

Those seven years I was with the *Statesman Journal* were the happiest of my professional life. For the most part I was on my own, free to develop my own stories. Larry provided me with guidelines on what to cover. I went to a lot of meetings held by city councils, the school district, port district, city and county planning commissions, and the weekly session with the Lincoln County Board of Commissioners. I was urged to work on stories before they came up as an agenda item for some meeting, to get at the story behind the story. What I really enjoyed was working on the hard news stories. Lincoln County had its share of shipwrecks, beach accidents, and capsized fishing boats. My first big breaking story was when the Cougar, a charter boat out of Depoe Bay on a tuna fishing trip, went down.

Five people were saved and four found dead after the boat sank 36 miles west of Newport. The survivors were in the water for 18 hours before they were rescued. I responded to the story first, and our managing editor John Erickson was in port at Newport on his boat when the story broke. He grabbed a camera and got a good photo of one of the survivors being taken from the helicopter to the emergency room. The editors wanted their star reporter working on the story, so they sent Alan

Gustafson down to Newport. I did share a byline with him on the front page story that came out the day after the sinking. I had been with the paper for a year, and I soon found out that maritime, fishing, shipping and ocean stories would take up a lot of my time. I really enjoyed working the docks, the fishermen and the port crew.

The Lincoln County Courthouse almost became a home away from home. I was there every Wednesday morning for the county commission meetings, and for stories involving the commissioners, assessor, treasurer, county clerk, the sheriff, county clerk and others. We were also big on elections. Stories had to be filed on candidates and their backgrounds, and measures. All of my stories were sent into the paper by my little Radio Shack laptop computer. I would file the election story, dial up the paper's number, activate the modem, and the story would fly over the telephone lines to Larry's desk in Salem.

On the big election nights, for the general and primary, I would have a helper, my granddaughter Sanie, who was about nine years old. About a year after we had moved down to Lincoln City, my daughter Jeanine and her husband Kim separated and were divorced. Jeanine was devastated. She and Sanie moved to Lincoln City into an apartment about a block away from us. The Taft Elementary School where Sanie began attending classes, was just across the street from our place. Sanie would come over to our house for lunch every day, and she spent more time with us than she did at home with Jeanine.

They had been in their new apartment for a few months when one night we heard a faint, plaintive call beneath our bedroom window. I looked out, and there was Sanie, under the street light, crying for Grandpa. I rushed downstairs, gathered her up and put her in bed with Carma. Sanie said her mother was drunk and acting crazy. I quickly dressed, and walked down to Jeanine's to see what was happening. Jeanine was standing at the kitchen stove, in a short T-shirt, naked from the waist down, trying to fry pork chops. She was fixing dinner for herself and Sanie at 11:30 p.m. I turned the stove off, led her to her bed, tucked her in, and said that Sanie was going to stay the night with us. Jeanine didn't remember anything the next morning.

Sanie is a bright child, and she was a hit with my colleagues at the courthouse on election nights. She would wait in the clerk's office for the returns to come out, and bring them to me so I could bang out the continuing story. The first big election she helped me with, an American Broadcasting Company political correspondent gave her an ABC press badge. Sanie wore it proudly at every election she helped me with.

For the most part, I developed most of the stories I sent in. Very few were on assignment from the editors. A lot of my time was spent in Newport, and at the county court house. My routine was to get there on Wednesday mornings early, before the regular commission meeting, have my coffee and doughnut in the lunch room. Then I would go to the bathroom.

One morning I was in the rest room, after my doughnut and coffee, seated on the commode completing my morning ritual, and reading my newspaper. I heard the door open, and then the click, click, click of high heels walking in. The door to the stall next to me opened and I spotted a pair of red high heels, slender ankles and trim nylon-clad calves.

"My God!" I silently screamed, "I'm in the women's can!"

I lifted my feet up in the air, so the occupant next door couldn't see my brogans.

The lady sat down with a rustle of skirts, slip and panties, tinkled daintily, and tore off the toilet tissue.

More rustling, she stands, opens the door, goes over to the basin, and washes her hands. It took a long time, maybe she was checking her makeup.

Click, click, click she walks to the door, opens it and the click, click, click recedes down the hall.

I lower my feet. Tear off the toilet tissue. Do my clean up. Bolt for the door. Check the urinals to make sure I am in the right place. Stop. Wash hands. Open the door and run into Lois Eddy.

"Have you forgotten something, Frank?" Lois giggled.

I said I hadn't, and then tried to stammer out what had just happened.
"You really must be upset," Lois said, "You forgot to put your suspenders up."

My suspenders were dangling down the sides of my pants below my sports coat. I took my coat off, pulled up my suspenders, and walked the few steps to the commission meeting, and sat down at the press table.

Just before the chairman gaveled the meeting to order, I heard click, click, click coming into the room. There stood a gorgeous brunette, in red high heels, ready to testify before the commission. I can't tell you to this day what she said. All I could see were the red high heels and the resounding click, click, click.

My discomfort was gleefully enjoyed by other reporters when I told them what happened. There were three of us who, although we worked for competing papers, became very close. Carmel Finley, the correspondent for *The Oregonian*, and Bill Hall, editor of the *Newport News Times*, then news director for Dave Miller's radio stations in Lincoln County, became good, fast friends.

I was only disappointed in Larry Roby and Dan Davies one time, and that was when they wouldn't run my "Frieda the Flasher" story. Frieda was the name of the lady of the evening who was driving the inmates of the county jail crazy. I gave her the name of Frieda, because of the nice alliteration with flasher,.

The mysterious Frieda the Flasher would show up at night under the floodlights in the county courthouse parking lot. The county jail was on the top floor. She would call to the guys upstairs and they would rush to the windows. Frieda would then unbutton her shirt, pull it open, and bare her breasts. The inmates would whoop, holler and cause all sorts of commotion. The guards would try to quiet them, to no avail, until Frieda stole away into the night. The deputies couldn't catch Frieda. It was driving the guards crazy.

I wrote it up as a straight news story, and Larry wanted to know Frieda's last name. I told him that it was a *nom d' guerre* that I dreamed up. Larry ordered me to try and interview the elusive Frieda, at least get her name right. I didn't want to spend my nights in a cold parking lot, working on a story that paid about $10, waiting for a woman who got her jollies from teasing cons, so the story died.

I still think it was a good story.

Weather is big news on the Oregon Coast. We have storms screaming in from the Pacific that have hurricane force wind gusts and dump a lot of rain. I usually had one or two big storm stories a month. Just before I left the paper, we had a storm that damaged some of the reconstruction work on the Yaquina Bay Bridge in Newport. One of the casualties was an outhouse, a Port-a-Potty on the bridge. The gusting gale blew a canopy off a pickup that was crossing the bridge, and about the same time the Port-a-Potty flew over the side into the channel below.

My answers to Larry, and the laughing city room crew were:

"No, there was no one in it."

"No, it didn't hit a fishing boat down below."

"No, they didn't recover it. The tide was going out. Last seen it was floating out to sea."

I learned much while working for Larry Roby, Dan Davies, and Andrea Howry I was realizing a dream that I had in my mind ever since I was a kid. I was 70 years old, and felt like a kid. I never failed to get a big charge when I got a page one story, or one of my pieces was picked up by the wire services.

One such feature was one I did on cranberries. Every November and early December I was asked to write several features that could be used during the holiday season, when many of our reporters were off and when we had slow news days. I had heard from good friend Jim Hawley, who was the county's emergency services director and an amateur radio operator, about a couple near Yachats who raised cranberries. That is sort of an unusual crop, so I arranged an interview with them. When I met and interviewed Sam and Carol Dorning, it was the beginning a great friendship. Sam had a good-sized cranberry patch that started from a bunch of plants he threw away after visiting his old home in Washington. The plants took hold and thrived. Then Sam and Carol had to pick them and get rid of them. That was easy.

Sam and Carol were ham radio operators, and active with the Oregon Emergency Net (OEN) emergency readiness network that was established during a devastating Oregon flood after WWII. Every summer Sam and Carol hosted a big picnic that lasted an entire weekend. OEN members would bring in their campers, trailers, and motor homes and make it a big weekend. Sam and Carol would hand out packages of cranberries to their OEN friends, and that became a tradition over the years. I wrote the story about the ham-radio-operating, cranberry-growing Dornings, and the Associated Press picked it up. Carol wrote to me and said that they were flooded with clippings from friends all over the United States, copies of the article.

When I interviewed Sam and Carol I told them about my background as a radioman in the Marine Corps, my career in civil aviation, and my radio background. They insisted that I was made for ham radio and that I should get my license. They told me about Bill Eidenschink in Lincoln City, a man who conducted free classes in amateur radio licensing. It wasn't until the cranberry story broke that I promised Sam and Carol I would take the classes. I did.

With a lot of help from Bill, Bryce Spence and Carl Schmauder. I earned my licenses, and did it in a short time. I went from novice to extra class, the highest rating, by taking an examination every month. I was afraid of the Morse code, but I bought some practice tape, and soon I had my speed back up. When I went in for code testing, they started me out at 15 words per minute, and I aced the exam. Then they said I should try 20 words per minute. I told them I hadn't copied that speed for 40 years, but I would try. I took the test, answered the multiple-choice questions, and passed, barely.

Ham radio became a big part of my life. I had never really had a hobby, other than approaching writing and photography as an avocation. Writing and photography were my life, and I didn't considered them hobbies. Bill urged me to become a volunteer examiner, helping give radio amateur examination. He also got me involved in teaching ham radio classes. For a couple of years, Bryce Spence and I conducted classes, until interest fell off. One my students was daughter Jeanine. Jeanine and current boy friend Dave Parker began taking classes from Spence and me.

Big changes were being made at the paper. I found out that I was about to lose my freelance status. One of our stringers had brought suit against the *Statesman Journal*, claiming that we were really employees and should have benefits. I didn't want to have any part of that. I was a freelancer, working on my own, under contract, and I wanted to stay that way. I started out as a free lancer almost 40 years before, and I wanted to remain a freelancer. I knew that I had to make a decision, but something came up that helped me make up my mind.

Rolf Glerum, the Portland principal in Rocky Marsh Public Relations, an old friend, called me and asked me if I would be interested in doing some consulting work. He said that the Confederated Tribes of the Grand Ronde Indians of Oregon had a monthly newspaper that needed some work. He wanted me to work with their staff and redesign their publication. So I hired out as a consultant with the Grand Ronde tribes, came up with a new format, and coached the staff on writing and editing.

It was tough saying goodbye to the *Statesman Journal* and a job that I loved. I knew that the consulting work I would be doing would also involve a lot of writing and photography work. And it did.

After 11 months my work at Grand Ronde was finished. I took over as editor of the Lincoln County Amateur Club Newsletter, something that I have continued, and a duty that I enjoy.

The idea that we would move to the coast to foil taking on any new family responsibilities was a doomed thought. Jeanine and Sanie had moved down to be close to us during a very trying time in their lives, and they stayed. Rosanne followed. She rented an apartment in Lincoln City, lived there for two years, then returned to Portland. She missed her friends in the city. Carma's youngest brother Zane Morrison, and his wife Joyce, moved to Lincoln City in 1994. Zane, a banker, had lost his job through a merger in Salt Lake City. Our family's physical, mental and spiritual cores would be tested from 1995 through 1997.

On June 26, 1995, about 10 p.m., the phone rang and it was Joyce. She was crying and said that Zane had collapsed, was lying on the floor and she couldn't wake him up. I told her to call 911 and I would be over right away. I dashed out to the car and sped to their apartment. I started CPR and mouth-to-mouth on Zane until the medics arrived. They rushed him to the hospital, barely alive. He was pronounced dead two hours later. Zane had an aortic aneurysm that had ruptured.

In June of that year, Jeanine had been complaining of flu-like symptoms. She sent Sanie up to Portland to stay temporarily with Rosanne. Jeanine became so ill that she asked to come out to our house to recuperate. I was glad to have her there. For several months I had been urging her to go to the doctor, because she had not been feeling well. Jeanine kept putting it off, and I really think she knew something was drastically wrong with her. For the last six months she had become a regular at our Sunday morning meeting of recovering alcoholics, and she was proud of her sobriety. Two days after she came out to our house, Jeanine collapsed on her way to the bathroom. I called the ambulance, and they rushed her to North Lincoln Hospital. Within two hours she was back in the ambulance on her way to Oregon Health Sciences University in Portland to the intensive care unit. Jeanine had acute myolegenous leukemia.

Melanie rushed down to Portland, and the family all gathered. We stayed in a Portland motel close to the hospital, as we all took turns being with Jeanine 24 hours a day. On the night of July 1 Jeanine was alert, in pain, but we could see that she was deteriorating rapidly. I kissed her goodnight, left, turned around in the corridor, and blew a kiss to her.

"I love you, Papa," she called.

Shortly after I left she went into a coma. On July 2, 1995, in the early afternoon, the family decided to remove all of the life support systems, and let Jeanine go. She was suffering so much. Melanie said that she wanted to with her sister to the end. I took Carma back to the motel. Within 30 minutes the phone rang, and Melanie said that Jeanine was gone. A crazy kaleidoscope from their childhood flashed through my mind. Jeanine and Melanie flying kites in Bountiful, swimming in Bear Lake, proud in their Easter dresses, sleeping together in their crib, and all four girls singing the wonderful love generation songs, with Jeanine on her guitar.

Jeanine's memorial service was at the club in Lincoln City. We conducted it as if it were a regular Sunday morning meeting of recovering alcoholics. I closed my eyes and saw her sitting at a table at the far end of the meeting room-smiling, nodding at the comments, happy and content. My beloved Jeanine, my Neenee, was gone, like my June, but she remains alive within me.

The toughest thing I had to do was write Jeanine's obituary for the Oregon papers. Lisa, who was living in Walla Walla, wrote one, with Joann Rasussen's help, for the *Union Bulletin*. Lisa told of what a great actress Jeanine was, and of her accomplishments in the theater. I was very proud of Lisa. I knew she was hurting, but she sure helped me.

As Christmas approached I got a call from Rosanne who said she was worried about Sanie, who had stayed with Rosanne after Jeanine died. Sanie was depressed, and getting back into drugs and alcohol. She was having a difficult time because she missed her mother so much. So just before Christmas, I went up to Portland and picked up Sanie. She and I bought a Christmas tree, decorated it, and I strung colored lights all over the front of the house and the yard. Being with her grandpa and grandma at that time was important to her, and Sanie began to snap out of her depression.

After the holidays I took Sanie down to the Taft High School's alternative high school in Lincoln City. She registered for classes at First Resort, and graduated in one year, with honors. Sanie took up where her mother left off, and began studying for her ham radio license. She passed her Novice and Technician exams then took the test for five words per minute Morse code. I paced outside the exam room like an expectant father. She passed the test, and ham radio became a big part of her life also. She was my sidekick, and I think that closeness did a lot to get us through the grief.

In late March of 1996 I got another dreaded phone call. It was Reisa, a friend of Rosanne's, who was living with her. In a bad insulin reaction, Rosanne had a heart attack. She died early in the morning of March 29. Like an automaton, I called the family, and waited for Sanie to get home. I tried to get her on her little hand-held ham radio she kept with her, but she had it shut down. When she got home I told her. She held up surprisingly well, and really gave me a lot of support. Carma was devastated, and really laid low physically, as she was when Jeanine died.

Rosanne, like her father and her sister, was battling alcoholism. During the last few years of her life she was trying hard to stay sober. She also tried joining with other alcoholics in a common effort to stay sober. She kept trying and trying.

We held Rosanne's memorial service at a funeral home in northwest Portland. We conducted it the same way as Jeanine's memorial, a meeting of recovering alcoholics. Family and friends filled the chapel to overflowing. Scores of Rosanne's friends, mostly from Portland' gay community were there. Tearful testimonies praised her humanity, her caring nature, her writing, and the things she had done for her friends. Most of my grandchildren were there: Sanie, Ian and Katie, Timmy and Jennifer and dozens of other kids. My brother Tony, Carma, Melanie and Lisa made sure that all of the youngsters were helped with their grief. Rosanne, who had no children of her own, became a surrogate mother for several kids, and the kids gravitated to her. She was a mother to them, a confidant, advisor, and friend. When Tony, Melanie, Lisa, Carma and I talked about Rosanne's death we agreed on one thing: Rosanne had to see for herself how Jeanine was doing. Forever the caring older sister, the one who looked over her younger sisters, she made the ultimate decision-to go where Jeanine was and make sure she was being well cared for.

In those trying times, those two painful years, not once did I think of taking a drink. A miracle had happened, and I didn't know it. After the numbness of grief began to fade, I finally was able to accept that I had been given a great gift,what my friend Marcus Johnson, the hippie doctor, calls "the clarity of sobriety." It came from somewhere. I think it stems from being sober, finding faith, recognizing and admitting my faults, and trying to help other alcoholics.

Writing helped me through this terrible time. Writing, photography and amateur radio allowed me to become involved in activities that absorbed my complete attention. For me, writing takes a lot of concentration, as does working in a darkroom, or building a transceiver, a little combined radio transmitter and receiver, from a kit. I am grateful that I have those activities.

When my consulting work was finished with the Grande Ronde tribes, I was approached by two men who were developing a coastal tourism publication, Todd Blickenstaff, a venture expert, and Jeff Spink, a business manager, asked me to write all of the copy for the new monthly publication. Roger Swanton, a Gleneden Beach graphic designer, would design, layout and prepare the magazine for publication. It was a new challenge, but I enjoyed working under deadline again and doing all sorts of stories about the Oregon Coast.

I thought that most of my misfortune was behind me, but I was mistaken. In September 1997 it was time for my yearly trip to Southern California. This time I was not only going down to make my yearly visit to see Lada, but I was going to attend a big reunion for all of the classes of Beaumont Union High School.

I made the trip alone, because Carma was not feeling very well. I flew into Ontario, rented a car, and drove to El Monte. I had a nice visit with my aunt, who was bedridden with arthritis. She was being lovingly cared for by her companion Sister Bea. I left El Monte early in the morning of September 19, 1997, a Friday. I wanted to get to Beaumont so I could see June Cassidy and Joaquin Lara before the reunion. When I left El Monte it was still dark. As I drove by March Air Force Base the memories began streaming back. That was where I went for my flying cadet exams, flunked, and then I went into the Marine Corps. The highway I was on was built when Grandpa Smith was pumping water from the ranch to the contractors building the road.

I drove past the ranch, and tears filled my eyes. I could only recognize the row of scrubby tamarack trees that lined the old driveway to the ranch yard. The sun was blazing up from the east horizon. I braked as a huge truck in front of me slowed. The truck sped up as it approached the freeway exit. The sun flared up from atop the bridge blinding me. The rear end of the truck loomed up, at a dead stop in the middle of the road. I stomped on the brakes, and slid violently into the truck's trailer.

"I am going to die in the same spot I played as kid," flashed in my mind.

The front of the mini van that was partially under was crushed under the rear of the truck's trailer. I felt as if I had been kicked in the stomach by both Charlie and Nellie. I managed to crawl out of the van, hunched over, trying to breathe. Someone, I think it was the truck driver, led me around to the rear of the van, made me sit down with my back against the rear wheel. I still couldn't get my breath. It only took moments for an ambulance to arrive. The paramedics strapped me onto a stretcher and loaded me into the ambulance. I could hear the medic talking on the radio with his dispatcher, then personnel in a hospital emergency room. It was then that I found out I was on my way to the Loma Linda Medical Center. I felt that if I could just get my breath back I would be okay, but I realized that maybe something else was wrong. The medic kept asking me if I felt as if I were going to pass out. I told him no, that I felt O.K. except for the pain in my diaphragm and lot being able to breathe normally. He intensified his calls to the hospital, and I overhead him say my blood pressure was going down.

They really rushed me from the ambulance to the emergency room, and the doctors and nurses took all of the information, and asked who they should call. I gave them my home and Melanie's numbers. They gave me some sort of a shot, and I was in and out of consciousness, but I remember X-rays and a CAT scan. The emergency room surgeon told me that I had internal bleeding, and they would have to operate on me to stop it. I knew then that it was pretty serious.

"What do you think my chances are, Doc?"

"What do you think"" he replied.

"About 50-50?"

"You keep that thought, and you will be O.K.," he said.

The next thing I remembered I was being wheeled down a long corridor, towards a bright white light. I was in a hazy enough state to question if I was going through a near-death experience, and approaching the hereafter. It was only the brightly lit operating room. I prayed. In my continuing journey of recovery from alcoholism I was told that I should make prayer a daily habit. But in my prayers I should pray for God's will and the power to carry it out. I should pray for others, not myself. I could pray for myself, if others would be helped. That thought came through strongly to me then. I asked God to spare me, because so many were depending on me. There was Carma, and Sanie, Lisa, Melanie, and the grandchildren. I didn't think that it was time for me to go and leave them. Carma had been having memory problems for the past three or four years, and the condition was not improving. Sanie was still in school, and I was her main emotional anchor after her mother and Aunt Rosanne died. So I asked my God, who I didn't understand, to let me stay for a while.

I awoke in the intensive care unit. Daughter Lisa, three inches away from my face, was gazing into my eyes. I winked. She cried, and Carma rushed over to my side.

One of my fellow alcoholics told me that coincidences were God's way of getting our attention. Coincidence carried Lisa and Carma to my bedside. When I left Oregon to fly to California, Lisa, who was living near Eugene, Oregon, thought it would be a good idea to visit Carma. It was Lisa who picked up the phone when Loma Linda Hospital called and told them of my accident. Carma and Lisa packed immediately, were driven to Portland where they jumped on an airplane and flew to Ontario. Carma never could have been able to take the trip by herself. They took a taxi from the airport to a motel next door to the hospital, and stayed there until I was released.

Lisa said that when she and Carma arrived at Loma Linda the doctors told her to prepare her mother for the worst. Things did not look too good, they didn't expect me to survive. After I roused from the anesthetic I began to improve at once. I had tubes running down my throat and nose, had a respirator helping me breathe, and an IV pumping liquid and pain killers into me. I was in intensive care for about 36 hours, fully aware of what was going on, then moved to the surgery ward. Right after I got there, the nurse came in, got me to my feet, and I took a few halting steps. When I saw my belly I almost passed out. I had an incision running from my chest to my groin. The nurse said the more I walked the sooner I would get out. I had a morphine pump running into me. All I had to do was push the little button when I felt pain. The only problem was that I never did feel too much pain, only discomfort and stiffness, after I got out of surgery. They took the morphine pump away from me. The nurse said I wasn't using it, so away it went.

Lisa had taken care of all of the things like notifying family and friends of my accident and condition, and the insurance carriers. Sanie, at home in Panther Creek, contacted my ham radio club friends, Father Mell Stead at St. Augustine's, and editors of publications I was writing for. I recovered quickly. Dr. Richard Catalano, the surgeon who operated on me, checked on me regularly. My primary nurse, Susie Parker, she who spurred me into exercise, had a lot to do with my recovery. Susie was pleased with my response, and said, "Not many men 74 years old have recovered from such an accident." My old school friends, Joaquin Lara and June Bourgignon Cassidy, made the trip down from Beaumont to visit me. They bore the news of the big reunion, and wondered why I didn't show up. Cousin Jimmy King, and wife Pat, who live in Camarillo, California, also visited me. Those visits meant a lot, and I was ready for discharge five days after I had been carried into the Loma Linda University Medical Center.

Lisa pushed me in a wheelchair from the hospital to the motel two blocks away. We were to fly back to Portland the next day. I was wearing a hospital nightgown, one of those wonderful contraptions that are put on backwards with the split up the back. I needed clothes. All of mine had been cut off of me in the emergency room. Getting to a department store to outfit me was a problem, then I hit on a possible solution. Lisa called a nearby Catholic church, and told them I needed clothes to fly home in. The pastor told her to call St. Francis Monastery in Redlands, a community of the Byzantine Brothers of St. Francis. I talked to Brother John Gray, and within an hour he was knocking at the motel door with his arms full of clothes: two pair of pants, shoes, shirts and socks. They all fit, except I had to roll the pants legs up. Brother John was very gracious and asked if they could help me in any other way, if I needed a ride to the airport. We had already made arrangements with the motel to catch our plane the next morning. It all seemed to fit. It was the Franciscan priests and sisters who were so important in my early life. Now when I needed help as an old man, it was the followers of St. Francis who came to my aid. I will be forever grateful to those wonderful Catholic brothers of the Byzantine Rite, not only for the clothes, but they prompted me to recall my heritage, my early church days, my family and their love.

My gratitude didn't stop there. When we took off from Ontario we departed to the east and climbed up over the San Gorgonio Mountains, close to Old Grayback, and I could see Beaumont nestled between the two great mountains, San Gorgonio and San Jacinto. I even managed to pick out Grandpa's and Grandma's cherry ranch, and the spot where I kissed death on the cheek. I silently said my own prayer of Thanksgiving, and we climbed steeply into the blue skies and headed north to our Oregon home.

I remain on a journey, just like the one my family and I took in the old Maxwell across the country in 1923. My dad was running away from alcoholism, poverty and a painful childhood. He, like my mother, Grandpa and Grandma Smith, and Lada, found a new home. Since I was very young, I felt that sense of not belonging, despite my great loving family. I began my own journey seeking that belonging when I first tasted the sweet cherry wine, and the musty heartiness of home-brewed beer. The loss of faith, sinking into the arms of alcoholic degradation, discovering my belief in a power greater than myself, and a joyful start on recovery has evolved into great trek into the frontier of my destiny. As friend Gary continuously reminds me, "It's not the destination that's important. It's the trip."

About the Author

Photo by Charlie Smith, K7GI

Frank King has been a free-lance writer for more than 40 years. He has written thousands of newspaper, magazine, and journal articles. He is currently a columnist for the *Oregon Coast Guide*, and a newsletter editor.